1:33

by Bruce Henderson
and Sam Summerlin

COWLES

Photographs, courtesy of *Look* magazine, by Phil Harrington, Doug Jones, Archie Lieberman, Maurice Terrell, Stanley Tretick, and John Vachon. © Cowles Communications, Inc.

Excerpts from "Memories of a Tragic Day" reprinted by permission of *New York Post*, copyright 1963, New York Post Corporation.

Excerpts from *Understanding Media: The Extensions of Man*, reprinted by permission of McGraw-Hill Book Company, Copyright © 1964 by Marshall McLuhan.

Excerpts from "When Castro Heard the News" by Jean Daniel reprinted by permission of the author, © 1963 *France Observateur*.

For Cheri, Laurie, and Mark

B.H.

For Sandi and Tony

S.S.

. . . in the hope that the young generation, bruised and bewildered by this decade of assassination, may find some perspective within this book that will help them overcome.

PREFACE

Classical historians calculate that it took two weeks, in an age of the chariot and galley, without telegraph, radio or television, for word of Julius Caesar's violent death in the Roman Forum to reach Alexandria, Egypt, 1,300 miles away. But within five minutes of that fateful announcement in Parkland Hospital in Dallas, Texas, on that unforgettable day in 1963, the words "President Kennedy died . . ." had flashed into every region of the globe. Only in our age, when miracles of communications have electronically joined the earth's population into one family, could such a shock wave have jolted the world with such speed.

Much has been written about the details and possible causes of the disaster of November 22, 1963. In the preoccupation with such concerns, however, perhaps insufficient attention has been paid to another interesting dimension of the tragedy—how people reacted to the news of John Fitzgerald Kennedy's death, why they reacted as they did, and what was the influence of that tragic event on the nation and on the world. We suggest that such a compendium may well be a valid addition to the recorded history of the assassination.

Into the mind of virtually every rational human being alive on that November 22 was seared the memory of that instant when he or she first heard the news: the President of the United States was dead of an assassin's bullet. In this volume, we offer a catalog of recollections of a shaken world to that event.

The importance of the reactions lies, however, less in the reactions themselves than in what they represent.

We write neither as psychologists nor as sociologists, but rather as journalists; there are experts far more qualified to speak on the subject than we. Nonetheless, it seems to us that on the basis of the evidence—including the writings of behavioral scientists themselves—the responses to the assassination of John F. Kennedy reflect two significant aspects of contemporary human civilization. One is man's continued tendency to become dependent upon leader figures, and his sense of loss and fear at the disappearance of such symbols. The second is the heightened immediate effect that instant communications have given the assassination of a political leader. Both phenomena, we believe, have contributed to the emotional effects that the assassination of President Kennedy has had on the American people.

In our concluding chapters, we offer an assessment of the effects of Kennedy's death on history to date—and its possible effects on the future. The latter area of conjecture includes what seem to us some of the questions—and dangers—raised by the spectre of political assassination in the electronic age, not only for the United States but for the rest of the world as well.

Human reaction to assassination and the problems that such events pose for society today were, of course, tragically reemphasized by the shootings in 1968 of the Rev. Dr. Martin Luther King Jr. and Robert Francis Kennedy. Like reruns of an incredible nightmare, the murders of these two political figures opened old wounds and worries. The first major milestone, however, in this grim succession of catastrophe was the killing of John Kennedy, President of the United States of America, leader of 200 million Americans, and commander in chief of the world's most powerful democracy. Any discussion of responses to, and effects of, the outbreak of political assassinations in the United States must logically begin with the slaying of President Kennedy.

We were struck by the crystalline clarity with which people remember their first reactions to the news of President Kennedy's shooting and death. To be sure, many of the details of that tragic day are fading from memory, and the only conscious impressions left are those that made the sharpest imprints. Yet those imprints appear to be indelible. What each person remembers varies, but the images are the ones that each brain, because of its own unique interests and impulses, captured in consciousness.

The fact that many of the persons mentioned herein expressed grief does not mean that this book should be interpreted as a posthumous eulogy to Kennedy's record as chief executive; the evaluation of his stewardship must spring not from the tears of tragedy but from the hard eye of history. In our endeavor, we have selected those recollections that, in our estimation, most eloquently mirror a moment whose shock was matched only by its impact on our times.

We are most grateful to those who shared with us their recollections, permitting themselves to be recorded for others to read. To the names mentioned in this book we wish to add those of the many persons both in the United States and abroad who have contributed to this work in various invaluable ways. Without their understanding and help, *1:33* could never have been achieved. Our thanks go to:

The staff of Research Reports, Ann Novotny, Susan Hartung, and Lorraine Abraham in New York, and Jessica Silvers, Los Angeles; Hal Gulliver, Atlanta; Tom Henshaw, Boston; Joan Pinkerton and Michael Shamberg, Chicago; Tom Johnson and Val Imm, Dallas; Jerry Buck, John Cunniff, Corinne Deutch, Alberto A. Quevedo, Gil Scott, Charles Storer, and Cynthia Summerlin, New York; Gary A. Claxton, Omaha; Wilbur Martin, Col. James Munson, Bob Horton, and Robert L. Robinson of the American Psychiatric Association, Washington; Oscar J. Serrat, Buenos Aires; Aly Mahmoud, Cairo; George Arfeld, Caracas; Richard O'Regan and Elke Jessett, London; Kevin B. Kelleghan, Mexico; Michael Parry, Nairobi; Joe McGowan, New Delhi; Allan Jacks and John Moore. Rome; Bob Tuckman, Saigon; Rodney Pinder, Tel Aviv; Henry Hartzenbusch and Ken Ishii, Tokyo.

Acknowledgment is paid to those who permitted their published works to be quoted in this book, and we extend our special appreciation to Dr. Paul B. Sheatsley and Dr. Jacob J. Feldman of the National Opinion Research Center; Dr. Fred I. Greenstein, associate professor of government at Wesleyan University, Middletown, Conn.; Dr. David Kirschner, New York psychologist; Dr. George R. Krupp, New York psychoanalyst; reporters Jean Daniel, Melvin Durslag, Ralph McGill, Judy Michaelson, and Don Sullivan; Hodding Carter, editor of *The Delta-Democrat Times*, Greenville, Mississippi; Relman Morin, and Marshall McLuhan.

Our appreciation also goes to Myrick Land of *Look,* whose interest was intrumental in bringing this book to fruition; to Mrs.

Francine Klagsbrun of Cowles, whose enthusiasm for the idea was decisive; to Nat Brandt of Cowles, whose perceptive editing enhanced the organization and structure of the book; to John Starr, for his enduring confidence in *1:33*, and to James Keogh and John T. Elson of *Time*, and Sam Blackman, Ben Bassett, Keith Fuller, Stanley M. Swinton, and Webb McKinley of The Associated Press for their patience and understanding in this endeavor.

The Authors
New York City
July 30, 1968

CONTENTS

PROLOGUE
Friday, November 22, 1963

Father Oscar Huber made the sign of the cross on the President's forehead with his thumb, moistened with holy oil. "Eternal rest, grant unto him, O Lord."

* * *

Malcolm Kilduff, a press aide, walked into the nurses' classroom. His eyes were red and he held an unlit cigarette in his hand as he faced the clamoring newsmen. Reading from a piece of paper, Kilduff said:

"President Kennedy died at approximately 1 P.M. Central Standard Time today here in Dallas. He died of a gunshot wound in the brain."

Amid the turmoil, a circular IBM clock on the drab, aseptic-green wall at Parkland Hospital marked the hour of

1:33

How did November 22, 1963, begin for you?

Where were you that day at 1:33?

What thought or words came to you at that moment that seem impossible to forget?

What did you do in that fleeting instant?

THE DAY

November 22, 1963, dawned as a normal day in what had become a chronically abnormal world.

In the United States, the people of history's strongest and most stable democracy, in the 187th year of its existence, were enjoying the fruits of its unique promise. Shop windows were festooned with fall and winter fashions. Wallach's of New York City and New Jersey advertised a new, narrow-brim hat model for men, the Lee Mark 64. Price: $11.95. In stores throughout the nation, Boston rockers—newly popular under the nation's Boston-born "rocking-chair President"—were selling in volume at prices from $19.95 to $29.95. On Broadway, crowds were snapping up tickets to "A Funny Thing Happened on the Way to the Forum," and in television land ABC-TV was rehearsing a new series, "12 O'Clock High." The CBS-TV schedule that morning featured repeats of "Our Miss Brooks" and "I Love Lucy," the new situation comedy of "Pete and Gladys," and, at 12 o'clock high, the soap opera "Love of Life."

At 10 A.M. on Wall Street, the clang of the opening bell signaled the start of the day's trading on that bulwark of the American economic system, the New York Stock Exchange. The approximately 2,500 men who populate the exchange floor—executives and employees of member firms, along with officials and clerks of the Exchange—went about their normal tasks. The market opened strong, with the Dow-Jones Industrial Average at 733.35, up slightly from the previous day's close. For the next two hours, volume was moderate and prices steady. Then the market started moving up again, strengthened by an announcement that a company suspended by the Exchange for failing to maintain minimum capital requirements had been reinstated. By 1 P.M., the Dow-Jones index had reached 735.87 points.

Americans were preparing for a festive Thanksgiving. College football squads held final workouts for the weekend's pre-Thanksgiving games. Among the biggest on the schedule was the Harvard-Yale contest, traditionally played on the Saturday before Thanksgiving. The Sky Chef Restaurant at Long Island's Idlewild Airport was offering a complete Thanksgiving dinner—roast turkey, gravy, cranberry sauce, and the trimmings, "all topped off with creamy pumpkin pie," for $3.50. Because Thanksgiving fell so late in the month, there was a mercantile squeeze between the day of thanks for the nation's bounty and the holiday celebrating the birth of Christ. Merchants emphasized that there were fewer shopping days between Thanksgiving and Christmas, and were advising customers to do their buying early. An advertisement in *The New York Times* that morning proclaimed, "If Christmas seems earlier this year— it is! 22 shopping days are all you have between Thanksgiving and December 25th—compared to 27 days last year. So shop now—the stores are ready, filled with more Christmas excitement than ever before."

In much of the nation, it was sunny and unseasonably warm. "Many persons strolled the streets as though it were early spring instead of late fall," reported *The Boston Traveler*. "The sun bathed the city and with the approaching holiday there was a feeling of well-being and contentment."

Along with the anticipation there was the morning's news quota involving tragedy. A 16-year-old Mineola, Long Island, youth pleaded guilty to illegally discharging a rifle, a bullet from which had critically wounded an 8-year-old boy. The teen-ager, a former member of a private rifle club, had fired the .22-caliber weapon from a second-floor window of his home when he spotted what he thought was a squirrel on a neighboring lawn. Approaching the lawn, the youth discovered the younger boy bleeding from a wound in the forehead.

In Jackson, Mississippi, a hearing had been set for Byron de la

Beckwith, a Greenwood fertilizer salesman charged with the rifle slaying of Medgar Evers, the leader of that state's chapter of the National Association for the Advancement of Colored People.

Dead that morning of natural causes were Dr. Francis A. Bartlett, 81, of Stamford, Connecticut, one of the world's leading authorities on shade trees and their care, and Robert Stroud, 73, the convicted murderer known as the "Birdman of Alcatraz" for his scholarly research into the diseases of birds while imprisoned on Alcatraz Island. Aldous Huxley, the distinguished English philosopher, was to die of cancer before the day was out.

In Washington, Democratic Senator J. W. Fulbright of Arkansas was denouncing a bill in Congress that would bar the United States government from underwriting commercial credit for the Soviet Union to purchase wheat. His opposition—joined by the Kennedy Administration—was couched in typically Fulbrightian logic. Unless Congress ceased restricting trade in "non-strategic" goods with Russia, warned Fulbright, who was chairman of the Senate Foreign Relations Committee, "we may, indeed, find ourselves in the same position in the free world which the Chinese find themselves in the Communist world. We and the Chinese will be outcasts, splendid in our isolated devotion to pure dogma." Fulbright said that he refused to "admit that Communist dogma, per se, is a threat to the United States." Coincidentally, the same day that Fulbright's words were published—November 22, 1963—saw the publication of a Moscow-authorized book, *Program of the Communist Party of the Soviet Union,* featuring a "special introduction" by Soviet Premier Nikita Khrushchev. In the edition for United States distribution, Khrushchev alleged that the party document could help Americans by acquainting them with Soviet "goals and aspirations." Moreover, the Premier declared, he was "firmly convinced of the victory of Communism" by what he innocently asserted was "not a plan of secret conspiracies or military threats but a plan for peaceful competition."

Gathering uncertain momentum at home was the series of antipoverty bills and similar social reform legislation engendered by the Kennedy Administration. In Washington, the president of the American Medical Association, Dr. Edward R. Annis of Miami, testifying before the House Ways and Means Committee, accused the New Frontier of underestimating the cost of its program of health care for the aged. Contending that the government's cost projections

for Medicare were "unrealistically low," he foresaw "the grim prospect of higher and higher taxes to protect the Social Security fund from an impossible new burden."

In an early symptom of the rebellious mood building in the nation, the self-styled Student Committee for Travel to Cuba, which had organized a trip to Fidel Castro's communist island in defiance of a State Department ban, announced that it was organizing another trip for the summer of 1964. In New York City, the cases of 120 persons arrested during demonstrations at a housing project had been presented to a grand jury. The defendants argued that, although their cases involved misdemeanors, they were before the bar of justice because of a "grave social problem."

Despite the fact that the Senate, on the day before, had passed a Kennedy-backed bill to increase the national debt limit to $315 billion —the third such increase in the year—the news that morning told of other Kennedy legislative proposals being in trouble. For one, the House Judiciary Committee had delivered a report on the Administration's civil rights bill containing no fewer than eight conflicting sets of views on the measure. Republicans were blaming President Kennedy himself for the bogging down of his program. A Washington dispatch on the morning of the 22nd quoted Republican congressional leaders as declaring that Kennedy's "legislative program is in a mess," and contending that the fault was not that of Congress but the Administration's own blunders. Senate GOP leader, Everett McKinley Dirksen of Illinois, asserted, "In the final analysis, it is President Kennedy's own mismanagement of his legislative program that has kept Congress in session since last January and everybody in Washington knows it." The Kennedy regime, chimed in the House Republican leader, Charles A. Halleck of Indiana, "adds up to almost total failure for what undoubtedly will be known as the three empty years. With the Democrats in control of the White House and every government agency, and with a two-to-one majority in the Senate and a three-to-two majority in the House of Representatives, Mr. Kennedy can have no alibi."

Former Vice-President Richard M. Nixon, who as the Republican Presidential candidate in 1960 lost to John Kennedy by a bare 118,550 votes, was joining in the criticism. On a business trip to Dallas the day before President Kennedy was to visit the city, Nixon charged that Kennedy's failure to control Congress, despite his Democratic majority there, "shows his lack of leadership much better than anything else." Nixon further taxed Kennedy with a record of nonachievement characterized by "brave talk but no action," with responsibility for a deterioration of policy toward Latin America and Southeast Asia, and with "what is apparently our permanent unemployment." "His public relations is tremendous," added Nixon, "but his performance is poor." The GOP leader concluded:

"I am going to work as hard as I can to get the Kennedys out of there. We can't afford four more years of that kind of Administration."

There was likewise unseemly dissension within Kennedy's own party. The press that morning reported a verbal blast by Democratic Senator Joseph S. Clark of Pennsylvania, in which he blamed the legislative stalemate on a complete breakdown of Democratic party discipline. In a speech on the Senate floor, Clark charged the party's leadership—meaning, ultimately, the President himself—with failing to discipline Democratic members of the Senate "establishment," principally southerners, who refused to support the program of the party "to which they profess to belong." Clark delivered his attack while announcing resolutions to force tax-cut, civil rights, and State Department money bills out of committees onto the Senate floor. Clark had also demanded that his senatorial colleagues act on another resolution, pigeon-holed for months, that was designed to change Senate rules in order to facilitate the flow of legislation. Adopting such changes, Clark argued, would be better than a "return to the days prior to 1961 when the majority leader spent his time in 'back-slapping, chest-jabbing and arm-twisting' "—a reference to the tactics reportedly employed by Vice-President Lyndon Baines Johnson when he had been the Senate Democratic leader. Mike Mansfield of Montana, Johnson's successor as Senate Majority Leader, declared that even he could not support Clark's discharge petitions, but he conceded that the Senate was indeed plagued by a "high degree of absenteeism," particularly among Democrats. Gazing around the chamber, Mansfield asked, "Why is the Senate not here this afternoon?" Replied Clark: "Because they couldn't care less."

Such was the atmosphere of political unrest on the morning of November 22, 1963. To be sure, every United States Administration is eternally on the receiving end of shot and shell, but in the case of John F. Kennedy the discord seemed particularly disruptive. Elected on a platform of "Let's get this country moving again," Kennedy was having serious trouble getting his own legislative proposals moving through Congress.

The overriding political mood of the nation was one of suspense, sharpened by rancor. Would the well-born, liberal Democratic, Roman Catholic President who had called for an array of new social welfare ventures at home and "bridge-building" overtures toward communism abroad succeed or fail in putting across his disputed programs? To what degree could he count on reelection in 1964 against a Republican party that was already mounting a counter-attack after its hair-thin defeat by Kennedy three years earlier?

Dominating the news that morning from around the globe was the seemingly endless struggle between the two principal political forces controlling mankind—totalitarian communism and those nations dedicated, with varying degrees of perfection, to the democratic ideal.

West Germany's Chancellor, Ludwig Erhard, was in Paris for talks with France's President, Charles de Gaulle. On his arrival in the French capital, Erhard had restated his conviction that a close Atlantic partnership with the United States was still important to both France and West Germany.

The Soviet Union had rejected a United States protest against the Russians' latest delaying of a Berlin-bound convoy on the East German autobahn. Scoffing at the protest as "unfounded," Moscow claimed that the commander of the American convoy had accepted a Russian demand that the number of military personnel in the convoy be counted. Simultaneously, the Soviet government newspaper *Izvestia* called for "warm friendship and cooperation" between the United States and the Soviet Union. In an editorial commemorating the 30th anniversary of the establishment of diplomatic relations between the United States and the Union of Soviet Socialist Republics, *Izvestia* blandly asserted, "Both our peoples want peace."

Over everything, as it had for more than a decade, hung the threat of nuclear holocaust. Possibly the most heartening word of the day was that the United States and the Soviet Union, despite their differences, had agreed on a code of legal principles to govern the exploration and use of space.

In the Middle East, three Russian fighter planes had shot down an unarmed Iranian aerial survey plane without warning 15 miles inside Iran's border. The incident set a record of sorts for diplomatic effrontery. Soviet President Leonid Brezhnev was paying an official visit to Iran at the time and was actually delivering a "good neighbor" speech before the Iranian parliament when news of the unprovoked attack reached Teheran. He expressed regrets.

In Africa's former Belgian colony, the Congo, Premier Cyrille Adoula's government was in the process of expelling the entire 100-member staff of the Soviet Embassy, accusing it of "collusion with a handful of Congolese agitators" based in the neighboring ex-French Congo.

In Latin America, the government of Venezuelan President Rómulo Betancourt had announced the arrest of 350 persons suspected of being pro-communist terrorists. The roundup followed an outbreak of shootings by snipers in the capital of Caracas that had left more than a score of victims dead.

Northward, across the Caribbean, a search was on for a lost American U-2 pilot whose reconnaissance plane—believed returning from a mission over communist Cuba—had crashed 40 miles northwest of Key West, Florida. The Pentagon discounted any possibility that the high-flying craft had been downed by Cuban antiaircraft missiles or MIG fighters. Radio Havana accused the United States Defense Department "of not wanting to say" what the plane was doing when it disappeared.

In Asia, the United States was reported to have halted supplying military weapons and ammunition to Indonesia's President Sukarno in retaliation for his belligerent policies toward Malaysia.

Cambodia's weathervane Prince Sihanouk, for his part, had requested that France replace the American economic aid that he had earlier demanded be canceled because of Washington's anti-communist stand in South Vietnam. Cheering the dyspeptic prince in his rejection of American help, Red China vowed "all-out support" for Cambodia in case of an "armed invasion instigated by the United States and its vassals."

In South Vietnam itself, Americans were in the early throes of the long and bloody struggle that was to follow. That nation's strong-arm president, Ngo Dinh Diem, had been assassinated three weeks earlier in a coup that some suspected had been inspired by the Kennedy Administration. Now, the military brass who succeeded Diem were flexing their own muscles by appointing a committee to investigate accusations that members of the Diem government had utilized "torture" and "murder" in dealing with political opponents.

At the same time, the military themselves were closing two Saigon newspapers with which they disagreed.

Apart from the Cold War, there were other events in the news that morning that amounted to a measure of man's folly and faith.

In Argentina, diehard *peronistas*—still fighting their battle eight years after the downfall of their exiled *lider*, former dictator Juan Perón—were blamed for a bomb-throwing binge in Buenos Aires. One mob shouting *"Viva Perón!"* burned a United States flag.

Iraq's premier of the moment, Lt. Gen. Taher Yahya, was forecasting the ultimate amalgamation of Iraq, Syria, the United Arab Republic, Algeria, and Yemen—not the first vision of a grand reunion among Arabs that had yet to see fruition.

Ethiopia's durable emperor, Haile Selassie, had charged neighboring Somalia with having "instigated and supported violations of Ethiopia's frontier," in another chapter of those two nations' private border dispute.

In Britain, the Labor party had shaken the ruling Conservatives by winning an important by-election in Dundee, Scotland, while in Japan, Premier Hayato Ikeda's middle-of-the-road Liberal-Democratic party swept to an impressive victory in a general election.

The Ecumenical Council of the Roman Catholic Church, in session in Rome, had pleased many of the world's 500 million Catholics by approving the use of vernacular languages for the church's liturgy, which had traditionally been celebrated only in Latin. Under the innovation, aimed at liberalizing Catholic forms of worship, an American priest giving the sacrament of penance could henceforth say, "I absolve thee from thy sins in the name of the Father and of the Son and of the Holy Spirit," instead of the traditional *"Ego te absolvo a peccatis tuis in nomine Patris et Filii et Spiritus Sancti."*

THE PRESIDENT

On the last morning of his life, the youthful President of the United States, bareheaded and without a topcoat, walked through misty rain toward a parking lot across the street from Fort Worth's Hotel Texas. There John Fitzgerald Kennedy spoke to a crowd of cheering Democrats who had not been able to get tickets to a breakfast being held for him that morning at the hotel. A few minutes later, he appeared at the fete sponsored by the Fort Worth Chamber of Commerce. Kennedy offered his now-famous apology for the fact that his wife was not with him, explaining that she was "organizing herself—it takes longer."

Mrs. Kennedy arrived a few minutes later, her entrance evoking enthusiastic applause from the 2,500 guests. Both the President and the First Lady were presented with cowboy boots, and Kennedy received a Texas hat. He declined to put it on in front of the audience but promised jokingly that he would wear it in the White House on the following Monday.

For Americans, the Texas hospitality and good-natured politicking of its President during his visit to the Lone Star State were part of the mundane beginnings of what was to be a stunningly disastrous day.

Despite his political and diplomatic frustrations, the handsome President, only 46 years old, remained a popular and appealing figure. Indeed, that morning he was in Texas to apply his person-

15

ality and prestige to help heal a schism in the state's Democratic party in hopes of ensuring Texas' 25 electoral votes in the 1964 Presidential contest. On the first day of his visit, riding in an open limousine with his lovely wife, he had been greeted by warm and enthusiastic crowds in San Antonio and Houston. In the former city —a center of space research in a space-conscious state—he delivered a politically popular pledge to continue the nation's program to conquer the "new frontier" of space.

At Houston, the President and Mrs. Kennedy had dropped in unannounced at a dinner-dance of the League of United Latin American Citizens, which the First Lady captivated by speaking in Spanish. Now, on the morning of Friday, November 22, the President and his wife were in Fort Worth, where they had spent the night.

It was to be a busy day for the chief executive: a luncheon address in Dallas, a party fund-raising dinner in Austin, and a final overnight stay as the guest of Vice-President and Mrs. Johnson at their ranch near Johnson City, prior to the Kennedys' scheduled return to Washington on Saturday.

After his breakfast speech in Fort Worth, the President placed a telephone call to former Democratic Vice-President John Nance (Cactus Jack) Garner, whose 95th birthday it was. Speaking from his home in Uvalde, Texas, Garner croaked, "Hello, Mr. President. God bless you. I hope you stay in there forever."

At 10:35 A.M., John and Jacqueline Kennedy left the Texas Hotel by limousine for Carswell Air Force Base near Fort Worth. There they boarded the Presidential jet for the short flight to Dallas, where they landed at 11:37 A.M. At the airport, youths in the crowd called out "Hey Jackie!" and pushed forward for a closer look, teen-age girls squealing over the presence of the President.

Despite Dallas' reputation as a conservative city, the welcoming crowd at Love Field was by far the largest that had turned out to greet the President on his Texas tour. Along the motorcade route toward the city's center there were scattered Goldwater signs, and one young man held up a placard that read, "Because of a high regard of the presidency I hold you and your blind socialist policies in contempt." But, on balance, the anti-Kennedy signs that might have been expected were almost nonexistent. One banner contended, "Mr. President, there is still hope in the South." A little farther on, two Negroes displayed a crudely printed sign that said, simply,

"Hi, Mr. President." At another corner, two schoolgirls hoisted a message pleading, "Please stop and shake our hands"; the President did.

At the Dallas Trade Mart, preparations were at high pitch for a gala, Texas-style luncheon. The Roman Catholic Diocese of Dallas-Fort Worth had issued a special dispensation allowing Catholic guests to eat meat, even though the consumption of meat on Friday was still generally prohibited for Catholics. Noting that sirloin steaks were to be served, the Rev. J. A. Schumacher, a spokesman for the diocese, explained, "Since most of the people at the luncheon will be non-Catholic, we felt that it would be easier to give a dispensation." As for Kennedy himself, Father Schumacher elaborated, the Catholic President did not need a dispensation. "Since he is commander in chief of the military," Father Schumacher said, "he is a soldier. The [church] law says that soldiers don't have to abstain."

The United States Secret Service had taken stringent precautions to safeguard Kennedy at the luncheon. On the previous morning Secret Service agents had poked through 5,000 yellow roses as they were being installed at the Trade Mart to ascertain that no bombs or other damaging weapons were included with the fragrant buds. Although chefs for the luncheon had planned to serve the President a special steak billed as the biggest and juiciest in Texas, Secret Service agents objected. Instead, they ordered that the President's steak be selected at random, by a Secret Service agent, from among the 2,000 steaks broiled for the entire guest list at the fete. "This was done for security reasons," a spokesman for the luncheon sponsors explained. "A would-be assassin couldn't be sure of poisoning the President's meal unless he put poison in every steak."

Heading for the Trade Mart, the President drove through friendly crowds into the downtown section of the city. Then, on a sun-bathed Dallas boulevard at Dealey Plaza, a fusillade of shots cracked out . . .

Slightly more than an hour later, at precisely 1:33 P.M. November 22, 1963, Central Standard Time, the acting Presidential press secretary, Malcolm Kilduff, announced that John Fitzgerald Kennedy was dead.

REACTION

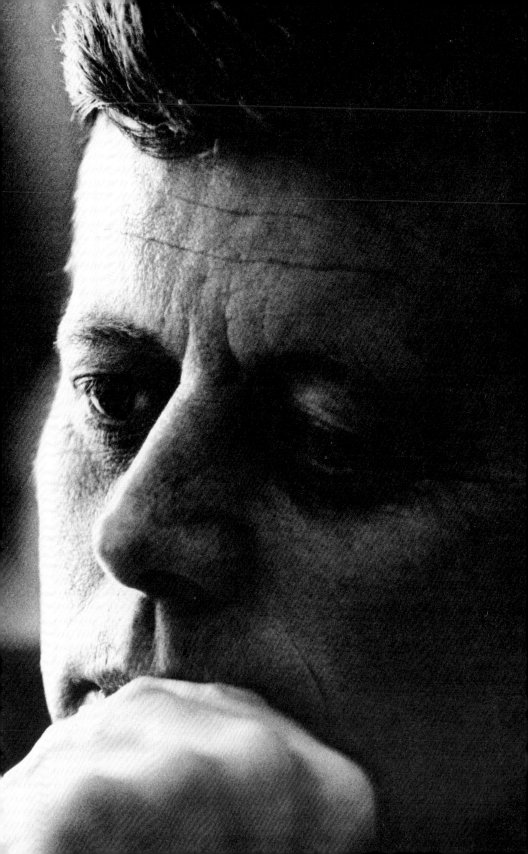

THE NEWS
IS FLASHED

The TV soap opera "As The World Turns" was spinning its saga of domestic turbulence into the homes of 6,800,000 American housewives midday of November 22, 1963, just as the program does five days each week over CBS.

On Manhattan's West Side, the network's anchor reporter, Walter Cronkite, was closeted at the CBS News headquarters. The veteran journalist was writing his commentary to accompany a film strip for his regular news program that evening. Ed Bliss, an editor on Cronkite's show, was in the general newsroom when his trained ear caught a pause in the clattering tattoo of the Teletypes arrayed along one wall. After an instant, the jangling ring of bells installed inside the machines sounded the alert that urgent news was coming. Keys came alive again, pounding out a "rat-tat-tat" of bulletins datelined Dallas. Bliss ripped the first bit of incredible news off one printer and ran toward Cronkite shouting that the President had been shot.

"We need you for a bulletin," Bliss cried out. Cronkite yelled back, "The hell with writing it. Just give me the air."

Cronkite dashed into a tiny, soundproof announcer's booth in a corner of the newsroom. At 1:40 P.M., Eastern Standard Time, CBS Master Control stopped "As The World Turns," substituting a visual announcement on the screen of a CBS special news bulletin. Then, in a trembling voice heard by millions, Cronkite announced:

"President Kennedy has been shot while traveling through Dallas."

It was the first TV bulletin of the shooting on the networks. Cronkite said later that his initial shock was mixed with the thought, "I can't break up. I must control myself."

A disturbing new age in TV journalism was born—one that might be termed the era of the televised assassination.

NBC in New York was rerunning an episode of "Bachelor Father" when staff announcer Don Pardo was handed the bulletin. He raced to an audio booth and was on the air by 1:45 EST.

William R. McAndrew, the director of NBC News, was lunching at the Louis XIV restaurant adjacent to the Rockefeller Plaza ice skating rink. A waiter spread the news of the shooting. McAndrew knocked over a glass of water as he rushed out.

NBC's Chet Huntley was having lunch with McAndrew's assistant, Julian Goodman, in the sixth-floor executive dining room of the RCA Building. A butler leaned over Goodman's shoulder and said, "The President has been shot." Goodman, who was later to become president of NBC, echoed most of America when he looked up and replied, "You're kidding." In another instant, however, he hurried out of the room and down the stairs to the floor below, where the broadcast operations control room for NBC's nationwide network is situated.

ABC news chief Elmer Lower was called out of a swimming pool at the New York Athletic Club. An attendant had advised him that he had an urgent call. Dripping wet, he heard the news from his secretary.

The all-encompassing eye of American television focused on the tragedy with incredible speed and breadth. The most unforgettable drama ever viewed began to unfold, minute-by-minute, hour-by-hour, and day-by-day, in millions of living rooms in the United States and abroad.

So great was the swiftness and emotional impact that for many, including some TV men themselves, all sense of time vanished. Charged with absorbing and relaying the first blitzkrieg of bulletins, Cronkite, after a time, could not remember whether he had been on the air one, two, or three hours. (He was actually on, during his first stint of reporting the tragedy, nearly two hours.) Several times the CBS News commentator, who had covered wars and countless tragedies, came close to breaking down at this catastrophe. Producer Don Hewitt at one point watched as Cronkite began aimlessly putting on and taking off his glasses. Hewitt decided that it was time to relieve the star newscaster, and network correspondent Charles Collingwood took over the microphone.

Cronkite left the newsroom and walked back to his corner office to call his family. When he picked up the telephone, there was a call already on the line. He heard a woman's voice ask, "Is this CBS News?"

Cronkite answered, "Yes." The voice went on, "Well, I just want to say that it's the worst bad taste to have Walter Cronkite on the air when everybody knows he spent all his time trying to get the President."

Cronkite asked the woman's name, then retorted, "This is Walter Cronkite, and you're a god-damn idiot." He slammed down the phone.

New York Times correspondent Tom Wicker heard the news that the President was dead over the radio of a parked car. He was walking across the lawn of Dallas' Parkland Hospital toward a press room that had been set up in a hospital classroom. "Ordinarily, I couldn't jump a tennis net if I'd just beaten Gonzalez," Wicker recalled. "That day, carrying a briefcase and a typewriter, I jumped a chain fence looping around the drive, not even breaking stride."

Within seconds, the news from Dallas had reached not only millions of Americans but the entire world. From the heart of Manhattan, The Associated Press and United Press International, the two largest news agencies in the United States, flashed the tidings around the globe to more than 100 foreign nations via underseas cables and radio signals, activating Teletype printers from Kuwait to Kuala Lumpur, from Alaska to Athens. Foreign news agencies, such as Agence France Press and the British-run Reuters, also transmitted the news to many parts of the world.

By incredible coincidence, the first TV broadcast beamed across the Pacific, from California to Tokyo, was scheduled to take place that day. Instead of a recorded message from President Kennedy, which was scheduled to inaugurate the broadcast, startled Japanese viewers heard the news of his assassination. During the ensuing four days of mourning, live American television was relayed by satellite for the first time into the Soviet Union. In Europe, 18 nations linked by the Continent's Eurovision network, and six of seven communist nations in the corresponding Intervision bloc, broadcast the Kennedy

23

tragedy live to their viewers, picking it up from across the Atlantic via the relay communications satellite Telstar. Only East Germany did not take the Kennedy program; instead, it showed a soccer match.

In effect, the globe-girdling TV tube had suddenly transformed Wendell Willkie's one world into one room.

Never had a moment so rocked the United States and the world. Across the nation, it was as though someone had yanked a giant electric plug. As one newspaper put it, "From this afternoon on, the day is black and the world is in mourning."

Business came to a near-halt. Conventions and executive conferences, courts, and legislative councils adjourned. As if by some unseen hand, flags on schools and other public buildings were lowered to half-staff. Traffic inexplicably thinned and slowed. Americans clustered in numbed knots around radios, television sets, and newspaper bulletin boards. Everywhere, the initial reaction was one of stunned disbelief, then consternation. Former Democratic Senator Herbert H. Lehman of New York called Kennedy's death "the greatest catastrophe our nation has suffered since the assassination of Abraham Lincoln." Said Senator Paul H. Douglas of Illinois, "We will mourn his loss. May I add, I hope this doesn't mean we're becoming a Latin-American country."

Paradoxically, the chill of death evoked an uncommon human warmth among the living. George Forsythe, a reporter for *The Boston Traveler,* observed, "Everyone seemed to talk a little more quietly and appeared to be a little kinder to each other. Complete strangers conversed in muted tones as they walked down the streets."

In millions of households, perplexed parents faced the problem of how to explain the murder of the President to their questioning children in terms that a youngster could understand and accept. Telephone operators, their switchboards jammed as thousands of Americans called each other, bawled unabashedly into their circuits. "Poor Jackie, poor Jackie," a woman murmured over and over in a Boston lounge. "To have him shot before her eyes. Those poor children." "Poor us," rejoined a man. "What does this do for the country?" Warned an executive in a downtown Boston office:

"It's not a man that did this, it's an idea. It can't happen here? Who said so?"

In McAllen, Texas, A. W. Plath died after learning of the assassination on television. According to officials, Plath, an elderly man, was watching TV when the news flashed on. "Oh, my God!" he said, and collapsed.

On hearing the news on the radio, Sutton Christian, 61, chief of the Hampton, Virginia, Institute news bureau, collapsed of a fatal heart attack.

There was an instant, widespread fear that there might be a conspiracy behind the assassination, or that it might spontaneously touch off more mayhem. An anonymous caller telephoned the office of Gov. Carl Sanders of Georgia, mumbling about Kennedy's death and hinting that Sanders might also be the target of violence. State police dispatched extra troopers to guard the Governor.

In Montgomery, Alabama, a force of state troopers surrounded the executive mansion of Gov. George C. Wallace. "Let's just say," a state official explained, "we're not taking any chances."

The murder of the President eclipsed what, in terms of numbers of victims, was a far greater tragedy that occurred the next day: a wind-whipped fire in a Norwalk, Ohio, old folks' home that took the lives of 63 men and women.

Likewise pushed out of the limelight was the Great Salad Oil Scandal, which broke that weekend but did not rise to wide public attention until weeks later.

The shooting caught the eastern half of the nation at the lunch hour. In Manhattan, New York Gov. Nelson A. Rockefeller was lunching with former Republican Presidential candidate Thomas E. Dewey. Rockefeller rushed back to his office to issue a statement of condolence.

In Jackson, Mississippi, a man walked into a restaurant and asked for the attention of everyone present. A hush fell over the luncheon crowd as he announced, "The President has been shot."

In New Orleans, Mayor Victor Schiro announced the news of the shooting at a luncheon of local civic leaders, but his audience refused to believe him. Finally, Schiro was reduced to saying, "No, I'm serious. It's true."

An unidentified man slammed a newspaper violently onto a desk in Manhattan's Criminal Courts Building and ran out of the room in near-hysteria.

"Dead? Who's dead?" asked a man standing in the lobby of a Newark, New Jersey, office building on hearing that someone had

been shot. Told that it was the President, he opened his mouth, but said nothing. Then he shook his head and walked away, head bowed.

In Nashville, Tennessee, a woman burst into tears on the sidewalk. "I can't stand it," she wept. "It's just too terrible. He was the best President we ever had."

For millions, entertainment no longer seemed fun. Even honky-tonks, normally immune to national issues, turned off their juke-boxes, and their patrons went home. Along Baltimore's stretch of nightclubs, strip-tease shows, girly magazine stands, and shooting galleries, the neon lights went out and blaring music ceased. Scores of major sports events—including the Harvard-Yale football game that was one of Kennedy's favorites—were called off. Broadway theaters closed. The Metropolitan Opera canceled its evening production of Wagner's "Götterdämerung." The Boston Symphony Orchestra was in the midst of its regular Friday afternoon concert when the news hit; conductor Erich Leinsdorf broke off a Handel concerto that the orchestra was playing and led the musicians in the second movement—the funeral march—from Beethoven's Symphony No. 3. The more than 2,600 guests stood with heads bowed. The three major radio and TV networks suspended entertainment broadcasting for the rest of the day and night. Movie houses from coast to coast canceled showings of "Cleopatra," a box-office hit of the day.

In Hollywood, where John Kennedy had been more popular than any recent predecessor because of his own wit, charm, and interest in the arts, artistic sensibilities were destroyed. On a Hollywood set, actress Audrey Hepburn was rehearsing the song "Wouldn't It Be Loverly?" for the movie version of "My Fair Lady." She burst into helpless weeping, and the rehearsal was suspended.

Actor Jack LaRue, filming "Robin and the Seven Hoods," collapsed on hearing the news, and was rushed to a hospital with a suspected heart attack.

Jack Lemmon sat in stunned silence in his dressing room on the set of "Good Neighbor Sam." Filming of the comedy was broken off abruptly.

Mourned Sammy Davis Jr.: "I can't believe it happened. Every member of every minority group in the world should thank God for a man who made things a little better while he lived."

James Garner, performing a comedy scene for the movie, "The

Americanization of Emily," began crying openly. "I can't go through with it," he said.

Actor James Stewart, visiting in Colorado, deplored the killing of a "vital, intelligent" President, terming it "a tragedy of terrifying proportions."

For perhaps the only time in his public life, the irrepressible Bob Hope, who has helped millions of American troops laugh through the tragedy of war, was himself crushed. Only two months earlier, Hope had received a Congressional medal from the President for services to the nation, and the President and the comedian, who shared the same birthday, had exchanged quips. Barely coherent, Hope said, "It's unbelievable. I mourn with all America and the world. I am too shocked to make a statement."

Part of the shock stemmed from the inability of many Americans to conceive that their President had been so suddenly and violently eliminated. In a Falls Church, Virginia, department store, an announcement of the tragedy was made over the public-address system. The reaction, according to one shopper, was "fantastic." "Clerks were just walking out of the store. . . . People were in a daze. . . ."

On college campuses, students simply failed to show up for afternoon classes. "I have never seen so many people break down before," said a faculty member at the University of Tulsa.

In the lobby of the Oklahoma state capitol, a woman stood wringing her hands and whimpering, "What's going to happen to our country now?"

For the moment, political affiliations vanished. Republicans joined Democrats in eulogizing the murdered President and calling for national unity in such a moment of crisis. Governor Rockefeller of New York, who had already announced his candidacy for the GOP nomination to oppose Kennedy in the 1964 Presidential election, called off a planned campaign trip to New Hampshire. "This is a shocking and terrible tragedy for the nation and the world," said Rockefeller. "May God grant strength and guidance to Lyndon Johnson as he assumes his grave responsibilities under these tragic circumstances."

Two former Republican Presidents echoed the expressions of grief. Said Dwight Eisenhower: "I share the sense of shock and dismay that all Americans feel at the despicable act that resulted in the death of our nation's President." Commented Herbert Hoover: "I am shocked to learn of President Kennedy's assassination. He loved America and has given his life for his country. I join our bereaved nation in heartfelt sympathy to Mrs. Kennedy and their two children."

At his home in Independence, Missouri, Harry S. Truman—the last person to succeed to the White House at the death of a President, and himself the target of an assassination attempt by a band of fanatic Puerto Rican nationalists in 1950—was initially too stunned to speak. He later issued a statement saying, "I am shocked beyond words at the tragedy that has happened to our country and to President Kennedy's family today."

Roger M. Blough, chairman of the United States Steel Corporation, and the man against whom John Kennedy clashed in the 1962 steel price showdown, declared, "It is unthinkable to me that such a thing can happen in America these days. I am shocked and deeply grieved."

Victor Lasky, author of *JFK: The Man and the Myth,* the best-selling book that was bitingly critical of the President, canceled three scheduled TV appearances and twelve lecture engagements. "As far as I'm concerned," said Lasky, "Kennedy is no longer subject to criticism on my part." The Macmillan Co., which published the book, suspended its promotion and distribution. "We consider the book inappropriate at this time," a Macmillan spokesman explained.

Senator Barry Goldwater of Arizona declared, "It is both shocking and dreadful that a thing like this could happen in a free country. The President's death is a profound loss to the nation and the free world."

The militantly conservative John Birch Society expressed condolences. In a telegram to Mrs. Kennedy, Robert Welch, the organization's founder, said, "On behalf of the council of the John Birch Society, I wish to express our deep sorrow at so untimely a loss to our nation of its youngest President." The Communist party of the United States offered a propaganda-tinged unction. "All true Americans, in tribute to your husband," it said in a message to the President's widow, "will not only condemn this political murder but also will rededicate themselves with greater strength to the struggle for the democratic character of our country."

Negroes were especially anguished. For them, it was the loss not only of a President but also of a savior figure, of one who had resurrected the American Negro's desire for social and legal equality again to the level of national attention. A. Philip Randolph, Negro president of the Brotherhood of Sleeping Car Porters and a leader in the civil rights movement, said, "Today, President John F. Kennedy, who was the second emancipator of black people from the serfdom of racial segregation, has been struck down by an assassin's bullet. Negroes face a challenge to rededicate their lives to complete the unfinished business of American democracy for which two presidents have died."

There were, of course, some exceptions to the general mourning. Pro football games were to play on Sunday of the tragic weekend to capacity crowds. In Woodland, Georgia, white schoolchildren applauded. In Manhattan, the late Black Muslim leader, Malcolm X, in a remark nine days later widely interpreted as referring to the assassination, declared, "Being an old farm boy myself, chickens coming home to roost never did make me sad. They've always made me glad." James R. Hoffa, president of the International Brotherhood of Teamsters, was in Nashville. Appearing on television, Hoffa told his Tennessee audience that the assassination made his bitter foe, Attorney General Robert F. Kennedy, "just another lawyer."

For many, however, the energetic President, cut down in the flower of life, loomed larger than life. A man in New Haven, Connecticut, said, with a catch in his throat, "I felt as if he was my brother. But he was more than that—he was our President."
Describing the national mood on that Black Friday, The Associated Press spoke of "citizens who felt the sick emptiness, the helplessness that death brings, especially the death of one who counted for so much to so many. . . . But there was more than that for many, a kind of stunned immobility, a desolation for which there were no words. . . . And it came so suddenly, so violently, so unexpectedly, this death of a young President. . . . The implications were in the faces, the eyes, the gestures of people."
The overwhelming response among the American people was summed up with childhood simplicity by Michele Canty, a fourth grader in Quincy, Massachusetts. Wrote Michele:
"There was no gayness in the United States the day it happened."

Abroad, a shadow was also cast over strange and distant lands. Indeed, the reaction was hardly less acute—a measure of the importance that the American Presidency holds for the world, and of John Kennedy's particular mystique.

In Buenos Aires, newspaper sirens wailed in woe. A teen-age girl in western Argentina collapsed in a trauma from which she has yet to recover.

African tribesmen gathered to hear the news from their chiefs.

In Ireland, John Kennedy's ancestral home, electric lights were switched off and candles lighted.

In London, Piccadilly Circus went dark, and a funeral bell tolled. In English pubs, as news of the assassination blared from radios, Friday evening crowds pushed back their pints of beer, abandoned their dart boards, and drifted away.

On the Continent, Frenchmen cried and Italians prayed. West Berliners marched in mourning. Denmark's liberal newspaper *Politiken* exploded in nihilistic bitterness, declaring, "It took twelve years and a world war to kill a bandit like Hitler. Just three years is what this decent and fine man got. The world must still be an evil place."

Even the communist camp was saddened. As the funereal TV panorama came in from America, a Russian woman television commentator burst into tears. Muscovites buttonholed Americans in the Soviet capital to express condolences.

Across Asia, normally impassive Orientals expressed unabashed grief. Indonesia's President Sukarno, often a vociferous critic of President Kennedy, interrupted the installation of a new Cabinet in Jakarta when word reached the palace, and ordered a moment of meditation. Although it was a holiday in Japan, people poured into the streets to snap up newspaper extras reporting the tragedy. In a village north of Tokyo, the skipper of the destroyer that had cut Jack Kennedy's PT-boat in two mourned, "The world has lost an irreplaceable man, for there is no other President who worked for peace like he."

President John Fitzgerald Kennedy was dead, but life and the world had to go on. Back in Dallas, as the President lay dying the afternoon of November 22 in Trauma Room One at Parkland Hospital, sitting just outside the room, appropriately unnoticed in the confusion, was an unobtrusive man named Ira D. Gearheart. There is no public record to show that he was even in Dallas that day. His mission, as always, was secret.

Gearheart was an Army warrant officer but wore civilian clothes on assignments in order to blend inconspicuously with the entourage that accompanies the President on trips outside Washington. His revolver was out of sight. By his hand rested a brown leather brief-case nicknamed the "football" or the "black box."

Inside that case were coded messages by which the President, and only the President, could order missiles armed with nuclear bombs against an attacking enemy. This silent courier's sole task was to keep those codes always within the quick reach of the commander in chief.

Gearheart had flown to Dallas with President Kennedy and was in the motorcade that turned into the nightmarish dash to Parkland Hospital. He waited outside Trauma Room One, silent but watchful.

At the moment that John Kennedy was pronounced dead, Gearheart quietly rose from his seat, picking up his briefcase. He walked past the Emergency Room desk, pushed open the door to a surgery room and stepped inside. There, behind drawn shades, sat Vice-President Lyndon B. Johnson.

Gearheart moved in close to the new leader he would shadow. Those few steps marked the first real, if not formal, transfer of Presidential power.

Also necessary were certain bureaucratic chores. The President of the United States earns $150,000 in taxable income a year. On the last working day of each month a paycheck is made out to him in the old, gray-stone Treasury Annex on Pennsylvania Avenue and sent across the street to the White House.

On November 22, 1963, John Fitzgerald Kennedy's pay was stopped at two o'clock in the afternoon, Washington time, because he had completed only 14/24ths of a computerized day's work. For the remaining 10 hours of that day, the Presidential salary was paid to Lyndon Baines Johnson.

There was a time when it took rather longer for word of the demise of a leader to get around, both in his own land and through-out the known world, and when the details of the event were far less complete. The speed of the news was that of a runner, a horse, a carrier pigeon, or at the caprice of an ocean wind. The relative emotional impact on the people was undoubtedly deep even at the late moment of revelation, yet they could hardly have had the sense of immediate involvement as today—and certainly society as a whole was not affected nearly so quickly. A survey of reaction to the assassination of John Kennedy, carried out by the University of Chicago's National Opinion Research Center, indicates that within 30 minutes of the President's being shot, 68 percent of all adult Americans knew of the event; by six hours later, fully 99.8 percent of them had learned the news.

The Institute for Communication Research at California's Stanford University studied the diffusion of the news of John Kennedy's shooting in a northern California city. "All of those interviewed were informed by the broadcast media or by other persons," the institute's report concluded. Underscoring the remarkable speed with which the word spread, the Stanford researchers found that 88 percent had heard of the shooting prior to the death announcement.

Political leaders, predictably, were among the first to become aware of the social implications of the video revolution. As early in television's development as the period of the Korean War, the late South Korean Premier Syngman Rhee unhesitatingly granted exclusive interviews to correspondents for TV networks, although often rejecting talks with reporters of printed media. The shrewd old strongman was so enamored of TV that he installed a huge set in his pagoda-roofed palace on a green hillside overlooking Seoul, despite the fact that South Korea as yet possessed no television station and the TV signals from neighboring Japan did not reach Seoul.

Social scientists and historians, for equally logical reasons, have also been avid speculators about the effects of the cathode tube on civilization. Probably no happening in this sphere of study has galvanized more conjecture among them than the assassination of John Kennedy. One, Richard Selcoe, an assistant professor of history at Union College in Cranford, New Jersey, stated:

"History is filled with dramatic events which no doubt people have used as benchmarks or check points for their own relatively insignificant activities. One can imagine ancient Egyptians asking: 'What were you doing when the Red Sea parted?' Our own national events have also provided a modicum of such incidents. . . . Lexington and Concord, Gettysburg, Pearl Harbor, and, of course, presidential assassinations.

"No one would claim that the assassination of John F. Kennedy was any more dramatic than that of Lincoln, or that by itself it had any greater effect on the minds and hearts of the people. Evidence gathered in the century since Lincoln's funeral train went from Washington, D.C., to Springfield, Illinois, certainly indicates the depth and breadth of emotionalism released by Booth's deed. Nevertheless, the events of November 22, 1963, do constitute a unique experience for the American people, it seems to me. The uniqueness stems from what has been called by some the 'communications revolution.' The ability of almost all people to see the great events almost as they occur has changed the psychological effects of these events. A comparison with the aforementioned assassination of Lincoln might serve to illustrate the differences.

"At the outset, it can be seen that both Lincoln and Kennedy died amid atmospheres of raw hatred and grievous tensions. (Granted that technically the Civil War had ended, it is still obvious that the 'nation's wounds' to which Lincoln had recently made reference, were still bleeding in a very real sense.) Also, both men had aroused deep-seated passions—pro and con—by their handling of executive affairs. Moreover, thanks in great part to the telegraph, the whole nation in 1865 was soon apprised of the terrible events; every newspaper in the North and some in the South carried as detailed accounts as possible. Hundreds of thousands of mourners saw the funeral train as well.

"But the nation in 1865 could not literally pause as one man and contemplate the awful occurrence, as could be done in 1963. Reading about what allegedly happened at Ford's Theater does not have the same impact on the beholder as seeing the confusion at Dealey Plaza, played and replayed. Further, when Booth died in that barn, no one, save a few participants, saw it. On the other hand, probably 20 million persons saw Lee Harvey Oswald die at Jack Ruby's hand.

"The point is that Kennedy's death became the nation's tragedy in a direct way much more than Lincoln's. The events of November 22, 1963, had a hypnotic effect. From the time of the first bulletin to the playing of taps at Arlington on Monday, November 25, a great many Americans sat figuratively glued to their sets, mesmerized by the unprecedented scenes of human mayhem and mourning. In fact, it becomes for me, among others, a lost four days."

In the past, the reaction to an assassination, the feeling of personal involvement, was leavened by time and space. Not so today. The impact television had on reaction to the assassination would seem to have been confirmed, at least in principle, by a survey made for the National Opinion Research Center by Drs. Paul B. Sheatsley and Jacob J. Feldman. In their report on public responses and behavior, the center's investigators concluded:

"The assassin's bullet that so abruptly ended the life of John F. Kennedy on November 22, 1963, created a public event unique in the lives of contemporary Americans. The networks of mass communications and personal contact spread the news with a speed that was in all likelihood unprecedented, and, instantaneously, public attention turned away from everyday personal concerns to the details and meaning of the improbable event. Probably never before were the sentiments of the American public engaged so deeply by a happening on the political scene."

"The unique character of the event," they continued, "centered around both its sudden swiftness and the personality of the man who was killed. Other events in recent times had some of the same elements, but not in the same combination. Attempts had been made upon the lives of Presidents Truman and Roosevelt, but no American president had actually been assassinated for more than sixty years, long before most current adults were born. Almost twenty years ago, within the memory of most of the public, President Roosevelt had died in office, but the Kennedy assassination was qualitatively different in two major respects: Roosevelt died of natural causes, while Kennedy was murdered; and Roosevelt, in his fourth term of office, was in his sixties, whereas Kennedy, in his first term and not yet fifty years of age, was the very image of youthful energy and vigor. Among contemporary public events, perhaps the closest parallel to the assassination, in its suddenness and its impact upon the population, was the unexpected Japanese attack on Pearl Harbor, which precipitated U. S. entry into World War II, but this event lacked the personal element that attended the unbelievable killing of the nation's President."

Thus it can probably be concluded, without overstatement, that never before in history had the death of one person exerted such an instant and powerful impact on the emotions of so many. Everyone experienced his or her own personal reaction to the death of John F. Kennedy, and the responses were as diverse as the myriad faces of mankind. Each individual's reflex was a result, in part, of his particular background and of his unique situation—all of which contributed to what amounted, in effect, to his private relationship with the President of the United States.

TEXAS

Dallas—Big D, perhaps the nation's proudest city—was plunged into the depths of an epic humiliation at being the site of the President's murder.

The audience at the Dallas Trade Mart—without any hint at the time of what had happened—was waiting impatiently for the chief executive's appearance as one o'clock came and passed. Most of the 2,400 guests had already begun eating when industrialist Erik Jonsson, the master of ceremonies, announced that something had happened to the President. "There has been a mishap. . . ." he said, and silence descended over the hall. Then, as the bewildered guests began to stir uneasily, Jonsson returned to the podium. "Ladies and gentlemen," he said, his voice tight with emotion, "I'm not sure that I can say what I have to say. . . . It is true. Our President and Governor Connally have been shot. We don't know how seriously."

The Dallas Times Herald described the scene that followed in the cavernous building:

"Then the crowd began to stir. Sobs were heard and now and then a high, near-scream echoed in the air. But the people mostly remained in their seats, whispering to each other in disbelief.

"They still did not know how seriously the President was injured. But a few transistor radios in the crowd, and the KRLD-TV mobile news unit parked behind the building, became command posts for news.

"And it was only a few, hushed minutes until the hall knew that this was the unbelievably worst news it could have heard."

A clergyman, the Rev. Luther Holcomb, pastor of the Lakewood Baptist Church in Dallas, went to the microphone. "Oh, God," he prayed, "none of us can find words to express the deepest feelings of our hearts. We realize it is a time of mourning, but we are relying upon the faith that we possess to see us through this most difficult period. Each of us comes with perhaps the most earnest prayer we have ever offered, for our President and our governor and their families."

The Times Herald account continued:

"After the oppressive first wave of silent shock, people began leaving the hall. Rows of steak lay untouched. . . . Dallas City Manager Elgin Crull, wringing his hands, said again and again, 'Nothing can be done, now, nothing.' Robert Cullum, Dallas Chamber of Commerce president, could hardly talk. 'It's . . . . horrible . . . . horrible . . . .' he said.

"A group of city leaders gathered below the speaker's platform and looked at each other in unbelief. C. A. Tatum could only shake his head. . . . Willis Tate, president of SMU [Southern Methodist University] said, 'I am so ashamed I am sick . . . . nauseated.' "

At the head table, the places set for the President and the First Lady—silverwear, china, and crystal—were untouched. Behind was the President's chair—an executive, swivel-type—empty.

State Senator Oscar Mauzy of Dallas, then a Democratic precinct chairman, had tickets to hear the Kennedy speech at the Trade Mart and met his wife there at the last minute. They were seated on the fourth floor.

"They were probably the worst seats in the whole house," he recalls. "When I got up there, I noticed that all the Republicans were seated in the good seats on the first floor and the Democrats on the third and fourth floors. As I recall, there were a number of jokes made about this. I, trying to be lighthearted and comical, said, 'Well, the reason for this is that spit doesn't travel horizontally, it travels vertically. They put all the Republicans on the first floor so that when the President is introduced and they get up to spit at him, they can't hit him. From up here where we're sitting, we could hit him, but, of course, we're not going to be spitting at him.' "

"And I said there was another reason," continues Mauzy. " 'If one of those nuts is down there with a rifle, and stands up to shoot him, they'll be easier to see down there on the main floor because they'll have to stand up to get a good shot at him, but up here they could just lean across the balcony rail and shoot at him.'

"At the time I made the remark, it was about five minutes before the President was shot.

"The first word we heard that anything was wrong came in the public announcement by Erik Jonsson, head of the Dallas Citizens Council and now the Mayor of Dallas, who said there had been an accident, that the President had been involved in an accident, leaving the inference that it had been an automobile accident.

"Well, in view of everything that had happened in Dallas in recent weeks and months, when Adlai Stevenson had come to the Memorial Auditorium and been insulted and spat upon, in view of what happened to Vice-President Johnson during the 1960 campaign here in Dallas, when he and his wife were assaulted and spat upon in the lobby of the Adolphus Hotel . . . and I was within six feet of them then . . . and in view of the climate that existed in Dallas at the time, I was apprehensive, I was fearful, that some of these right-wing nuts around here would try something. But I had also been confident that the Secret Service and the FBI were on their toes and were competent to protect the President. I was fearful that some incident might occur but I did not think it would be successful.

"I immediately got up and grabbed my wife and said, 'Let's get out of here. There hasn't been an accident, somebody's been killed.' It was pure intuition that my worst fears had come to pass."

By the time the Mauzys made their way down the several escalators through the crowds to the parking lot and their car, they had heard from an hysterical woman that Kennedy was dead.

"My next impression was that the right-wing nuts had just taken it upon themselves to destroy everyone who didn't agree with them politically. And I included myself in that latter group.

"As we got into the car and started out, I told my wife that when we got home, I fully expected to find Mary, the maid staying with our children, murdered and the two children dead. And I was sure they were looking for me, too.

"It was a totally paranoid thought, pure emotion. I didn't have any basis in fact for it . . . but that's what I thought."

As they drove home, the Mauzys passed the Texas Theater and noticed a commotion going on at the movie; they did not know it at the time, but it was the very moment when the police were arresting Lee Harvey Oswald. Everything was in order at the Mauzy home when they got there.

Mrs. David Richards is one of those durable persons known in Texas as a "loyal" Democrat. She always supports and works for the Democratic nominees, whoever the man and whatever the office. She had put in many hours during the 1960 Presidential campaign in her North Dallas precinct urging people to vote for John F. Kennedy. Although Richard Nixon carried conservative Dallas County by a landslide 149,369 votes to 88,876 for Kennedy, her efforts contributed to Kennedy's slim but crucial overall Texas victory of 1,168,230 votes to Nixon's 1,122,323.

She and other liberal Democrats in Dallas were understandably put out when they were not invited to hear Kennedy make his Dallas address at the Trade Mart. A last-minute appeal to United States Senator Ralph W. Yarborough of Texas—while he was in Fort Worth with the Kennedy party Thursday night—had paid off. Mrs. Richards, an attractive blonde woman in her mid-thirties, and a few other liberals were finally included among the 2,400 who gathered at the Trade Mart at noon Friday for steaks and the Kennedy speech.

"The people at the head table were, of course, the downtown establishment and the liberals felt as if they were unwelcome," she said. "We knew we were unwelcome. We'd had to raise hell to even get there."

Waiting for the President to arrive, she found that her mind was filled with trivia. Mrs. Richards was worried about the exotic birds and canaries flitting from the rafters to ferns and other plants in the giant room and she feared for her food. Many guests had transistor radios. Word passed from table to table on the progress of the motorcade as it wound its way through the downtown section.

"It had been in all our minds that something might happen. But not in any real sense did we think that anything might happen."

Then someone whispered to a friend two or three tables away that something had happened.

"It was just a tense place. I looked down and I saw the reporters running, on the ground floor, which was two or three floors below us. They were all running toward the back.

"This was the first sense I had that there was something wrong, or they wouldn't be running like that. We still waited a little longer. We were all frozen, and then the word started passing through that someone had been shot. Everyone was saying, 'Oh, no! Oh, no!' The girl next to me kept eating and I was terribly nervous. I couldn't figure why she'd keep eating like that when there was obviously something wrong.

"We heard that Connally [Gov. John B. Connally of Texas] was killed. My immediate thought was, 'Well, they finally did it—one of the right wingers had gotten through'—because we'd been to that Adlai Stevenson UN speech just a month before, where the right wingers were picketing and rattling bracelets while he spoke. The right wing was my immediate thought.

"Then someone got up and made an announcement. He said something like, 'There has been an unfortunate accident,' and that we were to go home.

"I had an immediate panic for my own safety, well-being. That was my immediate reaction, that I was afraid for myself. And I thought, 'I've got to get home.' I guess that's one of those returning-to-the-womb instincts, but I felt I had to get home. It was a panic.

"We all headed toward the escalator and then the word passed that it was Kennedy. Women began to cry. Still, my only feeling was I had to get home. It seemed like it was just a matter of . . . I had to protect myself . . . I felt like I had to protect the children . . . I don't know. We got to the escalator and at the bottom of it was an advertising sign display. As the people went down the escalator, they couldn't get off. The sign was in the way. So people started backing up and we all got mashed in there, with these crying and hysterical women. Then there really was a physical sense of danger, that we were going to be mashed on this escalator. Finally, some man at the bottom shoved the sign out of the way and we all kind of spilled out of the escalator.

"Someway, I found the woman I was with and we got to the car and I have no recollection of getting home. We obviously drove home. We got out of the Trade Mart and we heard the sirens but I didn't know where they were going. We heard on the radio that Kennedy was at the hospital. I don't remember just when I heard he was dead, it must have been on the radio driving home."

The next day the Richards' washed every window in their house, then went on a picnic just to get out of town.

A few moments before the Presidential motorcade reached Dealey Plaza in Dallas, 25-year-old ambulance driver Al Rike and his partner, Dennis McGuire, picked up a 20-year-old man who had suffered an epileptic seizure at the plaza site. The ambulance sped the patient to Parkland Hospital.

"We were standing around," Rike recalls, "trying to check in our man. Suddenly, all these guys came running in, raising hell with their guns. One man shouted, 'We need some stretchers,' and another said, 'Everybody clear out of here.'

"As I looked around, Vice-President Johnson walked in. He was so pale I thought he'd had a heart attack. I thought that was what all the commotion was about. But then they brought in Connally on a stretcher. He was covered with blood. And after him came a stretcher with a man's body on it. His head was covered. But I recognized Mrs. Kennedy, who was walking behind, holding on to the stretcher and crying. I realized then the President had been shot."

Rike and McGuire managed to deliver their patient, then waited around. "We were just standing there in all the confusion when a Secret Service man told us to stand by our ambulance. Then another Secret Service man told us to call our office and order a casket, which I did. Then they told us to go back to the Trauma Room where the President was. He was laying there, all bloody. When a priest gave the last rites, they asked us to leave the room, which we did."

Within a few minutes, Vernon Oneal, the owner of the funeral home for which Rike worked, drove up in a hearse bearing a coffin. Rike, McGuire, and Oneal carried the casket into the Trauma Room.

"Mrs. Kennedy was in there with us a lot," Rike remembers. "She asked me for a cigarette and I gave her one . . . it was a Salem. A Secret Service man lit it for her. I said I was sorry. She said, 'Don't be sorry for him. He wouldn't want it that way.' Then she left. It was hard. We wrapped him up in a plastic bedsheet. But his head was still bleeding so bad that I had to wrap two sheets around his head. We put a plastic sheet in the coffin, kind of lining it. Then we picked the body up, put it in the casket, tucked the sheet around him and closed the lid. When we picked up the body, I kept thinking, 'This is the President!' The feeling was like I get when we have to pick up some little child that has been hurt or killed, or a member of your own family. I have seen a lot of dead people, but this was something different. I wanted to cry, but I couldn't. I got all bloody and had a lot of cold chills.

"We took the casket to the hearse and loaded it on one side. We let down the seat on the other side so Mrs. Kennedy could ride with the body, and she smiled and thanked us. She never did break down then.

"The Secret Service men took over after we closed the door to the hearse. They drove it. We followed in the ambulance, and got back the hearse out there"—Love Field, where the casket was put aboard Air Force One for the sad flight to Washington.

The slaying brought Dallas to a halt. Its major department stores —Titche-Goettinger, Sanger-Harris, Volk's, Sears Roebuck, Jas. K. Wilson, and famed Neiman-Marcus—spontaneously closed. Dallas night life on that night was nonexistent. All movie theaters were shut, and the city high school championship football game was canceled. The Adolphus Hotel closed its Century Room, the Statler Hilton its Empire Room. The Crystal Charity Ball, one of the city's most glittering social events, which was to be held that evening, was postponed. The Dallas Civic Opera put off its opening performance of "A Masked Ball."

In one of history's insignificant but incredible coincidences, Richard Milhous Nixon, who so narrowly lost the Presidency to John F. Kennedy, was in Dallas on the day Kennedy was shot there. As the President dressed for his motorcade, Nixon rode unnoticed to Love Field and departed aboard an airliner for New York.

Nixon landed at New York's Idlewild Airport and talked with newsmen, while at that very moment in Dallas Kennedy was being accorded one of the city's most enthusiastic welcomes.

Answering reporters' questions, Nixon said that he believed Vice-President Johnson would be dropped from the Democratic Presidential ticket in 1964. Predicting that there would be "great pressure on President Kennedy to strengthen his ticket" by forsaking the Vice-President, Nixon added that Johnson had been an asset to the Democratic ticket in 1960 but that he was "a definite liability in Texas now."

After the airport interview, the former Republican Vice-President climbed into a taxi and headed for Manhattan. He will never forget that trip. The cab had reached 125th Street in Harlem when a man ran out and shouted that the President had been shot.

"My first words," Nixon recalls, "were, 'My God, it must have been one of those nuts.'"

John Newnam, an advertising man with *The Dallas Morning News*, had paused while on an errand to watch the motorcade bearing President Kennedy down Dallas' Main Street. Then Newnam strolled back to his office.

"Jack Ruby was sitting at my desk, waiting for me," Newnam recalls. "I handled the ads for his Carousel and Vegas clubs on a regular basis. Jack was leafing through the paper, milling around and just killing time, as he always did. Jack got to where he wrote his own ads, and was quite proud of the fact that he could write the copy himself.

"One of our people ran into the office and said, 'Kennedy's been shot.' We were just frozen. I looked at Jack and he looked at me. He didn't say anything at first. Then there was this expression of disbelief on his face, and he joined with all the others in saying how terrible it all was.

"Well, his ads were already in and he had paid me, so I didn't pay him any more attention. Our telephones were ringing off the hooks with people wanting to cancel all sorts of ads, because of the shooting, and we got real busy. It became utter bedlam."

The next morning, in the classified obituary column of *The Dallas Morning News*, between "Janosky Mrs. Anna" and "Lucky Carl Guy," appeared the following listing:

> KENNEDY
> President John F. Beloved husband of Jaqueline [sic] Kennedy, dear father of John and Caroline Kennedy. Parents, Mr. and Mrs. Joseph Kennedy, brothers Robert and Ted Kennedy, sisters, Mrs. Peter Lawford, Mrs. Robert Shriber [sic]. Remains forwarded to Washington, D. C. Friday.
> Oneal, Inc.
> 3206 Oak Lawn   LA 6-5221

The chagrin of the United States was magnified a thousandfold across Texas, home state of the man who was boosted into the White House by the bullet that killed John Kennedy.

Dr. Abner McCall, president of both the Baptist General Convention of Texas and Baptist-supported Baylor University in Waco, said, "It is not only the loss of our national leader at this strategic time, but a blow to the whole American tradition of freedom and self-government. The Baptists of Texas join the rest of the nation in sorrow for the family of President Kennedy and the future of our nation."

Mrs. Carole Johnson, 35, was at work in her cosmetic shop on West Berry Street in Fort Worth the day that the President was killed in Dallas. She gives demonstrations in the proper application of facial makeup, as well as in the business of selling cosmetics. She was working with a customer when a telephone call informed her of the shooting. She and her customer immediately got down on their knees and offered a prayer that Mr. Kennedy would live. Then Mrs. Johnson turned on a radio in her shop and heard that he had died. The customer quickly left. Mrs. Johnson recalls her condition as stunned, and says that she felt a palpable heaviness in her chest.

There were no more customers in her place on usually busy Berry Street until around 3:15 P.M., when a young, well-dressed woman entered and announced, "I'm here for my demonstration."

Still somewhat dazed, Mrs. Johnson replied, "But haven't you heard? Kennedy has been killed in Dallas."

"So what?" the customer said. "I have an appointment and I want my demonstration."

Mrs. Johnson mechanically went through the process of applying various cosmetics to the woman's face, all the while listening to the radio. When Mrs. Johnson finished the job, she was openly weeping. Her persistent client, who had been making small talk the entire time, finally said, "Oh, I shouldn't have insisted on your doing all this since you seem to feel so bad about what happened. Actually, the only bad part I can see is that now we will be stuck with Johnson for a President."

In Austin, site of the Governor's mansion, whose incumbent, John Connally, had been the President's host, there was mortification and chaos. "It is a sad tragedy," grieved Lt. Gov. Preston Smith, "leaving millions of Texans and other people in the country and world sad and shocked that something like this could happen in Texas or America."

President Kennedy was to have visited Austin that Friday evening to address a $100-a-plate dinner in the municipal auditorium. The shady, scenic state capital, also the home of the University of Texas (25,000 students), had awakened with a bright face that morning, confident that, whatever jeers or insults might befall Kennedy in conservative Dallas, he would receive the warmest welcome in Austin, one of the state's liberal Democratic centers. In 1960 Kennedy had carried Travis County, of which Austin is the seat, by a comfortable 5,000 votes out of 49,000 cast.

The press room in Texas' pink granite state capitol building was almost deserted as the five bells signifying a bulletin sounded on a Teletype machine. Seconds later it pounded out the news that the President had been shot in Dallas. The word quickly spread. One shattered reporter, trying to fix his mind on what reaction story he should pursue, could focus at first only on the lines in his new

herringbone suit, which he had bought earlier in the week for the purpose of covering the President. By 1:15 P.M. the press room was jammed with Texas politicians as well as correspondents. A man running for Congress on the Republican ticket who had based much of his campaign on vilification of Kennedy, his family, and everything that the President stood for showed up in tears and delivered a public apology for what he had been saying. When the word was flashed at 1:33 P.M. that the President had died, everyone left except the newsmen, who—as is their lot—began trying to find answers to such exceedingly peripheral editors' questions as what would happen to the money paid for tickets to the Friday night dinner.

Austin was affected more sharply than most Texas cities because not only did Governor Connally, seriously wounded in the Dallas gunfire, reside there, but also because the new President's LBJ Ranch was only 60 miles to the west. Elaborate preparations had been made for Kennedy's scheduled visit to Austin, and a crowd of thousands had planned to greet him at the airport. The city and its 200,000 residents were numbed by the tragedy.

Known throughout Texas as a hospitable, open-minded town because of the university students it receives and the state government that it hosts, Austin—named after Stephen F. Austin, who led the first American settlers into Texas—became silent and inward-looking on that Friday afternoon. A Dallas woman, Mrs. Wallace Ralston, was being driven to the Austin airport by her daughter at the time of the shooting. They were in a small foreign car that had no radio. They noticed people acting strangely. Some cars pulled to the side of the street, their drivers sitting motionless. They were listening to their radios, but Mrs. Ralston and her daughter had no way of knowing what had happened. The daughter stopped at a gas station for her mother to ask directions.

"I went in and there were four or five men sitting around a radio," Mrs. Ralston recalls. "They ignored my questions and I thought, 'How rude of them!' So we went to a cafe and the same thing happened, except that someone there told me about President Kennedy's being shot. He also told me how to get to the airport."

Mrs. Ralston boarded her Dallas-bound flight about 1 P.M., but it did not take off until hours later. By the time the plane landed at Love Field in Dallas, Air Force One had departed.

James E. Gardner, a chemistry laboratory technician at the University of Texas, was waiting in his office for his wife to meet him for lunch when he heard the first word of the shooting on the radio.

"My wife walked in and we listened for the rest of the lunch hour in a state of shock," he remembers. "Then she went back to work, neither of us having felt like eating, and I found that the tragedy was much harder to grapple with alone.

"After the announcement was made that the President had died, I felt I couldn't work. I wanted to get away, to get drunk, to somehow blunt this emotional storm that was almost making me sick. I went out of the Chemistry Building and headed unconsciously down the sidewalk toward a small tavern a block away. I met a dozen or so people on my walk and all appeared somber and thoughtful. As we met, we would stare briefly into each other's faces as if to verify that this thing was real and universally apprehended and not some individual and personal madness.

"I finished my beer and walked back out into the sunshine. I was inconsolably depressed. Though not particularly a Kennedy lover, I felt that the assassin had snuffed out the freshest breath of air our government had felt in a long time."

On Friday night, State Attorney General Waggoner Carr told an overflow crowd at a memorial service in the chamber of the Texas House of Representatives that he would do all he could to assist in securing the death penalty for the assassin.

Monday, November 25, was windy and cold in Austin. The sky was gray. A crowd of several hundred persons, bundled in coats against a norther that howled in from the Great Plains, gathered on the capitol grounds for a final memorial service. University of Texas bandsmen, their orange and white uniforms bearing black mourning bands, played funeral dirges. The ceremony was brief and simple. Associate Justice W. A. Morrison of the Texas Court of Criminal Appeals presided. The chill breeze ruffled his white hair as he said:

"We hang our heads in shame because he was assassinated while on a state visit here in our Lone Star State. In the future, we will be able to hold our heads high and look our fellow Americans in the face only if from this day forward we make ourselves citizens of this great Republic who are superior in every way, more dedicated in the American way of life, than the citizens of any other state in this Union.

"From this day forward, Texans must be known as progressive thinkers, just as was President Kennedy. We must abandon the ways of the Old South."

THE WEST

Clifford William Marx, the 17-year-old son of a Redding, California, sign painter, had been saving for three years to pay for a vacation trip to Europe after his graduation from high school. He worked part-time as a stock boy in a department store. John F. Kennedy was his idol. Clifford had been chosen by his class to be on the Welcome to Redding Committee that greeted Kennedy when the Senator had campaigned through northern California in quest of the Presidency.

The day Kennedy died, Clifford withdrew all his savings and flew to Washington for the funeral. He rode back home, cross-country, by bus.

Judee Wing, a ninth-grade pupil in a Bay Area junior high school in Oakland, California, wrote on that black Friday:

". . . Even the seagulls seemed to mourn his death.

"And the usual lunchtime chatter became no more than a whisper.

"Many solemn faces passed me on my way to class, and the room seemed dark and sad. . . ."

A Lewiston, Idaho, first-grade teacher, Mrs. Evelyn Powell, realizing the difficulty that her pupils would have in understanding the news from Dallas, told her class, "I want you to be good to your parents when you go home. The death of President Kennedy is something as serious and sad to them as the death of a member of your own family. So don't beg for a lot of things or ask for special favors. They'll be upset and you'll have to help them."

In Tacoma, Washington, J. (Bud) Nelson, a leader of the state branch of an ultraconservative group, the Citizens' Council of America, quit the organization, declaring that all the extremists must share the moral responsibility for the Kennedy tragedy. In his letter of resignation, Nelson said:

"Though it was a left-wing [Marxist] who wantonly assassinated our President . . . I feel that every radical, left and right, had his hand on the rifle butt and finger on that trigger. We are all guilty (morally) of fomenting hatreds of one sort or another, thus guilty of a common act of cruelty."

In Phoenix, Arizona, a distraught free-lance writer fired two pistol shots through the windows of the local office of the John Birch Society. Police said that the 33-year-old author admitted calling the headquarters of the organization shortly after the President's assassination and exclaiming, "I'll give you 30 minutes to get out of there." He then drove to the society's offices on Camelback Street, the police said, and fired a .357 Magnum twice through the window.

Melvin Durslag, sports columnist of *The Los Angeles Herald-Examiner*, deplored the fact that professional football games were held as usual on the Sunday after Kennedy died, with stadiums packed. The Pittsburgh Steelers played to a 17-17 tie with the Chicago Bears before the biggest crowd of the season at Chicago's Forbes Field. A sell-out crowd watched St. Louis defeat New York, 24-17, at Yankee Stadium. The last 1,500 tickets were sold just before game time at Philadelphia, where 60,671 watched the Washington Redskins beat the Eagles, 13-10. Washington coach Bill McPeak announced that the team was sending the game ball to the White House as a symbol of the deep feeling that the Redskins had for the late President. "I don't want to be morbid or corny," explained McPeak, "but I really feel our gang was playing today for President Kennedy and in his memory."

Columnist Durslag recoiled. He wrote:

"Extended mourning may be outmoded in the Space Age, but we still pause to wonder where dramatization ends and simple respect begins when noting the full schedule of professional football played while the late President lay in state.

"A football game at that particular time had the general flavor of a sick joke and it tended to symbolize the frightening trend toward self-indulgence in our culture . . . The fact that the games throughout the National League were well attended points up our original concern about people so self-absorbed, so coddled and so emotionally misanthropic that they are unable to forego little pleasures at a time that calls for at least a modicum of reverence."

The sportswriter quoted one man to whom he talked as saying, "I was shocked by the tragedy, and I feel as badly about it as anyone. But what can we accomplish by staying away from the football game? We can't do anything for President Kennedy now."

The columnist concluded:

"The argument is irrefutable. Nothing can be done for the late President, and in a world moving as swiftly as ours, it may be scandalously sentimental to expect more than token homage.

"But one weekend hardly amounts to a marathon bereavement, and it remains our feeling that, under the circumstances, people who had to pamper themselves with football were no credit to the breed."

Perhaps no group of individuals is more aware of its feelings, and more articulate in expressing them, than show people. For much of the American film colony, the news of the tragedy seemed incredible. Compounding Hollywood's shock was the special interest that the President had evinced for the theatrical arts, and his personal friendship with several stars. Kennedy was probably the only United States President who was an avid reader of *Variety*, which he received regularly.

Actress Donna Reed, for one, was rehearsing her television series, "The Donna Reed Show," on Stage I at Columbia Studios in Hollywood. "We were in the middle of the scene when the phone rang," she remembers. "It was another member of the cast saying that there was a report on the radio that Kennedy had been shot. We all stood still—stopped everything. Someone found a radio and we all clustered around waiting for the next piece of news. We stayed there until word came that the President was dead. I do remember weeping. And so did everyone weep. I remember saying, 'It's a terrible, terrible world.' That's an awful thing to say, but that's how I felt at the time.

"We closed down and several of us went to my husband's office. He was the producer of the show. We just sat there. No one said much. My husband and I knew him slightly. Then I remember my son called from boarding school and said, 'Don't you think we should go to church this Sunday?' The whole studio closed down. We were about the last to leave, and when we walked out onto Gower Street it was empty. And there was a silence . . . a silence like I've never heard before in a city. The silence was so sudden. We were bereft, devastated."

Groucho Marx remembers being at home that day and hearing about John Kennedy's death on television. "It didn't seem possible, like watching a movie," says Groucho. Nor could he understand why the President would go to Dallas when there had been so much concern for his safety there—"just to save John Connally's political life"—nor why Kennedy would ride in an open car. "A man of his age and position—what was he trying to prove, riding in an open car like a movie queen?" To Groucho, such an act was "false bravery."

George Burns was doing a guest appearance on Jack Benny's television show. They were on the set about to begin a scene. Someone came on the set and said that the President had been shot, and, as George puts it, "that ended us that day—that was the end of comedy for that day. Everyone was a wreck. Everyone started crying." He remembers that those on the set went to Jack's dressing room and just sat around in shock. Nobody could think of words. It was, says Burns, "like you were out of your mind—that this beautiful, handsome man parading down the street had been killed. Everyone loved him and his beautiful wife."

Director Billy Wilder ("The Apartment," "Roman Holiday," "Sabrina") recalls that he was in his office "working on some very, very insignificant comedy scene with my partner, I. A. L. Diamond, and my wife called. We stopped everything and just sat in my office and watched TV. I think we were working on 'Kiss Me Stupid' or 'Irma La Douce,' and that page, that yellow piece of paper, was left in the typewriter for two weeks, I can tell you, until the whole thing was over."

Actress Marie Wilson was home and heard the news on the radio. She felt so "badly because this beautiful, intellectual human being had been physically hurt—that he was physically hurt seemed the worst." She remembers having got tickets for her niece's birthday

54

to see "It's a Mad Mad Mad Mad World" that night. They went only because they already had the tickets. But the audience's reaction to the movie, Marie reports, was topsy-turvy; it laughed in all the wrong spots, reacted to other scenes in ways opposite to what was expected.

Lorne Greene, patriarch of the Cartwright clan on "Bonanza," was meeting with a banker. "We were just about to start talking when his secretary walked in and handed him a note. He read the note and then just sat there. He became white, the blood drained from his face. I asked, 'What's the matter? Are you sick?' He told me the President had been shot. After awhile people started running around, phones started ringing. I went out for coffee . . . to Pupi's, I think, on Sunset next door to the bank. I couldn't drink the coffee. I ordered pastry and couldn't eat the pastry. Finally I just went out and walked around."

Jerry Paris, director and a cast member (under the stage name Jerry Halper) of the "Dick Van Dyke Show," remembers that he was staging a scene with Van Dyke and Mary Tyler Moore at a rehearsal. It was a domestic scene in the living room. The show was about a birthday party for their son, and there were "a million" kids in the show. Dick and Mary were arguing about the party when "a prop man came in from the kitchen set and said the President had been shot. Everyone thought it was a joke—'Oh sure, you got to be kidding . . . Lincoln was shot, too.' But then the three of us ran into the kitchen. Carl Reiner came running in. He had heard at the same time upstairs on the radio. Rosemarie and Morey [Amsterdam] ran in, too. We all sat in the prop room listening to the radio. There Dick and Mary were, on stage arguing about a birthday party, and Bang, it happened.

"None of us felt like rehearsing after that. The show was called 'Happy Birthday and Too Many More.' It was the only show in the five-year history of the series that we shot without a live audience. We canceled Friday afternoon's rehearsal and the rehearsal for Monday because of the funeral. We usually shot the show on Tuesday nights with a live audience of about 500. But we canceled and shot on Wednesday without an audience. It was the only time we ever used canned laughter, which is a comment on the whole thing."

In Las Vegas, slot machines in the casinos were turned to the wall.

THE MIDWEST

Even if it had been a normal day, dinner would not have been ready. Charlene Minchow knew better than to start the evening meal until her husband walked in the door. There were chores to be done after he got home from work and she could not be sure how long they would take. And because she was six months' pregnant and Brenda was only nine months old, whenever possible Charlene tried to avoid unnecessary work, such as warming and rewarming the food. But it had been far from a normal day, and dinner was not ready for another reason.

The Great Plains autumn dusk was cold, well below freezing. The weather had made its contribution to the atmosphere of unreality. Before the norther had hit, the temperature had started out at a freakishly warm 60 degrees before sunrise. That was when her husband Dean's day had begun.

At 5:45 that morning, Dean had arisen to begin getting ready for work. Like many young farmers in the Pleasant Dale, Nebraska, community, he supplemented his crop income by moonlighting at a second job during the unproductive late fall and winter months. The winter wheat had been planted in September and was to lie dormant until spring, when it would grow until the harvest in late June or July.

The extra money was helping Dean gradually buy the equipment he needed to farm on his own. In fact, he wouldn't have been able to farm at all had he and his wife not lived with his parents. His father tilled his own land, but Dean had found 160 acres to use nearby owned by a retired couple who could no longer work their spread for themselves.

Lincoln, the state capital, was only half an hour's drive away. It was there that Dean worked as a receiving clerk for Lincoln Steel. His job was to check in all the structural steel stock that arrived by rail each day to be cut and welded into prefabricated frameworks for large buildings.

Early that afternoon, the wife of one of Dean's co-workers telephoned the news: President Kennedy had been shot! The word spread quickly through the plant.

"He probably won't die," thought Dean. He continued with his paperwork, feeling shocked at the fact that such an event could happen, but hopeful that the President would survive.

Then the word came on the plant's loudspeaker system: John Kennedy was dead. Although it was a long way from the 5 o'clock whistle, work ended at the plant for the day. "I'm not really worried about what's going to happen," Dean remembers saying. "They're pretty well on the ball. They'll get the Vice-President in there quick."

When Dean walked into the house that evening, he was not surprised that dinner was not ready. His wife was perched in front of the television set, and he joined her—his desire for food fading as the grim events of the day unfolded before them.

Dean and Charlene Minchow had never seen President Kennedy in person, although he had visited the state on occasion. But as they discussed the assassination, they seldom touched on the local political or economic effects that the tragedy might have. Instead, their words were more personal and philosophical.

"It makes you wonder why," Dean said to his wife. "It's easy to remember stories of other Presidents that have been assassinated. But when there is one killed in your own time, it kind of hits you. I don't understand why it happened."

"There are a lot of people killed every day," he continued. "In war, there are servicemen killed every day. But I guess we just don't think about it until there is somebody killed that's prominent in the world or somebody you know personally."

He paused and thought about his small daughter, his child on the way, and his family that would soon grow to four.

"If we're going to have people assassinating the President, we're going to have to have strong governmental control," he said. "We're going to have a police state to stop it. And then it won't be a democracy any more."

On a late Sunday afternoon—Father's Day, 1968—Ferdie Murphy Sr. sat on a metal lawn chair in the yard next to his white farm house near Troy, Ohio, a town of 10,000, 20 miles north of Dayton, on the western edge of the state, and spoke about the death of a President.

The industrial nucleus of Troy is Hobart Manufacturing, which makes welding equipment and kitchen appliances, notably Kitchen Aid dishwashers. But Troy is surrounded by sparsely populated, fertile farm country, and Ferdie Murphy, 56, has lived in the area all his life.

Enveloping his modest complex of house and barns are three fields planted with oats, beans, and corn. They total 200 acres and are set a mile back from the main highway on a dusty dirt road. A creek runs at the back of Murphy's property, and his two closest neighbors, who share the dirt road, are a surgeon and the widow of an executive at the Hobart plant. Murphy farms the widow's land for a cut of the profits. His gut tie with the Presidency is farm policy. Ferdie Murphy Sr. voted for Richard Nixon in 1960.

Yet Murphy had considerable respect for John F. Kennedy. "TV brought the candidates on a personal level," the Ohio farmer commented. "When I first saw him [Kennedy] on TV I figured he'd get elected because he's smarter." And Murphy readily supported Kennedy upon his election. "I'm a Republican, but that's beside the point. When he was campaigning I said to myself, 'If he's elected, I go along with him.'"

Murphy is short, stocky, and weathered from the sun. "I was picking corn," he remembers, "when Momma came out and told me." His first thought? "Now what the hell'd they shoot him for?" It was 5 P.M. and Mrs. Murphy had been informed by a friend's phone call.

Murphy did not rush to his TV set immediately after being told about the slaying. He just kept picking corn because he must squeeze his living from a fluctuating market. His margin of profit, he says, is not the crops but the 200 hogs a year he sells; their price can swing from $25 to $40 apiece depending upon demand. The government under Kennedy, Murphy felt, "was a whole lot better than the one we've got now."

Reminiscing about the assassination, Murphy reflected the dirt farmer's penchant for cautious understatement. "I read about Lincoln when I was a student in school," he said, "but this more or less sticks with you."

One of Murphy's four children, Ferdie Murphy Jr., 36, sat with his father and also spoke of the assassination. Murphy Jr.'s wife and two children played in the yard. His mother joined them. A clean-cut, crew-cut man, six foot two, the younger Murphy punctuated his statements with slashes of a well-muscled arm. He is a mailman. Like his father, he voted for Richard Nixon. The son concedes that "Nixon lost on the debates with Kennedy," but disagrees with his father on the candidates' respective intellectual merits. "Nixon was smarter," he says. "He just couldn't answer the questions."

Despite his preference for Nixon, young Murphy also says that "once the man [Kennedy] got to be President I supported him 100 percent. He was a good man and a good politician. He had money . . . He didn't have to be President . . . His youth made him seem closer to us.

The son can likewise pinpoint the moment that he was told of John Kennedy's death. "I was carrying mail in the 500 block of West Market street when a woman came out and told me. I went inside her house and watched some of the stuff on TV.

"I thought right away that some crackpot did it. Then I felt a definite sense of loss. JFK did more for us [mailmen]. We felt like he was doing something for us. It was the biggest loss in the last 20 to 30 years for government employees.

"He said what he thought. He wasn't wishy-washy. He was like one of your family. He had young children just like we do."

Then Ferdie Murphy Jr. expressed a chilling equation that has become almost rote in the United States:

"Anyone in public office is up to being shot."

US 30 fluctuates from two to four lanes as it crosses Indiana east to west. Once a jugular, it is now just an artery. An interstate highway is under construction parallel to it, and the durable Indiana tollway is not far away for through travelers.

Etna Green, Indiana, is about 120 miles east of Chicago on US 30. Its population is 550. In the middle of the town, on the highway, is White's Gas Station (PURE OIL). A square, spotless building with white porcelain walls, it is owned by Harold White, 42. He is a bland-looking, amiable man, with a sun-reddened bald head protruding from a white work shirt that is tucked into navy blue pants. In 1960, White voted for Richard Nixon.

"I was working and a customer drove in and told me about the assassination," he recalls. "I ran inside and turned on the TV. No-

body left that TV, that was for sure. I was even watching when Oswald was shot.

"I even remember what I'd been doing at the time—painting. It's still hard to believe. That's the stuff you read about in history books. That was the first time it ever happened in my lifetime. Of course now it's getting more common . . ."

An assassination, White says, "is always a great loss. Although Kennedy wasn't as popular as Bobby, it's a fact of the Kennedy image: John would have gained if he ran again."

Like many Americans, Harold White believes that there was a conspiracy that has not been solved. He has been to Dallas and driven the route of the fatal motorcade. But he is unsure of what the motive may have been.

Yet White was not worried about anarchy after the President was shot. "I still have enough confidence in government that it's going to go on. Nobody is that great that he can't be replaced."

Twenty-four-old Arlene Simms, a comely blond whose hair is piled in a beehive, is married, has two children and works as a waitress in the Melco Restaurant just outside of Hanna, Indiana (population 600) on US 30.

The Melco Restaurant is clean, the food is edible, and the place is homey. Posted about its walls are signs such as "CAUTION ADULTS PLAYING," "THIMK," "I HAVE TO WORK FOR A LIVING, WHAT'S YOUR EXCUSE?"

Mrs. Simms can't remember exactly when and where she learned that President Kennedy had been shot, but definitely recalls that it was the day of her mother-in-law's funeral. "Everyone was astonished and hoped he would get better. As soon as I got home from the funeral I turned on the TV."

Her memories of Kennedy's death are merged with those of her mother-in-law's passing. "It was a very sad day for us, something that tragic. He was so well liked and well loved. I definitely felt I knew him."

Arlene felt a kinship, too, with John Kennedy's youth, his children, his wife. Memories, she muses, "lingered on. TV kept it alive, kept giving a reminder. I remember the casket being pulled through the streets on the horse-drawn cart."

Arlene, of course, had read about Lincoln's death, "but when it happens in your generation it makes you stop and think what this country is coming to."

The assassination was most certainly a conspiracy, Arlene believes. "I don't ever think we'll find out who was behind it. It's something we'll never find out. Maybe our kids will read the answers in history books."

Rosemary Hertel is 22. In mid-June, 1968, she had just graduated from Drake University in Des Moines, Iowa, and was doing factory work until fall when she would start a teaching job in a town near her own, Fremont Center, Illinois.

Rosemary looks like a country schoolteacher. She has brown hair, clear skin, wears glasses, and is neatly but conservatively dressed. She goes to Chicago "whenever I have a reason to."

Fremont Center really isn't a town at all, not even a mailing address. But it is listed on the map as an hour's drive northwest of Chicago. It consists of a half-dozen homes, a farm equipment sales agency, and is surrounded by lush fields that run to the horizon. A mile away, nonetheless, splotches of housing developments are encroaching upon the land.

Rosemary lives in a farmhouse just off the main road. Behind it are two large barns, a new Pontiac Bonneville parked in one of them. Large cornfields are to the rear.

On the day of John Kennedy's murder, she was inside the high school that she attended in Mundelein, Illinois. "I was taking the Illinois state employment test. At half-time I heard someone whisper it to the test monitor. I was the only one who heard. I did real lousy on the rest of the test. I didn't believe it. Later they announced it over the P.A. system."

That night Rosemary had to work. She was a receptionist for a chiropractor, a part-time job that she held during high school. "A lot of people canceled their appointments," she remembers.

"It seemed like you lost a good friend. I saw him once [during a campaign visit] from a study hall window. Being in high school, I used to follow the Presidency quite closely." Watching the funeral on television, Rosemary felt, she said, a "dual sense of participation" in that she was "both observer to, and participant in, history."

"I don't think I wanted to forget about it, really. It's the first assassination I've ever known about firsthand. You read about things like that in history books. You usually say, 'Oh gee, that's too bad.' But this was different. To me, he was a young man being President. You know how old Eisenhower was—good old Ike."

In Sioux City, Iowa, Vaschia Michael Bohan, a dental technician, sat with his mother and stepfather, Stephan Sikerachi, watching the televised funeral cortege as it carried the body of the late President from the White House to the Capitol Rotunda. Sikerachi, 68, a Russian-born retired packinghouse worker, had been a United States resident since the 1920's. According to the police, Bohan claimed that his stepfather "cursed President Kennedy and the United States," and that a fight started after Bohan told the older man to be quiet. Bohan, the police added, said that in self-defense he grabbed a pair of scissors and stabbed his stepfather, who died.

In Cleveland, James Farmer of the Congress of Racial Equality was riding down an elevator to a hotel lobby when someone got on and told him.

"I felt as though the world had come to an end," Farmer recalls. "My first reaction was that the segregationists had shot him in Dallas. There was an early report that a Negro had been seen running from the scene and this almost killed us. But then it turned out that he had a child with him and was running for protection. . . .

"I immediately recalled the pictures of Kennedy sitting on the lawn with his children and it was impossible to believe he was dead and that such a thing could happen in America. I wondered how it would affect our cause, and, of course, I didn't know. I think it is still one of the greatest tragedies of our nation's history."

In Chicago, the reaction of Mayor Richard Daley, a close friend of the Kennedys and fellow Democratic politician, albeit of a less-genteel genre, was typical of that of millions of Americans. Told the news at a luncheon by a secretary, the normally tough-tempered mayor broke up emotionally and hastened away. Later he issued a brief statement saying, "I cannot express my grief," and ordered purple and black banners of mourning draped over Chicago's City Hall.

Other Chicago politicians were less at a loss for words. "This is more than an attack on the President—it is an attack on our system of self-government," declared Democratic Representative Roman C. Pucinski, of the North Side.

John M. Vitek, an Illinois state representative, said, "The first thing I thought of was why wasn't he in his bulletproof bubble? Why would they permit him to be exposed?"

"All the world should cry at this loss," asserted Gov. Otto Kerner. "We have lost our President, and the free world has lost its leader."

The tragedy had double significance for Kerner's wife: her father, former Chicago Mayor Anton J. Cermak, was killed in 1933 by an assassin's bullet intended for President-elect Franklin D. Roosevelt.

At State and Randolph Streets, a busy intersection in Chicago's Loop, several hundred persons who had heard rumors of the shooting of President Kennedy gathered to watch a billboard that flashes news bulletins. When the lights at first carried only political stories out of Washington, the frustrated crowd grew restless, almost angry. "Come on, come on," a man shouted.

At Michigan Avenue and Harrison Street, traffic came to a stop. A cab driver rolled down a window and shouted wildly at onlookers on the sidewalk:

"He's dead!"

"I thought he was crazy," said a reporter on the scene.

"I have only read about such things in history," mused a 25-year-old airline clerk in Chicago's Conrad Hilton Hotel. "I never believed it would happen again."

A middle-aged Negro man got on a city bus and announced to those already aboard, "The whites have tried to kill my President."

The owner of a small store in the Loop mourned, "He was a young man. . . . He had a brother killed in the war. . . . He was doing the best he could for everybody and he is dead."

"Poor Caroline," six-year-old Jennifer Stebbing, a Chicago first grader, said over and over. "Caroline has no daddy now."

"We think he is a martyr," asserted John A. McDermott, executive director of Chicago's Catholic Interracial Council. "He tried to rid our society of racial discrimination, and I hope that his murder will serve to remind all of us of the evil that is real in the racial problem. I hope his death will somehow unite the country."

On Friday night, about 100 members of the Congress of Racial Equality held a candlelight vigil in front of Chicago's Federal Building. The mourners stood in intermittent rain for more than an hour, cupping their hands around their candles against the wind and rain. Their feelings were perhaps expressed in an independent statement by U. S. Judge James B. Parsons, a Negro who was appointed to the federal bench by President Kennedy.

"Like Christ," Parsons said, "he died for the sins of religious and racial bigotry among us."

65

Reporter Don Sullivan of *Chicago's American* wrote a memorable account of one experience on the day of Kennedy's death:

"This is my story of a 528-mile train ride from Memphis, Tenn., to Chicago.

"It covers from 2 P.M. Friday . . . minutes after the President's assassination was announced, to 2 A.M. Saturday, when I debarked at Chicago's Illinois Central Station at Roosevelt Road.

"It's the story of people on a train and how they reacted to the news of the President's assassination.

"A Negro bus boy, in his 40's, said: 'Well, that makes two.'

"Asked for an explanation, he answered: 'I meant that's two Presidents who had died to free us.'

"The first one, of course, was Abraham Lincoln.

"As the train, the City of New Orleans, pulled slowly out of the Central Station in Memphis, a light rain began to fall.

"As the train slowly passed a fire station at the intersection of Main Street and Butler Avenue in the heart of the city, a fireman eased the American flag down to half-staff.

"As it reached half-staff, he secured the rope and saluted.

"I walked thru the train's 12 cars and stared into the faces of 123 people. Here's what I saw and heard.

"A middle-aged white man dressed in an expensive blue suit, leaned back in the crowded dining car. He smiled and said:

" 'Well, there's an awful lot of people made happy by this.'

"A Negro waiter stopped, stared at the man, and said:

" 'Why, you must be insane or sick! What's wrong with you?'

"The southern man was struck dumb. The other passengers turned and stared at him.

"The Negro stood rooted on the spot for a few seconds, and then turned, shook his head and said:

" 'This man is insane.'

"A middle-aged white conductor shook his head also, crossed his legs, and said: 'That Kennedy family is a tragic family.'

" 'Gosh, the oldest son, killed in World War II, a daughter mentally retarded, that little baby dies, and now the son is assassinated. That poor man. That poor mother.'

"The conductor said he voted for Nixon in 1960.

"A Negro businessman in gray suit and vest shook his head nervously.

" 'It's bad,' he said. 'It's bad for everybody. Bad for the nation. What must people think of us?'

"Someone in the club car finally received clear reception on a transistor radio as the train cleared Memphis.

"The first sound was 'The Star Spangled Banner,' played by a full orchestra as a station signed off the air.

"The passengers sat, listened, and looked as if they had been punched in the face.

"In another car two young men and a woman laughed and talked together.

"A third man, sitting apart, shook his head and criticized the levity.

"An older man sitting next to him smiled and said:

" 'You've got to learn to be more tolerant.'

"The train flashed thru a small whistlestop somewhere in Kentucky. Thru a rainstreaked window I caught a glimpse of four railroad workers, three white and one Negro, huddled around a radio in a dispatcher's shack.

"In Carbondale, the train stopped and a ragged, old news vendor tried to hoodwink passengers into buying Thursday's newspapers.

"He ran thru the train shouting: 'Paper! Extra! Extra!'

"No one bought papers. One man swore.

"An old heavy-set Negro woman said to her Negro woman friend, after the paper seller left:

" 'When they got Huey, the Louisiana papers were out an hour later.'

"At Champaign-Urbana, the train took on downstate editions of Chicago papers carrying details of the assassination.

"The 102 remaining passengers, bound for Chicago, clustered in and near the club car, borrowing a few copies of the papers.

"Nobody said much."

THE SOUTH

Across the South, where John Kennedy was the object of a special brand of love and hate because of his stand in favor of equal rights for Negroes, the reaction was—unsurprisingly—a mixture of grief and glee. However, in the pillared mansions of Birmingham's white aristocracy, as well as in the dilapidated shacks of Mississippi Delta Negroes, the first reaction far outweighed the second. Among some white racist extremists there were open expressions of satisfaction that John Kennedy was gone; in New Orleans several persons telephoned newspapers to express their conviction that the murder of the President was "God's way of solving the civil rights problem." But such a response was by no means unanimous among Southern whites. Nor was it, as the National Opinion Research Center survey indicates, even representative of the majority of them. Many white segregationists who bitterly opposed Kennedy were nonetheless appalled at the assassination of the President of the United States.

The reverberations in Atlanta, the South's queen city, were characteristic of those that swept the rest of the Old Confederacy.

Mayor Ivan Allen Jr. of Atlanta remained in his second-floor office at City Hall, pacing back and forth, as the tragic story unfolded from Dallas.

"He was such a young man, in the prime of life," Allen burst out. "He had everything to look forward to."

The mayor had canceled a trip to Washington that morning because of renewed desegregation demonstrations in Atlanta. Now, he called off a scheduled appearance on a local television station and again made plans to fly to Washington—this time to attend Kennedy's funeral. "Atlanta mourns the death of a great President," Allen said in a telegram to Mrs. Kennedy.

On the mayor's orders, all offices in Atlanta's City Hall were closed and the American flag was lowered to half-staff. The City Hall superintendent, Howard Monroe, visited each of the building's 14 floors at the mayor's direction to notify employees that City Hall was shutting down.

"In almost every department, people were hovering around their radios," remembers Monroe. "I've never seen as much grief and shock registered on so many faces."

The Rev. Ralph David Abernathy was leading the civil rights demonstrations in Atlanta that had prompted Mayor Allen to cancel his original flight to Washington. Abernathy was immersed in the nitty-gritty details of sidewalk dissent; under his direction, the marches and picketing in Atlanta were aimed at a local department store, in protest against alleged job discrimination.

At the news of the President's death, the demonstrations halted. Abernathy, pastor of the West Hunger Street Baptist Church, described himself as "shocked and appalled" by the loss of a President who "in my estimation was one of the truest great Presidents of all time."

"He belongs to the ages, taking his place beside Abraham Lincoln, Medgar Evers, the six children who were killed in Birmingham, Alabama, and all those noble souls who died to make the dream of our democracy a reality for all people. We feel that President Kennedy was one of the great friends of civil rights and the cause which we champion."

The Rev. Martin Luther King Sr. was overcome by the news. Members of the Negro congregation at Atlanta's Ebenezer Baptist Church, where he was pastor and his son, the Rev. Dr. Martin Luther Jr., was associate pastor, flocked to the church as word of the shooting of the President spread. However, the elder King, a member of the congregation recalled, "walked out of the church in a daze."

His son, meanwhile, was at his home in Atlanta, talking on the telephone to the wife of his long-time aide, Abernathy. Suddenly,

Mrs. Abernathy interrupted the conversation and cried, "It's just come over—President Kennedy has been shot." King mourned, "We've lost a real friend to the cause."

Julian Bond, a young Negro who was to become the first member of his race in this century to win election to the Georgia Legislature, was, at the time of Kennedy's death, a militant staff member of the Student Nonviolent Coordinating Committee. In Negro homes throughout his district, Bond says, "there were three pictures—of Christ, King [Martin Luther Jr.], and Kennedy."

Bond was lunching at Paschal's Restaurant, not far from SNCC's national headquarters in Atlanta, when he got the news. Recalls Bond:

"Someone came by the table and said he was shot, but at first I thought somehow it was only a slight wound. I said, 'I hope he's not hurt,' and went on with my meal. Then, back at the SNCC office, they told us he was dead.

"The office was full of people, and somebody called someone he knew in Texas. We wanted to talk to someone about Lyndon Johnson, the new President. I don't know now who this was in Texas, but he said Johnson had ties in to the oil interest and that he had blocked any real liberal movement in Texas. I guess there were two emotions that day—real sorrow about Kennedy and real fear about what kind of man Johnson might be."

At Georgia State College, a block from the state capitol, the process of education came to a stunned standstill. A student from the college strode into Gov. Carl Sanders' outer office, seeking the latest information. "Everybody just walked out of the classrooms," he reported in agitation. "Everybody. Instructors and everybody."

In downtown Atlanta, on Peachtree Street, an electric ticker sign along the side of a building disgorged the news slowly and painfully. Passersby stopped and stared in disbelief as it spelled out: "President Kennedy has been shot . . . President Kennedy has been shot . . ." But the meager bulletin left unanswered the question on everyone's mind: Was the President alive or dead?

A Negro doorman stared, blinking, at the flashing sign. "Your thoughts just don't work at a time like this," he said. "I hate it. I just hate it. I just can't think about it."

A man who refused to give his name called *The Atlanta Consti-*

tution and exulted repeatedly, "I'm glad it happened. I'm glad it happened."

County Controller John F. Still reported that one of his "toughest auditors" wept bitterly upon learning that the President was dead. As for himself, Still commented to an acquaintance, "We shot him. Me and you. What have we done about these fanatical societies? We've sat here and let them flourish."

A middle-aged woman in slacks stacked boxes of Christmas tree icicles in an Atlanta variety store window, tears streaming down her face. A thin little Negro man pushed a broom along a downtown street gutter and looked around distractedly for someone to talk to. "Say the President's been shot bad?" he said, to nobody in particular. "Jesus, help us."

A group of men was leaving the Commerce Club in downtown Atlanta after lunch. Several of them stopped for a moment at the door. Georgia's young state insurance commissioner, James L. Bentley, emerged from the building and joined them.
"Did you hear the news?" Bentley asked. "The President has been shot. He was out in Dallas and—." The men held up their hands, interrupting him. They thought it was a joke in bad taste, yet not much different from many other anti-Kennedy jokes then in vogue. One of those present even started to remonstrate with Bentley. But then Bentley's grave face stopped them all. It finally sank in. He was not kidding.

At the county jail in Atlanta, a prisoner serving a term for murder wept when he heard the news.

During the fearful interlude between the first word of the shooting and the announcement that the President was dead, jurors hearing evidence in a divorce case at the courthouse inquired about Kennedy's condition. When the word came that he had died, the judge conferred with attorneys for both sides—then made the sad announcement in the courtroom. The jury asked for and got a recess.

Many Atlanta nightspots closed. "Nobody here feels like working," explained an operator of a downtown lounge.
Another lounge operator—appealing to an interesting form of

patriotism—insisted that he would maintain business as usual. "This is the one night we should stay open," he said. "It will show that our American way will go on, and no one man or one group can stop it."

The Georgia Tech football team was running through plays at a practice session in Atlanta that Friday afternoon. Coach Bobby Dodd's immediate response was: "I keep thinking about those pictures of Kennedy and his young son . . . the ones in *Look* magazine this week. They made him look so warm and so close to his family. To think that he has been murdered is simply too incredible to believe."

The tragedy did not stop Tech's scrimmage. The players nevertheless managed to gather scattered bits of information by trotting slowly past a transistor radio on the bench.

The publisher of *The Atlanta Constitution*, Ralph McGill, in his column of Sunday, November 24, 1963, told of the scene on an airline flight that preceding fateful Friday. Wrote McGill:

"Flight No. 55 out of New York to Los Angeles via Nashville, Memphis and Dallas was filled. . . There was a long line of passengers crowded into the big jet. Some said that a man carrying a small transistor radio had heard the President had been shot in Texas. The word spread. . . After a while the captain came on the communication system. . . In a tense flat voice he said, 'I regret to inform you that our President was shot at Dallas and that he lived only about an hour thereafter. He is dead.' There were gasps and exclamations of grief and horror. A woman began to weep. . . But way back in the forward cabin a slender man, wearing a matching shirt and tie and his hair worn long in the theatrical fashion, let out an impulsive cheer, which sounded louder in the silence of the plane. 'Whee!' he said. Eyes turned. The cheerer picked up a book and tried to read.

"Two seats ahead of him a tall man with a gray shock of hair unbuckled his seat belt, stood up, and walked to stand beside the man who had seemed so pleased. He said something inaudible save to the man to whom it was addressed. This man did not look up from his book."

Elsewhere in the Peach State there was also heartache and distress —and apparent elation.

Sixth and seventh graders in Woodland were reported to have

applauded when their principal, Joseph Parham, announced the news of the President's death. Parham fired off a letter to *The Atlanta Constitution* expressing shock. Wrote Parham:

"Do we indict the children? Of what can we accuse them? Whatever be our answer, we indict and accuse their parents a hundredfold."

For his remark, Parham was reprimanded by the Woodland City Council and ultimately resigned under pressure.

By contrast, in Marietta, a third-grade teacher, Miss Ellen Agerton, described what happened when the school public address system gave out the news in her classroom:

"Almost before I could stand up at my desk, the whole class was in tears. Then we had a little prayer about it and we all cried again."

In Rome, Ben Fortson, the Georgia Secretary of State, was presiding over a meeting of the state's Election Laws Study Commission. When the news of the shooting interrupted the session, Fortson arose and told those present:

"Get on your knees and pray for the President. Pray for the country."

Moments later, the President was dead.

A reporter for the student newspaper at the University of Georgia described the campus as "numb." "This is unbelievable," he wrote. "Everywhere I saw students crying."

The Governor of Georgia, Carl E. Sanders, was in his home town of Augusta.

"I was actually out at the Augusta National playing golf with Tom Rice, the president of Seaboard Railroad, and there were some other industrialists," he recalls. "We were either talking about industry for the state or something similar.

"What they did, somebody was sent out to me on the golf course. He very cautiously came over and told me, so the other men couldn't hear, that both the President and the Vice-President had been shot. I immediately left and went in and made a call to Atlanta. There, they told me only that the President had been shot. Somebody out of Macon, some idiot, had called [and] said they were going to shoot me.

"I just couldn't believe it at first. It seemed to be almost an unbelievable situation. Then, when I found out it was true about the President, I just felt sick all over, to be frank about it. I waited around a little while. Went back and told the people I'd been playing golf with. . . . It wasn't five minutes later that I was told the President had died. I immediately left the club and went home."

Sanders' reference to the threat against himself referred to a telephone call by an unidentified man, only moments after the shooting of Kennedy, to the Governor's office in Atlanta. The man asked Sanders' receptionist, Mrs. June Darby, whether the Governor's office was familiar with what had just happened to the President. "Well," the caller said, "we'll be seeing the Governor later on."

State officials were inclined to take no chances and dispatched an additional security force of state troopers to guard Sanders.

The little town of Warm Springs, where Franklin Roosevelt died, was particularly jolted by John Kennedy's sudden death.

"Everybody in town started calling everybody else," said Joe O. Butts, a Warm Springs grocer and former mayor. "Everybody was shocked and worried to death that something like this could happen."

The event set Warm Springs citizens to remembering not only FDR's death, but the day in 1960—October 10, to be exact—when Senator John Kennedy visited Warm Springs while campaigning for the Presidency. Butts recollected that Kennedy shook hands with everyone in sight. "He must have shaken hands with everybody within two miles of him, and he was smiling all the time."

L. Duncan Cannon, who was administrator of the Georgia Warm Springs Foundation at the time of Kennedy's death, also remembered Kennedy's campaign visit to Warm Springs.

"I'll never forget how my little girl acted," said Cannon. "She didn't want to wash her hands for two or three days after she shook hands with him."

For Thomas C. Chatman, an Albany, Georgia, Negro businessman, the day left a bitter mark. Involved in voter registration drives in the Albany area, which includes Terrell County, Chatman was being indicted in federal court the day that John Kennedy was assassinated. "I was actually in court and got the news at a 10-minute break just outside. You would have thought the judge would have recessed the court, but he didn't."

On a late summer night in 1943, 26-year-old Lt. (jg) Jack Kennedy, commander of PT-109, stalked a Japanese warship through choppy waters of the South Pacific.

In the dark, Kohei Hanami, 34, a lieutenant commander in the Japanese Imperial Navy, stood on the bridge of his destroyer, *Amagiri* (Heavenly Fog). His eyes searched for any hint of the enemy.

"Suddenly," said Hanami, "we spotted an object churning up white waves about 1,000 meters to our starboard. I realized it was a torpedo boat and cried out, '10 degrees turn, full speed ahead!' "

The destroyer sliced the fragile PT-109 in half. The small boat sank with a thunderous roar, flames from its fuel tanks spewing through the darkness.

Amidst the wreckage, the young American skipper tied a rope around a badly injured crewman, clenched it between his teeth, and towed the man to a nearby island. The strain on Kennedy's back from the experience plagued him the rest of his life.

The only PT-109 crewman lost that night was Torpedoman Second Class Jack Kirksey. Kennedy wrote to his widow:

"Your husband rode the PT-109 with me from the time he arrived in the Solomons area until that night of August 1st when a Japanese destroyer cut us in two.

"If a boat captain is fortunate, he finds one man in his crew who contributes more than his share—and through his leadership, builds morale and spirit up throughout the boat. With us, Jack Kirksey was that man—and he did a superb job.

"You have the consolation of knowing that your husband died in the service of his country."

Through the ensuing years, Kennedy had kept in touch with Mrs. Kirksey, who lived in Atlanta. He helped financially with the education of her son, Jack Jr., and she was a guest at his inauguration in Washington.

On the day that President Kennedy was shot, Jack Kirksey Jr. and Mrs. Kirksey's son by a previous marriage, Hoyt Grant, hastened to their mother's apartment to comfort her. She sent a telegram to Mrs. Kennedy, saying, "Our deepest sympathy to you and your family on the loss of your husband. Twenty years ago he had the sad duty of informing me of the death of my husband and his shipmate on the PT-109. We understand and share your feelings at this time."

The next evening, Mrs. Kirksey reported, the telephone rang. A

strange man's voice asked, "Are you the Kirksey connected with the Kennedys?"

She replied that she was and quoted the man as saying:

"So you're a nigger-lover, too. You'd better stay behind locked doors. We'll deal with you later." Atlanta police quickly stationed a guard to stay with the widow.

As in Georgia, the overall reaction of grief across the South was mixed with seeds of hate.

In Jacksonville, Florida, a television viewer called station WJXT and protested:

"I'm getting damned tired of hearing all the good things about Kennedy. Why don't you tell how he told the niggers they could disobey the law and run wild in the streets?"

There was also criticism. The Jackson, Mississippi, *Clarion-Ledger*'s Tom Etheridge, wrote:

"John F. Kennedy would probably be alive today if his brother had spent less time rounding up minority-bloc votes and more time rounding up dangerous subversives."

Interestingly, white leaders throughout Dixie who went too far in drawing parallels between the President's violent death and supremacist racial violence in the South soon found themselves slapped down. The vehemence of the rebuttals was a commentary on the philosophical gulf between a sector of southern opinion and much of the rest of the nation.

The Alabama state Democratic chairman, Roy Mayhall, reacting initially to the shooting of the President, contended:

"America has been on a drunken spree of hate, and we in Alabama share the blame. We have flaunted our disrespect for our government and our contempt for the courts. . . . We have vented our hate and malice on our elected leaders."

Subjected to angry denunciations by fellow members of the party's state committee, Mayhall issued a second statement that declared:

"The people of Alabama have nothing to be ashamed of but on the contrary can take immense pride in resisting the outsiders who would invade our state and stir up strife. . . . This communist-inspired element has been responsible for the violence threatening not only the people of the South but throughout the nation."

Similarly, former Florida Gov. LeRoy C. Collins, speaking in Columbia, South Carolina, in the wake of the assassination, branded all the political bloodshed in the United States—from the dynamiting of Negro Sunday school children in Birmingham to the murder of the President—"products of environments where hatred has been preached and lawlessness extolled." "It is time," he declared, "the decent people in the South, with all their might and strength, told the bloody-shirt wavers to climb down off the buckboards of bigotry."

Retorted *The Montgomery Advertiser*: "A swinish libel."

Alabama's Governor, George C. Wallace, was among those southerners who were publicly moved. Whoever fired the shots, Wallace averred, "must be filled with universal malice toward all. . . It is hard to believe that anyone would shoot at the President of the United States."

Gov. Ross Barnett of Mississippi, who, like Wallace, had crossed political sabers with Kennedy, telegraphed the President's widow:

"I am profoundly shocked and deeply distressed at the cowardly act which resulted in the death of President Kennedy. I extend my deepest and most sincere sympathy to you and your children. May God comfort and sustain you in your great loss."

Evangelist Billy Graham learned the news while at his Asheville retreat in the Blue Ridge Mountains of North Carolina. He disclosed that he had tried to reach the President to urge him not to visit Texas.

Only a week before Kennedy's trip, Graham related, "I had such a strong premonition that the President should not go to Texas that I tried unsuccessfully to reach him through Senator George Smathers of Florida. The Senator said that the President would get in touch with me later on. I wanted to talk to the President but it occurred to me that it might sound ridiculous to him, so I dropped the idea."

Charles Evers, who had taken his slain brother Medgar's place as Mississippi field director for the NAACP, was driving from Jackson to Natchez to attend a civil rights meeting. He heard the news of Kennedy's murder on his car radio. "I said, 'Oh, my God, not him.' "

A microcosm of southern reaction to John Kennedy's assassination was provided on Sunday, November 24, by the Greenville, Mississippi, *Delta-Democrat Times,* which is published by Hodding Carter, a racial moderate.

One front-page story presented a sampling of Greenville's comments. Among them:

"What surprises me is that the whole country said wonderful things about the President, repudiating what they said in the past few weeks"—a middle-aged woman shopper.

"I'll shed no tears. I'm glad he's dead"—another woman shopper.

"I'm sorry but he asked for it"—a local office girl.

"I'm sorry like the rest of the people. If Johnson carries out Kennedy's programs, then I'm very much against him"—a local tavern operator.

"It didn't affect me but it's a bad way for a man to die"—a peace officer.

"I think if this is the act of any group, it shows the depths to which our democratic society has sunk. We no longer can remove by democratic processes but must resort to animal methods"—a young busiman.

"A lot of them are happy that he is gone but why don't they say so . . . They hated him because he was good-looking, because he was young, and because he knew he was smart for his age. They hated him because he was Catholic. Nobody asked where Truman went to church. He loved the whole world and has done more for peace than any other man. He helped the poor people like me even though he was wealthy. A lot say they are sorry, but they are not"—a 73-year-old woman.

Another page one story in *The Delta-Democrat Times* reported:

"The startling news . . . sent many local residents streaming to Greenville churches despite a pouring rainfall and the threat of a tornado in this area . . .

"Many local workers wept unashamedly as they attempted to go about their daily office routines . . .

"A scheduled Greenville High School-Greenwood football game was cancelled here in deference to the late President and as a precautionary measure because of the weather. The game will be played Tuesday . . .

"School officials felt it better to have children in school where a proper atmosphere of respect could be maintained rather than dismiss school and have many school children 'enjoying a holiday' during a time of national mourning. But the reaction to the President's death was not entirely one of consuming grief. At least one local school child is reported to have applauded the somber news and many parties were held here and elsewhere Friday night."

Still another front-page story quoted local Mayor-elect Pat Dunne as saying, "The place to settle disagreements is at the ballot box and not with guns. I'm glad it wasn't a racist who did this thing."

Among liberal southerners the mortification was especially severe, and the eloquence with which they expressed their sorrow sometimes equaled or surpassed that of their northern counterparts. An editorial in *The Delta-Democrat Times*, observed:

"All words seem trite, for we have used them so often to cover situations of far lesser magnitude that their currency has been debased. We are a stricken people and nation bereft of the ability adequately to express our feelings . . .

"It is almost an insult to him, to his office, and his fellow Americans to speak now of the personal differences many of us had with some of his policies . . .

"It is a cruel coincidence that the first and latest Presidents to be assassinated had in common an unusual concern for humanity, and specifically for the downtrodden, abused Negro minority in our country . . .

"Perhaps from the icy shock of President Kennedy's assassination may come the kind of national unity this country so desperately needs. The worst has happened. Let us pray the best is to come."

THE EAST

The news of President Kennedy's assassination hit New York City, the nation's busiest and most sophisticated metropolis, like a wave of invisible, paralyzing nerve gas. The sidewalks of New York were suddenly enveloped by an almost funereal quiet. A hush fell over Times Square, the principal sounds being only those of creeping traffic and shuffling feet.

In a Times Square barbershop, 63-year-old Greek-born barber George Mishopoulos wept, explaining inarticulately, "I cry."

Somber crowds climbed the steps of St. Patrick's Cathedral as its bells began to toll.

Amid the skyscrapers there was an all-pervasive atmosphere of shock, disbelief, and consternation. In executive suites, tense corporation presidents and tearful confidential secretaries were riveted to TV sets. Two-martini lunches ended in spiritless gloom.

An incredulous crowd had gathered outside The Associated Press Building at 50 Rockefeller Center, reading the copy slowly unwinding from a clacking Teletype in a window: "He was such a young man, such a fine man," mourned an elderly woman in the group, shaking her head.

An Associated Press general executive, William C. Barnard, was walking back to the AP Building with Paul Neville, executive editor of *The Buffalo Evening News*, after having taken Neville to luncheon at the Mayan Room, a half a block away on West 51st Street. They noticed the cluster of people before the news ticker. "I thought, 'Oh God, the stock market's crashed again,'" recalls Barnard.

On learning that the President had been shot, Barnard rather hesitantly asked the visiting Neville, "Do you still want to take that tour of the fourth floor?"—the operational hub of AP's worldwide news-gathering and distribution activities. "Hell, no," answered Neville.

"I guess it was a pretty silly thing to say, 'Do you still want to go on and tour the fourth floor?' But I didn't know what else to say."

In Lower Manhattan's Federal Building, U.S. District Judge Dudley B. Bonsal, like many fellow magistrates across the nation, adjourned court. He stood, head bowed, while attorneys and spectators left the courtroom weeping and murmuring.

Outside New York's City Hall, a man impulsively began yelling, "I loved that guy! I loved that guy!" Policemen led the man away for medical observation.

A 60-year-old New York City cab driver, Joseph Kaufman, put a hand to his head and groaned, "Those dirty bums." Then he told his passenger, "As soon as I drop you off, I'm going home. I can't work any more."

Dancer Gene Kelly was in his hotel room on Manhattan's Park Avenue:

"I was alone rehearsing a number I was going to do at a surprise party that night for Jackie Gleason. A friend called and told me the news, and I turned on the television. I remember looking out the window onto Park Avenue. Traffic was stopping. I began to cry. I had known the President as a friend. I called my wife in California and said I was coming home. I was lucky enough to get a flight out two hours later, and I spent the next three days at home with my family. All we did was watch television and mourn."

Actor Walter Matthau was alone in his apartment in New York, listening to music on the record player:

"A friend called and said the President had been shot. I shut off the music and turned on the TV. Then it came across that he was dead. The shock didn't set in for awhile—till the Novocain wore off, about four hours later.

"I wandered around the city for a while, and then into a bar (which I never do). It was like being on another planet. I had three double Scotches (which I also never do), and then I really felt like I was on another planet.

"I went to my mother's for dinner and I remember arguing with my brother. He asked why I was taking it so hard, like my best friend had died. And I said, 'It *was* my best friend.' The tremendous identification I had with him—everyone had with him—like everyone's mother or brother had just died.

"Later I walked around with my friend who had called me and we said things like, 'Anyone worthwhile either never gets heard from or gets assassinated when he gets to the top.' We were all feeling sorry for ourselves as well we might be. And then over the next four days, watching all those bizarre events on television, it was like some fantastic script writer had gone berserk writing crazy things, and all those things were really happening. When you see things like that on television or in a theater or in the movies you have the privilege of just saying this is bad writing. But here was all this bad writing really happening."

Singer Barbra Streisand was shopping for a bracelet in an antique jewelry shop on Manhattan's West 47th Street:

"I remember all the radios were on and they were all saying he was shot, and I thought he must have gotten shot in the arm—I never thought it would be fatal. And one of the clerks said it was the head.

"And I thought, no, it couldn't be, it must be some Orson Welles trick. It turned my stomach and we, my business manager and I, had to get out of there. We went into the car, and we were driving and listening to the radio when the radio said slowly, 'John . . . Fitzgerald . . . Kennedy . . . is . . . dead.'

"It was such a shock, so incredible, it didn't leave any time to tell him you liked him, that he was a great President. Had he been alive a few hours, he might have known people cared.

"I was going to go somewhere, but I decided to go home. But first we pulled the car over on 57th Street and just sat. I was depressed for a long time. I felt terribly guilty about the bracelet, about being in a jewelry store then. . . He was really a storybook President."

Robert F. Wagner Jr., the Democratic mayor of New York, was told the news while at a luncheon with several other city officials. Heading back to City Hall in his limousine, the mayor barely spoke.

As his car stopped for traffic lights, pedestrians and construction workers who recognized him called out, "Is it true?" Wagner had the limousine halt at St. Vincent Ferrer Roman Catholic Church, at Lexington Avenue and 65th Street, and went in alone to pray. A week earlier, John Kennedy had been in New York for an address to the city's Protestant Council. "My wife and I then picked him up at the Carlyle Hotel," Wagner remembers, "and then we drove down to the Hilton. And he was talking about the campaign in '64 and somebody took a picture of the three of us, and the President sent it to me just after my wife died . . ."

At the United Nations, U.S. Ambassador Adlai E. Stevenson was advised of the news while lunching with members of the Chilean delegation. Frank Carpenter, press officer of the U.S. mission, hurried into the room.

"I went in and spoke to Mr. Stevenson immediately and asked him to excuse himself," Carpenter recalls. "At the door of the dining room I told him that the President had been shot and that it looked very serious. The expression on his face was one of complete shock, and he stepped back a moment. Then he went in and told a member of the delegation what had happened, and the word flew around the table."

Stevenson, who had been beset by a hostile conservative mob in Dallas a month earlier, commented, "It's too bad that in my old age, they couldn't have spent their violence on me and spared this young man for our nation's work."

Stevenson disclosed that he had expressed the view that the President should not go to Dallas. While crossing the street returning to the U.S. Mission building, Stevenson muttered, "Maybe I should have *insisted* that he not go to Dallas."

"We went into the elevator," Carpenter adds, "and on upstairs and then we rolled a portable TV set into the office. When the death was announced, there was immediate silence. Stevenson was quite poker-faced. His first thought was that he had to get some word of consolation to Jackie and the family. He dictated telegrams, then wrote out a statement of two or three paragraphs in longhand on sheets of white government paper."

In the UN General Assembly that afternoon, delegates led by the Soviet Union's Nikolai Fedorenko lined up and passed by Stevenson to extend condolences.

On Lexington Avenue a group of persons was peering at a small TV set in an appliance store window. A poignant description of their mood was given by John Ciardi in *The Saturday Review*:

"I could not hear the sound and I could half make out only a picture of a serious-faced announcer, but neither sound nor picture was necessary. The crowd had that look about it—how does one describe it?—as if each man had peeked around a corner of his own life and had been stopped by what he saw."

The first word of the shooting of President Kennedy reached the floor of the New York Stock Exchange—where no radios are allowed —at about 1:40 P.M. from brokers' offices by telephone to their clerks, who are posted around the edges of the two cavernous trading rooms. The result was pandemonium.

"The first thing I noticed was one of the members running over to a trading post, the type of guy who never runs," recalls George Hunter, a Stock Exchange official on the floor at the time. At the same moment, he caught another signal.

"You could tell something happened from the sound on the floor," he said. "You get a different tone. Almost like a baby crying, you know if he's hurt. After you've been here awhile you hear it and know something's going on."

Richard Callanan, another Stock Exchange employee who went to the floor with the first reports of the disaster in Dallas, also remembers the sound, "this terrific roar," which he heard when he walked through the door. "You couldn't define the noise. It was entirely different from the sounds normally associated with the market—a very high level and consistent level of sound, voices completely indistinguishable, of course."

"The annunciator boards went white," said Hunter, referring to the huge black panels on the walls of the trading rooms that clack out black metal plates with white numbers to notify the brokers on the floor that they have orders waiting for them.

A riptide of rumors and confused reports spread across the floor as brokers sought to execute trades and at the same time find someone with solid information.

"Trying to get the real story, that's what the real trouble was," Hunter says. "The market was going wild. It wasn't panic, but it was the nearest thing to it. It was an avalanche of orders, odd lots, everything. It really snowballed."

"Everybody was moving around at an exceptionally rapid pace,"

Callanan relates. "As I passed by several of the phone booths I could see the clerks writing out orders, and as much as you could see they were all red ones"—orders to sell.

At the information desk between the two trading rooms, supervisors of the Exchange were rushing up with slips reporting stock issues in which trading had been halted because of the enormous pressure of sell orders. In the Exchange lobby, the elevator starter was using most of the Exchange's nine elevators for fast shuttle trips to the seventh-floor members' dining room to bring brokers caught at lunch by the news back to the trading floor.

Hunter recalls, however, that he saw no one lose control of himself "except that one broker running" (running is not permitted on the floor).

The scene was also described in a special Stock Exchange research report on the effect of the assassination on the stock market. Calling the immediate reaction "a selling wave of panic proportions," the research paper reported:

"Shortly after the news of the shooting of President Kennedy became known, a deluge of sell orders hit the market. Prices weakened in a panic. By 1:49 P.M. the tape was one minute late. Communication lines between customers and their brokers and between member firms and the floor were overwhelmed. By 1:55 P.M. the tape was five minutes behind."

Finally, by about 2 P.M., seven governors of the Exchange, a bare quorum, were rounded up and a decision was made to close trading.

Walter Frank, vice-chairman of the Board of Governors; Exchange executive vice-president Edward C. Gray, and Exchange secretary John J. Mulcahy Jr. appeared on a small marble balcony overlooking the main trading floor. Gray, in the confusion, still had a cigar clamped between his teeth, forgetting the Exchange strictures against smoking on the floor.

At 2:07 P.M. Frank rang the gong once to halt trading, and, shouting over the bedlam on the floor, called out, "The Exchange is closed."

Because of the din, many traders did not hear either the gong or Frank's shout, and trading continued for about a minute after the gong until the word was passed to all corners of the trading rooms. When trading finally stopped, the tape was 13 minutes late.

Between the arrival of the first news and the closing, an estimated 2,603,000 shares changed hands, an average of almost 100,000 shares a minute, or five times the rate earlier in the day. Prices on the market—measured by the Dow-Jones Industrial Average—fell

21.16 points below Thursday's close. Concluded the Exchange research report:

"In statistical terms, the drop in prices on the New York Stock Exchange on November 22 was not as severe as in other major market breaks of recent years. But the intensity of the 27-minute sell-off that afternoon has never been matched. By closing the market 83 minutes early, the Board of Governors of the Exchange averted what could have become the worst one-day decline in history."

At the time of the closing bell, the announcement had not yet been made that President Kennedy was dead. Yet the stock market response to the shooting itself was a reflection of the nation's initial shock and confusion. Hunter says that "the question really was whether, because of the pressure business, people realized the implications."

For Boston, the President's home, the tragedy was like a death in the family. "It's as though there isn't a smile left anywhere in Boston," wrote a reporter for *The Boston Traveler*.

As those familiar with Boston society can attest, the Kennedy clan was never really accepted by the city's Back Bay Establishment— the aloof, Protestant bluenoses, many of them descended from colonial New England families, who make up Boston's Brahmins. The Irish Catholic immigrants of Joseph P. Kennedy's origin were beyond the pale.

For all that, Joseph Kennedy had succeeded in getting into Harvard at a time when, as one Bostonian puts it, Irish Catholics "were just tolerated." That citadel of learning in Cambridge, near Boston, later schooled his four sons. From Harvard's ivy-covered halls his second son, John, lured into public life the McGeorge Bundys, the John Kenneth Galbraiths, the Edwin Reischauers, and other intellectuals who, as New Frontiersmen, spawned a new Boston inner sanctum that rivaled—and in many ways eclipsed—the Brahmins on Beacon Hill. Thus, John Kennedy as President symbolized a certain background—the idealistic, often naïve, but relentlessly intellectual "Harvard circle" of thinkers, dreamers, and planners.

For members of this academic in-group, the rise of John Kennedy to power in Washington altered their cloistered lives forever; his fall was a devastating personal loss. Their reaction is perhaps typified by Reischauer, who was Kennedy's ambassador to Japan:

"I was in Japan at the time. My wife [a Japanese] had a tremendous admiration for Kennedy. After his death, she was so disillusioned, so little attracted by Johnson, that she was eager [for me] to leave the job. I told her that we couldn't leave, that we were needed now more than before."

In Boston's plebeian precincts, bars and restaurants were full but the patrons strangely silent. "What the hell is the world coming to?" said one customer. He began crying softly.

In another bar, a man sat drinking heavily as a radio played "Hail to the Chief." He stared at it hypnotized but winced when it began broadcasting recorded excerpts of Kennedy's speeches. "God, I can't stand to hear his voice," said another man. "I've been trying since yesterday to get drunk and I can't."

Two women—one elderly, her hands worn from toil, the other a matron wrapped in mink—stood on the sidewalk at Charles Circle listening to a transistor radio, their paths briefly joined by grief.

From Boston Common, a 105-mm. cannon boomed every half hour in mournful salute, by order of Gov. Endicott Peabody. Said one Bostonian: "They ought to stick the bastard who shot him in front of it."

Mayor John F. Collins ordered City Hall closed.

Students of Roman Catholic Boston College gathered in the school's library to pray for the repose of John Kennedy's soul. Organizations ranging from the Bunker Hill Monument Association to the Massachusetts branch of the Catholic Daughters of America canceled meetings.

The symbols of mourning appeared everywhere. Churches were draped with crepe. Department stores drew curtains across their Christmas-decorated windows.

Scores of persons filed by the house where Kennedy was born, at 83 Beals Street in suburban Brookline, stopping to read its bronze plaque. Visitors also trekked to Brookline's Holyhood Cemetery to pray at the Kennedy family burial plot, one man arriving at three in the morning, the police officer on duty at the cemetery noted.

In South Boston, a giant billboard stood mutely bordered in black, displaying only the legend, "NOVEMBER 22, 1963."

To Boston's Roman Catholic hierarchy, the first Catholic President of the United States was not only a political favorite son but a spiritual protégé. Richard Cardinal Cushing, who officiated at John and Jacqueline Kennedy's marriage in 1953, and who delivered the sermon at Kennedy's inauguration, declared:

"Every inhabited section of this earth is in sorrow over the terrible tragedy that deprived our country of one of its greatest Presidents, and the world of one of its most courageous leaders.

"My heart is broken with grief . . .

"John Fitzgerald Kennedy, known to me for a lifetime, loved by me as a devoted friend, has laid down his life for us all. . .

"Greater love than this no man hath. . .

"May the martyrs of all time lead him into paradise. . ."

Local leaders of other faiths were equally eloquent in their eulogies.

Said New England Methodist Bishop James K. Mathews:

"We must all bear a measure of responsibility in view of our unwillingness to be the people our religious heritage demands we be."

The Rev. Albert J. Penner, president of the Massachusetts Congregational Christian Conference, said, "This act reveals the awesome power of evil in our society and the depth of malice in the human heart."

Praising Kennedy as "a genuinely religious person and as a bona fide spokesman of Americanism," Rabbi Joseph S. Shubow of Boston's Temple Moshe added:

"From now on it will always be Lincoln and Kennedy, just about a century apart, who have clasped hands in an effort to unite the human families as the children of the One True God, as fellow human beings, as American citizens, black and white, yellow and brown, Catholic, Protestant and Jew, in one universal embrace of a divine will to live together in honor and peace.

"President Kennedy, *alav ha-Shalom* [peace be unto him]. . . "

By the day after the funeral, even in Boston, life was slowly returning to usual. Thoughts again turned to Christmas shopping. Unemployment offices in the city reopened for a busy day, receiving 16,000 persons who had been scheduled to pick up their checks.

"The sun will rise again," said the Massachusetts lieutenant governor, Francis X. Bellotti. "Life will go on, but it will never be the same."

THE CAPITAL

In Washington, the great engine of government of the United States was severely jarred by the assassination of its President, but it never missed more than a few beats—or its essential stability. The psychological concussion, nonetheless, struck the nation's capital like a bombshell.

Virtually every Federal agency came to a temporary halt as employees were dismissed an hour or more early. "There wasn't any work being done anyway," explained an official of the General Services Administration.

Stunned crowds gathered outside the iron picket fence in front of the White House to stare at the executive mansion whose incumbent would rule from there no more.

The Secret Service stationed a guard in the office of Speaker of the House John W. McCormack; the 71-year-old Massachusetts Democrat was next in line to succeed to the Presidency after Vice-President Johnson. McCormack was eating lunch in the House restaurant when reporters told him the news. "My God! My God!" he exclaimed. "What are we coming to?"

Compounding the shock for a time was a rumor that swept the capital that Johnson had suffered another heart attack. The report was hurriedly denied by Frank Valeo, secretary to the Senate Democratic majority bloc, after a check with the White House.

Johnson described his own reaction in a statement to the Warren Commission on July 10, 1964:

"It was Ken O'Donnell [a White House aide] who, at about 1:20 P.M., told us that the President had died. I think his precise words were, 'He's gone.' . . . I found it hard to believe that this had happened. The whole thing seemed unreal—unbelievable. A few hours earlier, I had breakfast with John Kennedy; he was alive, strong, vigorous. I could not believe now that he was dead. I was shocked and sickened."

It was just after 2:30 P.M. in the Pentagon. Friday at the sprawling headquarters of the U.S. Defense Department is usually the most relaxed day of the work week. Like executives of any huge corporation, the "brass" of this huge military nerve center, where 27,000 persons are employed, try to clean up their desks for the weekend. Thus, the principal physical activity under way on that Friday afternoon consisted of the last, frantic preweekend paper-shuffling.

In the Pentagon press room, there was an air of boredom. It was quiet, and, AP Pentagon correspondent Fred Hoffman remembers, "there weren't any messages from the office to be answered." An enlisted Navy journalist, in Hoffman's words "a young kid who'd gained quite a reputation as a practical joker," stuck his head in the door.

"Hey," said the sailor. "The President's been shot!"

"Go soak your head." "Yah, knock it off." "Nuts." "Funny, funny."

No one believed him.

As moments passed, however, something stirred the reporters' curiosity. Maybe it was a sudden increase in human traffic toward the Defense Department wire service machines just across the hall. Somebody went to look.

Within the concentric walls of the Pentagon, behind cordons of top-secret security personnel, are the so-called "war rooms" of the American military commands. The rooms connect the President, the Secretary of Defense, and their trusted inner circle with farflung bases around the world. Orders that could spell life or death in this nuclear age flow through these Pentagon communications hubs.

In military parlance, the war rooms are called operations centers. There is one for each of the three services—Army, Navy, and Air Force—to coordinate the actions of its respective branch. Highly trained men, working in shifts around the clock, sit in front of giant consoles. On small, slick-surfaced boards that look much like a child's magic-marking slate, are posted the names of all key defense officials and their exact whereabouts, whether in their offices or on a trip. At each console controllers' fingertips are jack plugs that can put him into instant touch with any U.S. military base or command. From an adjacent soundproof room, fitted with a long table and deep leather chairs, the decisions are actually relayed. Telephones plugged into the table where the secretaries, the generals, and admirals sit allow them to speak to a commander anywhere in the world, while the graphics of strategy—slides of maps and charts—are flashed onto a screen to pinpoint any pertinent data.

On the day that President Kennedy was in Dallas, Secretary of Defense Robert S. McNamara was meeting in the Pentagon with a few of his top advisers. In the group were Deputy Defense Secretary Roswell Gilpatric, Presidential aide McGeorge Bundy, and Dr. Jerome B. Wiesner, on leave from the Massachusetts Institute of Technology to serve as Kennedy's science assistant. The meeting was interrupted when an aide walked in and, without saying a word, handed a slip of paper to McNamara.

"As he read it," Wiesner says, "McNamara looked so frightened. He looked so upset, his face was white. The only thing I could think of was: Someone has dropped a nuclear bomb. McNamara read the note, then he stood up at the end of the table, and for a long time he didn't say anything. Then the note was passed around. As I recall, it was Ross Gilpatric who finally said to me, 'I think we should tell you. The President has just been shot.'"

The meeting broke up hurriedly. The Secretary asked Bundy to dispatch a message to Secretary of State Dean Rusk, then flying over the Pacific with five other Cabinet members for trade negotiations in Japan. The Joint Chiefs of Staff canceled a scheduled afternoon meeting with a visiting delegation of West German military leaders and hastened into emergency session. The Pentagon chiefs have standby power to order the nation's defenses from DEFCON Five (the name for normal peacetime status) to DEFCON One (an all-out war alert).

As the top brass gravely studied the situation, confusion and momentary fears were sweeping through Washington. Just as Lyndon Johnson had initially suspected that the shooting might be part of a subversive conspiracy, so did some officials in Washington momentarily speculate that the slaying might be a prelude to an attempted overthrow of the government.

The darkest fears soon vanished. Through the war rooms' maze of

95

communications, Secretary McNamara and the Joint Chiefs of Staff ordered all United States bases around the globe onto an alert, but no extraordinary alarm was sounded. As part of their normal operations, bombers of the Strategic Air Command were already flying within range of prearranged potential targets, while others warmed up on runways at key bases. In underground silos and launching pads were more than 500 intercontinental ballistic missiles capable of raining destruction on any attacking enemy nation, while Polaris submarines armed with nuclear-tipped rockets patrolled under distant seas.

But not a shot was fired except in honor of a fallen commander in chief. At every American army base, in every part of the world, one artillery gun boomed on the half hour from reveille to retreat on the day after John Kennedy was assassinated. It was a cannon's dirge for a lost leader, characterized in General Order No. 50, which was read at parade formation to all troops, at all bases, and was the official Defense Department announcement of Kennedy's death.

In the brief communique, Secretary McNamara said:

"The world has lost a gallant spirit whose championship of freedom and opportunity will be recognized in history. All members of the armed forces whose welfare was his concern can pay no better tribute to his memory than to carry on in the tradition which he shared, of which he was so proud."

The national Capitol, meanwhile, was quickly closed to tourists. The House of Representatives was in recess for a long weekend, but a few House committee meetings were under way; they were adjourned. One group in session was the Ways and Means Committee, which was conducting a hearing on medical care for the aged —one of John Kennedy's pet legislative projects. The hearing was suspended for a week.

Congressional critics of the President were as appalled by the assassination as were his supporters. House Republican Leader Charles Halleck labeled it "an unspeakable crime against all the people of this country."

Georgia's venerable Representative, 80-year-old Carl Vinson, had been a member of Congress when a stroke felled President Woodrow Wilson, when President Warren Harding died in office, and when death struck President Roosevelt. Vinson could have expected to experience no such additional tragedies of state; only four days earlier he had announced that after his current year in the House—his 50th—he would not seek reelection.

The white-maned Georgian, dean of the House and chairman of its Armed Services Committee, was in his office that afternoon when a clerk of the committee came in and told him that President Kennedy had been shot. Vinson went at once to the House Speaker's office to confer with him. Later, Vinson declared, "I am stricken with horror and grief," terming the day "the most tragic in the history of our Republic." Vinson was at the airport early Friday night when Kennedy's body arrived from Dallas.

A fellow Georgian, Representative Charles L. Weltner of Atlanta, was driving back to his Washington office from lunch. "A man saw my Member of Congress tag," he said, "and stopped me and told me the President had been shot. I didn't believe him. At the next light, I pulled alongside a car and asked what had happened. They said the President was in critical condition. I still couldn't believe it."

The Senate was desultorily debating federal library services. By coincidence, the President's youngest brother, Democratic Senator Edward M. (Teddy) Kennedy of Massachusetts, was temporarily presiding.

One of Teddy Kennedy's aides approached the dais and whispered the news in his ear. "No!" gasped Teddy. He immediately left the chamber, and Senate Majority Leader Mike Mansfield of Montana recessed the body "pending developments."

Before the Senate adjourned—and before the President's death had been announced—the Senate chaplain, the Rev. Frederick Brown Harris, a Methodist, led the chamber in prayer:

"Our father, though Thou knowest that this sudden, almost unbelievable news has stunned our minds and hearts, as we gaze at a vacant place against the sky, as the President of the Republic goes down like a giant cedar green with boughs goes down, with a great shout upon the hills, and leaves a lonesome place against the sky, we pray that in Thy will his life may still be spared.

"In this hour we cry out in words that were uttered in another hour of deep loss and bereavement: 'God lives! And the government at Washington still stands.'

"Hold us, we pray, and the people of America, calm and steady and full of faith for the Republic in this tragic hour of our history.

"God save the state and empower her for whatever awaits for the great world role she has been called to fill in this time of destiny."

In a sermonette of his own, Oregon's Democratic Senator Wayne Morse declared, "If there was ever an hour when all Americans should pray, this is the hour."

Georgia Senators Herman E. Talmadge and Richard B. Russell were in the Marble Room off the Senate chamber with several fellow senators. A page boy strode in and said, "The President has been shot."

Talmadge repeated the words for several senators who had not understood. Those present hurried to gather around wire service Teletypes, or rushed for the Senate secretary's office in search of more information.

"I had a numb feeling all over," said Talmadge, "pretty much the same as I experienced in combat in the South Pacific."

The Senate's 33 Republican members unanimously expressed their profound sorrow. The GOP bloc, led by Everett Dirksen, passed a resolution that, although touched with rhetorical flourishes, was undoubtedly a genuine expression of Republican sentiment:

"Whereas Almighty God in His infinite wisdom which passes all understanding has seen fit to take from this nation our distinguished Chief Executive, John Fitzgerald Kennedy, who according to his lights and his talent gave to this nation and to the world the benefit of his wisdom, his prudence, his experience, his courage and his leadership, and

"Whereas the late President John Fitzgerald Kennedy, as a former colleague in the United State Senate, maintained with the Republican members of the Senate of the United States a cordial and understanding relationship which endeared him as a friend and a fellow public servant,

"Be it resolved that the Republican conference of the United States Senate, speaking for all Republican members, express their profound regret and sorrow over his untimely and tragic passing, and as a token of our recognition of his service that we extend to Mrs. Kennedy and to all of the family our sympathy and heartfelt sorrow in this tragic hour, and that a copy of this resolution be tendered to Mrs. Kennedy and to the family of the late President in their hour of bereavement."

In a separate statement, Dirksen advanced the belief that only a deranged mind filled with hatred could have cut down "a great leader of the greatest nation on the face of the earth."

Republican Senator George D. Aiken of Vermont issued a personal prediction.

"This will have an unimaginable effect upon this country and the world," he said. "Much of our thinking will have to be redone."

The Congressional Record for that day was bordered in black.

The nine Justices of the United States Supreme Court were in a closed conference, considering appeals that had been argued during the week, when they heard the news from a court aide. The conference was immediately adjourned.

Chief Justice Earl Warren, describing himself as "stunned and shocked," rushed out a statement asserting, "A great and good President has suffered martyrdom as a result of the hatred and bitterness that has been injected into the life of our nation by bigots. . ."

Throughout the capital, diplomatic receptions and other social functions were canceled. Condolences poured in from foreign diplomatic missions. Announcing that Israel had ordered three days of national mourning, Israeli Ambassador Avraham Harman said:

"The people of Israel today are plunged into mourning and join in the sorrow and grief of Americans. The assassination of President Kennedy is a great blow to the whole world."

French Ambassador Herve Alphand declared that "the tragic death of President Kennedy has deeply moved the French people. . . He died as a soldier."

"It is in this terrible hour," said Yugoslav Ambassador Veljko Micunovic, "that the life work of John F. Kennedy to attain a better, more just and happier world, which would be founded on the cooperation and peace among nations, emerges to its fullest measure."

The Council of the Organization of American States, convened by council president Gonzalo Fazio of Ecuador, eulogized President Kennedy for "his enduring contribution to the cause of Pan Americanism." The OAS ambassadors then stood for a moment of silent tribute.

British Ambassador Sir David Ormsby Gore—a personal friend of the President and his wife—said, "This horrible, wicked, and sinful act has deprived not only the American people but the world of a great and wonderful man."

From across Lafayette Square opposite the White House came the mournful tolling of the bells of historic St. John's Episcopal Church.

Promptly, however, the reins of government responsibility were picked up again. With six Cabinet members on a jet plane over the Pacific en route to Tokyo, their seconds in command took over. Acting Secretary of State George W. Ball, substituting for Dean Rusk, summoned an emergency meeting of top State Department officials. Among the department's acts, it sent out formal notifications of the President's death to the heads of all diplomatic missions in Washington, and to all U.S. ambassadors abroad.

After the first moments of shock in the nation's capital, the consternation was balanced by instinctive confidence that government would go on.

"In the face of so sudden a tragedy," Senator J. W. Fulbright said, "we should be thankful that we have tested institutions of government which will continue to function in an orderly manner. We are also fortunate that President Johnson is a man of long and broad experience in government. Confronted with this tragic emergency, all Americans should unite behind our new President and demonstrate the strength of democracy to ourselves and to the world."

And Texas Republican Senator John G. Tower said that "there are no words to express my shock and dismay. . . Our Republic has survived these crises before, in other places and in other times. The knowledge that it will also survive this crisis, however, does not lessen our remorse that such a blow should be struck to our nation."

As always, there were the bizarre occurrences.

Malcom B. Kilduff, President Kennedy's assistant press secretary, was on the Dallas trip because his superior, White House press secretary Pierre Salinger, was flying to Tokyo with the Cabinet mission for talks with Japan. Kilduff had the task of announcing to the press and to the world the death of John Kennedy. Kilduff remembers well one of those isolated little instances that are nothing more than inconsequential passing moments in one's life but remain forever etched in the mind.

In the wake of the assassination, he had been awake for most of two days and nights, numbed by the tragedy and his own role in those historic hours. He had flown back to the White House with the body of the President. The nation watched as all television networks recorded the mourning in Washington.

On the third day after the tragedy, in his White House office, Kilduff's phone rang. "I remember it so well," he says. "It was a lady from Louisiana."

" 'Hello,' she said. 'I think it's just terrible—all these things we see and hear on television.'

"I told her, 'Maybe you'd better turn it off.'

" 'But it's the only enjoyment my children get!'

" 'Then maybe you'd better turn it back on,' I told her. I was trying to be nice. But it was sort of unreal.

" 'But it's the only enjoyment my children get. Honestly, what they're seeing is so upsetting to them. With all the cartoons taken off, and with the theaters closed and no other entertainment, just what am I to do with my TV set?'

"Lady," Kilduff remembers saying, "you can take your television set and—." The rest of his reply is unprintable.

In front of the White House, a lone picket appeared parading with a hand-painted sign that read:

"I warned JFK and God punished him."

Hickory Hill, the sprawling McLean, Virginia, home of Robert F. Kennedy and his large family, was a perennial gathering place for men of the New Frontier. On the afternoon of November 22, 1963, Kennedy had taken two guests home, U.S. Attorney Robert Morgenthau of New York City and Morgenthau's chief assistant, Silvio Mollo. Kennedy took a quick swim in the backyard pool, then rejoined his guests.

"We were eating lunch by the pool," Morgenthau says. "I had gone down to Washington for a meeting on organized crime, and the Attorney General invited me and my assistant out for lunch. The four of us, and Ethel, were eating tunafish sandwiches. It was nothing elaborate.

"I remember there was a man who was working on the house, hanging shingles, and he had a transistor radio. He ran over to Mrs. Kennedy and told her the radio said the President had been shot. We first thought the man didn't know what he was talking about. The phone by the pool had rung—it all happened simultaneously—and that's why the Attorney General didn't hear the work-man."

The caller was J. Edgar Hoover, director of the FBI, with an urgent message for Kennedy. While the President's brother listened to Hoover, Morgenthau recalls, "Kennedy's reaction was one of horror, I would say. We saw the Attorney General clap his hand to his mouth and turn away, and we knew it was true. Kennedy then said, 'The President's been shot in Dallas. It may be fatal.'"

The group all went inside the house. "We sat downstairs and watched the television. Kennedy was upstairs, where he had a bat-tery of telephones. I remember on the television they had just said there was nothing new to report, and Kennedy walked in and said, 'He's dead.' That's all he said. He walked out, and I didn't see him again for quite some time.

"I'd always thought that there was a possibility that Robert Ken-nedy would be assassinated, but I never thought it would happen to JFK. That thought had never occurred to me. But I guess when it happens once, you figure it can happen again."

THE KENNEDY
COMPOUND

Those hurt the most were those closest to the President—his friends and family.

At Hyannis, Massachusetts, the Cape Cod community whose "Kennedy compound" was the clan's vacation headquarters, even those who were strangers to the Kennedys reacted as though they had suffered a personal loss. All day Saturday dozens of local citizens stood watch by the cream-colored family plane, the Caroline, at the Hyannis airport to demonstrate their grief. One young mother, who had lived in town for three years but had never seen the President, stood vigil for seven hours in the gusty wind.

Throughout the weekend, the streets of Hyannis were almost deserted. "I haven't sold a loaf of bread all afternoon," said a baker. "I don't care."

A postmaster listlessly sorted mail.

The News Shop at Longwood and Wachusett Avenue was closed, its window darkened. One wing of the red-and-white shop had just been given a new white shingle roof; here, on those long summer evenings now gone, John Fitzgerald Kennedy used to bring Caroline and her friends in a golf cart to buy candy.

Hyannis Police Chief Albert L. Hinckley recalled how considerate the President had been to him and his men. "I remember the morning after the election just before the President started for the armory to make his acceptance speech," Hinckley said. "There was hardly anyone around and the President came over and shook hands with each one of us, thanking us for our help. There were about 15 or 16 men of our department there and he knew many of us by name."

Standing at the airport, State Senator Allan F. Jones, a Republican, remembered that "I even double-dated with him once right after the war."

Wyville J. Keveney, whose father had been an upholsterer for the Kennedys, told of an incident the preceding summer that, for the younger Keveney, typified the warmth and humanness of the slain President:

"As I remember it, the President had played a few holes of golf at Hyannis Port and as he was getting into his car he called his caddy over and said, 'Get in and I'll drive you to the camp.' The boy hopped in and the President drove him to the caddy camp, but he didn't just drop him off.

"The President got out and went into the camp and they were just having dinner so he said to the caddy master, 'I have always wanted to know what the caddies eat for dinner. Do you mind if I join them?' The caddy master, of course, was delighted and the President of the United States sat down to supper with the caddies."

The Rt. Rev. John J. Cavanaugh, president emeritus of the University of Notre Dame, had for years been a close family friend and confidant of the Kennedys. The square-jawed, bespectacled Roman Catholic priest was at his residence in South Bend, Indiana, when he heard the news from Dallas.

He was sitting in his room, reading Dante's *Inferno*. It was not long before the telephone rang. Sargent Shriver, husband of President Kennedy's sister Eunice and director of the Peace Corps, said, "The family would like you to come to Washington."

That very afternoon, Father Cavanaugh flew in a private plane from Indiana to the nation's capital.

On the afternoon of the assassination, John Kennedy's two children, John Jr. and Caroline, were taken to the home of Mr. and Mrs. Hugh Auchincloss, stepfather and mother of Jacqueline Kennedy, for dinner. They returned to the White House that night.

Early Saturday morning, the two children came downstairs from the executive mansion's living quarters with their mother for a mass for the dead, celebrated by Father Cavanaugh. Caroline only four days later would be six; John-John's third birthday would fall on the day that his father was buried in Arlington National Cemetery. The mass that morning was a private service, held for the dignified widow and children, Robert Kennedy and his wife Ethel, and a few other relatives and intimate friends.

After conducting the private mass in the White House, Father Cavanaugh was transported in a government plane to Cape Cod, to comfort the ailing patriarch of the Kennedy clan, Joseph Patrick Kennedy Sr. The 75-year-old Kennedy was a semi-invalid, partly paralyzed by a stroke that he had suffered two years before. His life was confined mostly to a wheelchair.

Mrs. Rose Kennedy, the President's 73-year-old mother, was playing golf alone at the Hyannis Port Golf Club when her son was shot. Jimmy Piersall, a celebrated outfielder for the Boston Red Sox in the 1950's, was playing one hole behind her when he heard the news.

"I was living in the Cape at the time, right in Hyannis Port about a block from the Kennedy compound," Piersall says. "My children used to play with Bobby Kennedy's children, and sometimes we'd go into the father's, Joe Kennedy's, pool. He kept it so hot, God love him, about 92 degrees.

"I was playing golf that morning on the front nine with some friends. One was an undertaker, another was a doctor, and a businessman. The undertaker and the doctor had come down from Fall River to play.

"Mrs. Rose Kennedy would come alone several times a week to play. She would drive up in her car and play just two holes, ending up where she parked her car. She might play those same two holes over and over again. We had watched her that morning for awhile, and then gone past her. We got to the 15th hole, and saw some Secret Service men go flying up the road to where Mrs. Kennedy was playing. There were lots of roads, maybe because the course was right next to the water, and you could get away if the water were to rise.

"Then the groundskeeper came up to me and said that the President was shot in the head. The doctor and the undertaker said that if he was shot in the head, he was dead. The Secret Service took Mrs. Kennedy away in their car, and left her car there. We went into the clubhouse, which was filling up with newsmen within minutes. They were all asking how I felt, and naturally I felt awful. Within hours the town was mobbed, and several newsmen who were my friends stayed at my house."

Workmen at the Kennedy compound heard the report of the shooting on a radio and told the family. The tragic tidings were withheld for the moment from the "Ambassador," as the family called the elder Kennedy in tribute to his days as the American envoy to the Court of St. James's on the eve of World War II. He was cared for by his devoted niece-companion, Miss Ann Gargan, and around-the-clock nurses.

Late Friday, as a blustery, November sou'wester whipped across Nantucket Sound, Rose Kennedy was seen taking a solitary walk along the beach, which for so many years had been the favorite playground of her large family. The entire clan had planned a reunion for the approaching Thanksgiving, when the President was going to carve the turkey.

Hyannis Port was cloaked in an eerie fog when Rose Kennedy arose early Saturday morning. With Ann Gargan, she rode in the family's chauffeured limousine to St. Francis Xavier Catholic Church. Mrs. Kennedy was dressed in black, a heavy veil trimmed in grosgrain partly concealing her face. She was met at the door by the Rt. Rev. Leonard J. Daley. It was a few minutes before 7 A.M. Looking at the assembled television and still cameramen, she said, "I know you have to do it, but I wish you would not take any pictures. The boys will be here later. I want to get back home and have breakfast with Joe. He doesn't know yet."

The white clapboard church was almost empty as the pastor escorted Mrs. Kennedy and Miss Gargan down the center aisle and seated them in a pew a few rows from the front, near the pew where Rose Kennedy's son, the President, used to worship. The mass was said at a blue-and-white altar donated by the Kennedys in memory of their first-born son, Joseph P. Kennedy Jr., who was killed in World War II when his plane exploded on a volunteer mission against a German V-2 base. On one side of the altar is a memorial to the French saint, Joan of Arc, and on another is one to Britain's Saint George. According to the pastor, the family chose the two saints to symbolize the fact that their son died over the English Channel linking France and Britain.

Jim Richer, an elderly parishioner, took his seat in a pew a row or two in front of Mrs. Kennedy, on the left side of the aisle. That morning, tears streamed down his cheeks. "I've been coming here every morning for the last four years," he said, "and whenever she's on the Cape, Mrs. Kennedy is always right there behind me."

Mrs. Kennedy stayed for the second mass, then was escorted out through a side door to the car that drove her home for breakfast with her husband. As his mother departed, Ted Kennedy arrived for the morning's third mass, accompanying his sister Eunice Shriver. They had flown to Hyannis from Washington. By the time they emerged from the wooden church, the sun had burned off the fog and haze, and the fall morning was crisp and bright.

At the trigabled Kennedy manor, Ted Kennedy had been selected by the other members of the family to tell his father the news about Jack. There was concern for the father, frail from his stroke, so a Boston neurologist, Dr. Russell S. Boles, stood by in the elder Kennedy's room. Also present were Rose Kennedy and Father Cavanaugh.

At 10:10 A.M. Saturday, Ted Kennedy, only 31, the freshman Senator from Massachusetts, slowly climbed the stairs and walked into the second-story sitting room where his father liked to look at the waters of Nantucket Sound. Ted sat down and told his father what had happened in Dallas.

The elder Kennedy, Dr. Boles said, showed no visible emotion as he listened. "He took it very well. He showed tremendous courage. They all have."

Behind the white-shingled, sprawling manor on Irving Avenue, a flag was raised to the top of a pole, then lowered to half-staff. As they watched the scene, the townspeople of Hyannis knew that the Ambassador had been told, that the entire family was in mourning.

Not quite three years earlier, in the Boston section of Dorchester, Mrs. John F. Fitzgerald had watched with unbounded pride, on television, as her grandson raised his right hand to take the oath of President of the United States of America. As he laid his hand on her Bible, which she had loaned him for the occasion, Mrs. Fitzgerald exclaimed, "Isn't he wonderful? That's my boy!"

John F. Kennedy's maternal grandmother, the mother of Rose Kennedy, the widow of Boston Mayor "Honey Fitz," had lived to see her "boy" inaugurated to the nation's highest office. Nine months after the tragedy of Dallas, at the age of 98, she died. She was never told that death had called her illustrious grandson ahead of her.

THE AMERICAS

John F. Kennedy, as other American presidents before him, maintained friendly ties with his nation's closest neighbors, Canada and Mexico. With his wife by his side, he paid a three-day state visit to Ottawa less than five months after his inauguration. The trip was Kennedy's first outside the United States after becoming President, and it symbolized the particular ties of partnership that have existed between Americans and Canadians for more than 100 years.

Kennedy had returned to the White House with a painful reminder of his sojourn. While planting a red oak during a ceremony on the lawn of Government House in Ottawa, the President had tossed eight shovelsful of dirt into a hole prepared for the tree. The exertion aggravated an old back injury. For some time afterward, Kennedy sat more often than usual in his rocking chair.

Canadian Prime Minister Lester Pearson was having lunch with his wife at the state residence in Ottawa when his executive assistant called from Parliament Hill with the news that President Kennedy had been shot. The Prime Minister rushed to his office. He received word of Kennedy's death while on his feet in the House of Commons speaking of the Dallas shooting.

"The world can ill afford at this time to lose a man of courage," Pearson later told Commons. He said that Canada, more than any other nation except the United States, would share the latter's grief.

The Toronto Stock Exchange closed after the floor was thrown into a panic of selling. Operations in the Winnipeg grain exchange stagnated as traders forgot their business and crowded around the tapes for news of the tragedy. Then a plunge in grain prices began when sudden declines were reported on the Chicago exchange, and Winnipeg shut down.

Said a Negro in Toronto:
"Thank God it wasn't a Negro."

The Kennedys enjoyed special popularity in Latin America, which *El Presidente Norteamericano* had called the most crucial area in the world for the United States. With his brunette, Spanish-speaking *señora*, John Kennedy had won the emotional hearts of *latinos* who accorded him thunderous receptions on visits south of the border. To all but the professional *gringo*-baiters among the Latin Americans —the communists and rabid rightists—the President possessed that magic quality, *simpatismo*. And despite the debacle at the Bay of Pigs, which shook the faith of many a Latin American leader in the New Frontier, Kennedy's Alliance for Progress was hailed as the most inspiring move toward greater hemispheric cooperation since Franklin D. Roosevelt's "Good Neighbor" policy.

In Mexico, as Abelardo Monges Lopez, a 70-year-old physician, can testify to, the reaction was total shock. Dr. Monges Lopez had lived through the Mexican Revolution of the early 1900's. He can remember when a hero of that struggle, General Alvaro Obregón, was assassinated by a religious fanatic in 1928 after winning the presidency for a second time. The assassin, José de Leon Toral, was an artist. While the President-elect, who had earned the wrath of the Roman Catholic church in Mexico, was attending a banquet, the man approached with some sketches. Obregón was inspecting them when the artist pulled out a gun and shot the general in the back.

"The mood in Mexico, in the wake of that assassination," Dr. Monges Lopez recalls, "was one of fear. We were afraid that there would be new shooting, new revolution. We all locked ourselves in our houses."

Three and a half decades later, in 1962, the doctor switched on his TV set to watch President and Mrs. Kennedy as they arrived in Mexico City for a state visit. "As I looked at the television, I noticed Kennedy's face when he got off the airplane. He wasn't sure just how these people in a foreign nation would receive him. He was wary, careful, and you could see him feeling the mood of the crowd. Then, as [Mexican] President Adolfo Lopez Mateos gave his reception speech, and Kennedy answered, you could see him relaxing, noticing the mass of people there to receive him.

"As Kennedy came down the airport boulevard to the city, his car was stopped constantly. He reached out to shake hands with people who wanted to touch him. It was absolutely incredible. The motorcade was so slow that the program was delayed for hours. I have never in my life gone out to see a public figure arrive in Mexico. But in this case, I was so surprised at the reception I was watching on television that I literally couldn't believe it. I turned off the set and I walked out and down to the Paseo de la Reforma, because I wanted to see it for myself. There was such a mass of people there at Reforma that I turned around and went back home. I was convinced it was true.

"I had consulting practice that afternoon, but the nurses didn't come to work. The next day they came to tell me they had gone to meet the President when he arrived and they had thrown flowers at him and at Jacqueline. I was flabbergasted that these women, normally restrained and mature, in their 30's, had acted so much like schoolchildren, rushing out to see that public figure. The only previous time that any crowd like that had turned out for a foreign personality was when Lindbergh came down."

A year later, while the Kennedys were riding through Dallas, Dr. Monges Lopez was at a wedding celebration. "We had just come from the church, and there was a lot of dancing and happiness at the house when we arrived for the wedding dinner. We were all inside and having a wonderful time when someone came in with a radio and we all heard that Kennedy had been shot. Well, everything stopped. There was a hush, and then they all left the party. We went home and turned on the television, and for the next four days that's all we did." (The programs, from the United States, were being transmitted live to Mexico.)

"My first reaction," the doctor continues, "was: How could they shoot such a popular man? Once again, Mexico was abandoned as it was when General Obregón was shot. But this time it was different. The next day, Saturday, I got up from the TV set and went to look out the window. The streets were deserted. I was afraid that if we left the cars out they would be stolen. There wasn't a policeman in sight. So I called my son and my son-in-law and told them to put their cars in the garage, because the streets were empty and no one was outside, even though it was broad daylight. The entire country was in mourning. Mexico City came to a complete standstill. Just about every Mexican cried and cried, day after day."

In Buenos Aires, the sprawling (population 7,000,000), sophisticated capital of Argentina, the buildings of major newspapers are equipped with sirens that are sounded on only the most extraordinary occasions, such as the end of a war abroad or the conclusion of a revolution at home. On November 22, 1963, the sirens blew for the passing of *Juan* Kennedy.

For more than a fourth of her life, Maria Elena Tello has been in a coma. The best medical minds in Argentina cannot agree on why the dark-haired young girl has remained, year after year, in a deep sleep.

Maria Elena was only 15 when tragedy struck her. One of nine children, she lived with her parents in a suburb of San Juan, a dusty city that lies in the foothills of the towering Andes mountain range almost a thousand miles west of Buenos Aires.

Her father, Cosme Tello, 66, is a day laborer. His wife, Rosa Bustos de Tello, tends the children and their humble dwelling.

In November of 1963, Maria Elena had almost finished her primary schooling and was enrolled in a sewing course. To her family and friends, she was a normal, healthy, and happy teen-ager.

"One afternoon, while visiting a friend's house," her mother remembers, "Maria Elena heard on the radio the news of *Señor* Kennedy's assassination. My daughter screamed and fell to the floor, crying so much they had to put her to bed. A few hours later, she seemed to have overcome that crisis. But she remained very depressed. I got to the house which she was visiting late that afternoon and found her very nervous and having dizzy spells.

"A neighbor gave her a tranquilizing injection, but it didn't have any effect. The next day we took her to a doctor, whose diagnosis was that Maria had suffered a strong nervous shock. He prescribed more injections. But my daughter did not improve.

"Two days later we took her to Mendoza [approximately 80 miles from San Juan and the largest city in western Argentina] where they subjected her to all kinds of analyses. The doctors couldn't agree on a diagnosis. We went back to San Juan and put her in Rawson Hospital, in a psychiatric ward.

"Maria Elena kept getting worse. She cried constantly, kept having dizzy spells and vomited. She pleaded that I take her out of there.

"Finally, the doctors said the best thing was to take her home. We didn't have much comfort, so we moved her to the house of one of my married sisters. She continued to suffer pains, which became complicated with convulsions and periods of rigidity. One afternoon, after taking a pill, she went to sleep and never woke up for any length of time again. I guess by then it was the end of November."

Maria Delia Tello, a sister of the stricken girl, recalls that on hearing the news of Kennedy's death, Maria Elena "suffered a tremendous blow, since she always had been fascinated with the life and work of the great President. And she also admired Mrs. Kennedy, whom she called *muy hermosa* [very beautiful]."

Since then, Maria Elena has been taken to clinics, psychiatrists, psychoanalysts, psychologists, and neurologists in San Juan and Buenos Aires. They have never been able to decide on the nature of her illness or the chances of recovery.

A few times, Maria Elena has regained consciousness for brief moments. She has recognized her family, said a few words, and then dropped back into her strange sleep.

The governor of her home state had Maria Elena flown to Buenos Aires in an ambulance plane in November of 1967. During the entire flight, she seemingly remained in the coma. Admitted to the Center of Medical Investigations of the University of Buenos Aires, she was subjected to rounds of further examinations and analyses, before being flown back to San Juan, her condition unchanged.

Mrs. Tello says that on one occasion her daughter awoke briefly and told her:

"Every night I talk with Kennedy. He is in a box of crystal."

In inflation-ridden Brazil, where the strike is almost as sacred as the samba, employees of two strike-bound Rio de Janeiro TV stations rushed back to work to transmit the sad news of John Kennedy's death.

From the shantytown *favelas* that cling to the lush green hillsides encircling Rio's harbor the poor climbed down from their shacks and thronged to churches.

At Rio's shrine of Saint Therese, worshipers traditionally leave candles burning as symbols of their prayers for romance, for relief from pain, or for victory by their favorite soccer team. That night in November, 1963, the candles were for Kennedy.

At St. Croix in the Virgin Islands, a newly founded newspaper, *The Virgin Island Times,* had been staging "dry runs"—making up issues of the paper but not actually going to press—for three months while the editor trained his staff. When the news came of Kennedy's assassination, the editor dropped plans for a later debut and inaugurated the first daily newspaper in the islands' history, in order to record that moment of larger history.

In Caracas, the soaring, bustling, overgrown oil boom town hard by the Caribbean, taxi cabs attached black steamers to their antennas. This was the city where Richard Nixon had been set upon, spat at, and almost killed by a communist-incited mob. This was where John Kennedy received one of the most wildly enthusiastic receptions of his career.

Only six months before, Venezuelan President Rómulo Betancourt had himself escaped violent death by only the barest of margins. While being chauffeured in his black limousine along a boulevard outside Caracas, he was severely burned when a car parked by the roadside exploded from charges hidden inside the vehicle. The Venezuelan government accused Rafaél Leonidas Trujillo, dictator of the Dominican Republic, and a long-time enemy of Betancourt, of plotting the latter's assassination.

After the attempt against his life, Betancourt was advised by his physician to take a *siesta* after meals. On November 22, he had just finished lunch with his Cabinet ministers at Miraflores, the presidential palace. With his ever-present pipe clenched between his teeth, the short, stocky Venezuelan leader walked to his second-story suite, slipped into his pajamas, and gave orders not to be awakened.

Downstairs, his press officer, Ali Caccavale, was sifting through his notes from the Cabinet session. One of his jobs was to edit the daily official press bulletin, which always grew fatter on Cabinet days.

A Zenith Transoceanic radio, tuned to a Caracas station, rested on his desk. An announcer suddenly broke into a jazz record to read the first dispatch from Dallas. Caccavale spun the dial knob, got the same news from another station, then telephoned the Caracas bureaus of the major news agencies for confirmation.

Even a President must be disturbed sometimes. Caccavale rushed up a flight of stairs to Betancourt's private suite. Risking the President's easily provoked wrath, the press aide knocked and went in. *"Señor Presidente, las agencias noticiosas dicen que el Presidente Kennedy ha sido herido de un balazo en Tejas y está muy grave!*

[Mr. President, the wire services say that President Kennedy has been shot in Texas and he's in very poor shape!]"

Betancourt sat up, stunned. No South American leader had been closer to Kennedy, ideologically and personally, than Rómulo Betancourt. As a statesman who was a middle-of-the-road builder—uncomprisingly rejecting dictatorship of left or right as an instrument of social advance—Betancourt had been a chief architect of the Alliance for Progress, which was predicated on evolutionary reform by democratic government. Later, after the news of Kennedy's death, the Venezuelan President called in reporters. Standing in the patio of his presidential palace, Betancourt started to read a message of condolence. He broke into tears, could not go on, and handed the slip of paper over to an aide to finish.

A sharp ring of the telephone broke into Fidel Castro's animated dialogue with a French journalist, Jean Daniel. The two were eating lunch in the living room of Castro's villa at Varadero Beach, a sun-splashed resort 72 miles from Havana.

A secretary, garbed in the olive-green guerrilla uniform of Cuba's communist revolutionaries, picked up the receiver. He turned to Castro. Cuba's puppet President, Osvaldo Dorticós, had an urgent message for the bearded Prime Minister.

Daniel remembers clearly how Castro got up, walked to the phone, listened for a fleeting moment, and then barked back into the telephone, "*Como? Un atentado?* [What's that? An attempted assassination?]." Castro turned to Daniel and Cuban aides in the room. He said that President Kennedy had been shot in Dallas. Then he exclaimed in a loud voice into the phone, "*Herido? Muy gravemente?* [Wounded? Very seriously?]."

Castro hung up, slumped into a chair, and repeated three times, "*Es una mala noticia* [This is bad news]."

Daniel described the scene:

"We got up from the table and settled ourselves in front of a radio. Commandant Vallero, his physician, aide-de-camp, and intimate friend, was easily able to get the broadcasts from the NBC network in Miami. As the news came in, Vallero would translate it for Fidel: Kennedy wounded in the head; pursuit of the assassin; murder of a policeman; finally the fatal announcement: President Kennedy is dead. Then Fidel stood up and said to me: 'Everything is changed. Everything is going to change. . . . I'll tell you one thing: at least Kennedy was an enemy to whom we had become accustomed. This is a serious matter, an extremely serious matter.'

"The Miami station observed a moment of silence, and then broadcast the 'Star-Spangled Banner.'

"Strange indeed, was the impression made, on hearing this hymn ring out in the house of Fidel Castro . . ."

Castro told Daniel, "Now, they will have to find the assassin quickly, but very quickly; otherwise, you watch and see, I know them, they will try to put the blame on us for this thing."

Later, Castro invited Daniel to accompany him to visit a state farm.

"We went by car, with the radio on," Daniel recalled. "The Dallas police were now hot on the trail of the assassin. He is a Russian spy, says the commentator. Five minutes later, correction: he is a spy married to a Russian. Fidel said: 'There, didn't I tell you; it's my turn next.' But not yet. The next word was: the assassin is a Marxist deserter. Then the word came through, in effect, that the assassin was a young man who was a member of the 'Fair Play for Cuba Committee,' that he was an admirer of Fidel Castro. Fidel declared: 'If they had had proof, they would have said he was an agent, an accomplice, a hired killer. In saying simply that he is an admirer, this is just to try and make an association in people's minds between the name of Castro and the notion awakened by the assassination. This is a publicity method, a propaganda device. It's terrible. But you know, I'm sure this will all soon blow over. There are too many competing policies in the United States for any single one to be able to impose itself universally for very long.' . . .

"Quoting the words spoken to him by a woman shortly before, [Castro] said to me that it was an irony of history for the Cubans, in the situation to which they had been reduced by the [U. S.] blockade, to have to mourn the death of a President of the United States. 'After all,' he added, 'there are perhaps some people in the world to whom this news is cause for rejoicing. The South Vietnamese guerrillas, for instance . . .'

"I thought of the people of Cuba, accustomed to the sight of posters like the one depicting the Red Army with maquis superimposed in front, and the screaming captions 'HALT, MR. KENNEDY! CUBA IS NOT ALONE . . .' I thought of all those who had been led to associate their deprivations with the policies of President John F. Kennedy."

At the southernmost tip of the Western Hemisphere, Raphael Ouaknine walked on the deck of a U.S. Navy research ship, which was shrouded in the foggy, eerie twilight of late spring in the Antarctic. It was November 22, 1963, but the seasons are reversed south of the Equator. The temperature was comparatively mild—around 32 degrees above zero—but a 24-knot wind from the west whipped against Ouaknine's hooded, pile-lined jacket. The vessel, the Eltanin, named for a Northern Hemisphere star, her hull strengthened to plow through ice, maneuvered through the choppy waters. The ship had sailed from Valparaiso, Chile, to the Antarctic. Ouaknine, 26 years old, was born in French Morocco, but now was seeking to become an American citizen and was an electronics technician for Alpine Geophysical Associates, a private company working for the National Science Foundation.

"It is perpetual twilight down there that time of year," Ouaknine recalls. "Sometimes when you wake up and go on deck, you think it's 8 o'clock in the morning, and find out it's like 10 o'clock at night. But I'll never forget that November night.

"There were about 40 scientists on board, and about 40 crewmen. Most of us were on deck. We were taking a core. That's a piece of pipe, 22 feet long, which we send to the bottom of the ocean floor with cables to take up mud samples for the geologists. Well, somebody who had been chatting with a ham radio operator in the States came out on deck and yelled, 'Kennedy's been shot in Dallas!' No one wanted to believe it. On board ship, we're used to rumors, like someone saying, 'We're going to Tahiti.' That keeps the morale high. So we thought he was a joker. The captain said he didn't know anything. But an hour later, the radio officer was monitoring MSTS— the Military Sea Transportation Service shortwave—which sends messages to all Navy ships, and the report said that Kennedy had been shot.

"The captain got his copy of the messages, and called all of us into the conference room. He told us it was true. The ship's whistle blew, the captain ordered the flag at the stern put at half-mast, and we stood for two minutes of silence. Then the whistle blew again. We had some foreigners aboard, scientists from Latin America, and there were tears in their eyes.

"I remember I felt that something great had just disappeared. I had a lot of time to think, and I wondered, 'How could it happen? Who shot him?' "

Reflecting their special sense of loneliness, Ouaknine adds, "All week long, those from the States were calling home on the radio-telephone, asking questions like, 'How come this happened?' "

119

WESTERN EUROPE

It was 7:33 P.M. in London when the news was flashed . . . 9:33 P.M. in Moscow . . . 11:33 P.M. in Karachi . . . and in the Far East a new day, Saturday, had already begun; it was 2:33 A.M. in Saigon, 3:33 A.M. in Peking . . .

Tom Ochiltree, a veteran foreign correspondent, was high over the Atlantic Ocean, flying back to his London base after home leave:

"The big Pan American jetliner flying from New York was 45 minutes from landing at London Airport when its captain, Gene Vaughan, switched on the public address system. He said: 'Ladies and gentlemen, I have an announcement of importance to all of you. President Kennedy has been shot and killed.'

"Airline captains are paid, among others things, to keep their emotions under control. Captain Vaughan made the announcement in a matter-of-fact and unemotional voice.

"All the same, his words had the effect of an electric shock on the passengers aboard the plane. They had finished cocktails and dinner, and most of them were dozing when the incredible words snapped them to attention.

"One woman began to sob softly. Another stared for several minutes at the ceiling, an expression of disbelief stamped on her face.

"One of the hostesses in the galley in the aft part of the jet cradled her head in her hands. But she quickly realized that her professional duty did not leave room for a display of emotion.

"There was almost no conversation among the passengers during the rest of the flight into London. Everyone seemed too stunned to speak."

At the moment of Captain Vaughan's announcement, 20,000 feet below the graceful jet lay the green shores of Ireland, the lights of cities and towns flickering in the early evening darkness. The sad tidings were already spreading from Dublin to Cork, to Limerick and Wexford and Dunganstown. And the word reached New Ross, the town that an Irish emigrant named Patrick Kennedy—John Fitzgerald Kennedy's great-grandfather—had left in the mid-19th century to seek a new life in America.

Auctioneer John V. Kelley of New Ross recalls that "people heard the news on television, and immediately they ran to neighbors who did not have sets and told them."

In County Wexford, where the President of the United States had relatives, the churches soon filled with mourners, praying for the man they proudly claimed as "Cousin Jack."

Dunganstown is little more than a cluster of farmhouses, and in one of these humble dwellings lived Mrs. Mary Ann Ryan, 62, known to the townspeople as "Widow Ryan." A Kennedy before her marriage, she was a third cousin to John Kennedy—and the President's closest relative in the homeland of his ancestors.

That evening, the Widow Ryan and her daughter Josie knelt in prayer in the kitchen of their farmhouse. Mrs. Ryan was too distraught to speak. Josie, fighting back the tears, said, "We were listening to the radio and were stunned by the announcement. Mommy and myself said a prayer for him. That is all we could do."

A Roman Catholic priest called on Mrs. Ryan. As the knell tolled from Ballykelly Church, he said, "Never again will we see his smiling face."

From miles around, Ryans and Kennedys trekked to Dunganstown to try to comfort the Widow Ryan. But nothing they did or said could stem her tears.

Only five months earlier, the same clans had gathered to greet President Kennedy when he visited the birthplace of his great-grandfather, and the widow, a stocky woman windburned by life on a farm, had played hostess to her illustrious cousin. Along with other, more distant cousins and relatives, she had laid out long tables covered with cakes and pies. Mrs. Ryan served tea to her guest. He took two lumps of sugar, ate a sandwich, and cut the cake she had baked for him. The exuberant President had said that he came "3,000 miles and three generations" to claim his heritage, to see where Patrick Kennedy started life before emigrating to Boston.

Celebrating, the clans called their visitor "Sean" (Irish for John). It was the biggest, most festive family reunion that anyone around Dunganstown could remember.

On the night of November 22, 1963, however, New Ross, Patrick's birthplace, became a ghost town. For the period of mourning, shades were drawn on the houses. Shops were closed. All sports and social functions were canceled.

And in Dunganstown, after the commiserating relatives left, the Widow Ryan sat quietly with her daughter and their priest before a fire in the little cottage where they had served tea to Sean.

President Eamon de Valera probably spoke for all Ireland that evening when he said:

"No one could have done more, for no man has more to give than life itself. John Kennedy died because he so ardently welcomed the burden of supreme authority on that chilly afternoon three years ago. Had he been less devoted, less determined, he need not have fallen to an assassin's bullet. The mediocre are suffered to live. It is those who stand head and shoulders above their fellow men who invite the hatred of the demented."

In Ireland, tradition dictates the manner of mourning the death of an "exile," as the inhabitants call someone of Irish descent who lives far from his homeland. The custom is for the mourners to put lighted candles in the front windows of their homes. Through the night of November 22, 1963, all electric lights were switched off in many Irish homes, and candles burned in tribute to the departed son of Ireland.

A tiny lamp still burns on a parlor wall in the Ryan home in Dunganstown. The lamp, with only the strength of one candle-power, casts its modest glow over a picture of John Kennedy. Directly beneath the lamp is a horsehair sofa, which one visitor described as "the kind that winds up in a farmhouse attic most times after the sheen wears off." No one sits on that sofa anymore. It is where President Kennedy relaxed that sunny June day when he visited his cousin, Mary Ann Ryan.

The British Broadcasting Corporation broke the news in London, where young John Kennedy had lived when the clouds of World War

II were gathering in Europe and his father was Ambassador to the Court of St. James's. On the evening of the President's death, the BBC broadcast bulletins from a newsroom, then projected on the screen a spinning globe, with organ music in the background. A few moments later, the BBC returned to its regular programming, broadcasting the comedy show of Harry Worth and Dr. Finlay's Casebook.

Irate television viewers besieged the BBC's Lime Grove TV center with telephone calls, denouncing the broadcasting of comedy instead of more news about the tragedy. "Our duty officers handled 64 calls of protest," one harassed BBC executive said. "The switchboard had to deal with the rest and they say there were hundreds." Later, an American comedy program was scrapped.

London's other network—Independent Television News—was broadcasting a Dr. Kildare-type program called "Emergency—Ward 10" when word of the President's death came. The network cut off the situation drama and broadcast bulletins alternating with somber music. In contrast to the BBC, an ITN official reported, "We had about 600 calls, most of them to thank us for our treatment of the news but some to complain that we weren't going ahead with our normal programme."

Although every newspaper on Fleet Street had an obituary on President Kennedy in its library, the BBC did not. Columnist Pat Williams of *The London Observer Weekend Review* asked why, and was told with British aplomb, "We only have obits on *older* people."

Sir Winston Churchill, stooped and drawn by his 88 years, grieved at home for his young and now departed friend. With his wife "Clemmie," Churchill peered at television that evening, long past his bedtime. The aged lion summoned a growl within him the next day, pronouncing the assassination "a monstrous act which has taken from us a great statesman and a wise and valiant man."

"The loss to the United States and to the world is incalculable," Sir Winston declared. "Those who come after Mr. Kennedy must strive the more to achieve the ideals of peace and human happiness and dignity to which his Presidency was dedicated."

In Piccadilly Circus, the flashing lights were blacked out for three hours in honor of John Kennedy. Only twice before since World War II had the famed lights been dimmed—during electric power emergencies.

The great tenor bell of Westminster Abbey, last heard at the

death of King George VI, echoed on Saturday, a gray-worsted London day, tolling once each minute for a full hour. Traditionally the tribute is reserved for British monarchs when they are laid to rest in the Abbey. This day, the bell tolled 60 times for the great-grandson of an Irish potato farmer.

In Larnarkshire, Scot workers at an American-owned factory walked off their jobs, protesting that a two-minute silence called by their superiors failed to demonstrate proper respect. "Our factory should have closed—for the half-day, at least," one worker said.

At a London pub called the White Swan, Mrs. Breda Harris said, "Everyone just stopped drinking when it was announced. Even the boys with Beatle haircuts—they just said, 'Leave the radio on.'"

A sign was posted in a Brighton pub: "There will be no singing tonight."

In Soho, London's nightclub district, one customer wearing the traditional billed cap of the British working classes, sighed, "My word, something always happens just before Christmas."

Soccer teams postponed matches. When play resumed, the players wore black armbands.

In London's Old Vic Theatre, actor Sir Laurence Olivier strode forward after a performance of Chekhov's "Uncle Vanya" and addressed the audience:

"Out of respect for President Kennedy, may I ask that there be no applause."

The audience and the rest of the cast then arose and stood with Sir Laurence as the theater orchestra played "The Star-Spangled Banner" and "God Save the Queen."

The British Prime Minister, Sir Alec Douglas-Home, was driving to the south coast of Sussex to stay the weekend in Arundel Castle, the ancestral home of the Dukes of Norfolk. He learned of the shooting in Dallas at a stop on the road and turned back for London. "There are times in life," said the Prime Minister, "when mind and life stand still, and one such is now."

Harold Wilson, leader of Britain's Labor party, was at a political rally in North Wales. Police escorted him to the BBC's studios in

Manchester to air a statement of regret. Shortly afterward, Wilson himself received an assassination threat and was given a strengthened guard by Scotland Yard.

The deputy chief of Wilson's Labor party, the volatile and emotional George Brown, broke down and burst into tears in full view of the camera during a televised program of tributes to the late President. Brown's party called for an explanation of his demeanor. The uproar over the incident prompted a cartoon in *The Daily Express*, which portrayed a man and a woman in a pub, the man saying, "Trust that Harold Wilson to slap down the only member of his party who bears some resemblance to a 'uman being."

At Buckingham Palace, Queen Elizabeth was "shocked and horrified," and ordered a week of court mourning. The Queen's Counsel, appearing in High Court, wore "weepers" in mourning for the late President. "Weepers"—white cuffs worn with a black coat—earned their name from the fact that, in feudal times, a gentleman who wept over some personal tragedy would dry his eyes on the broad cuffs of his coat or jacket.

Over the halls of Parliament, and across the British Isles, the Union Jack was lowered to half-staff.

The British press bemoaned the American President's passing with all the articulateness of the people who gave birth to the English language.

" 'Assassination,' Disraeli declared with the sublime confidence of the Victorian high noon, 'has never changed the course of history.' Can we be so confident now?" asked *The Liverpool Daily Post*.

The London Daily Herald bitterly noted:

"The Stalins of the world must die in their beds. It is the Lincolns and the Kennedys who are shot down."

Across the English Channel, a chilling drizzle fell on Paris that evening. President Charles de Gaulle was in his private apartments at the Elysee Palace when an aide brought the first bulletins from Dallas. De Gaulle switched on his TV set. Himself twice the target of assassination attempts, the towering French leader seemed to his aides to turn pale and drawn when he heard the news that John Kennedy had died. De Gaulle summoned his secretarial staff and dictated a statement of condolence, saying "President Kennedy has died like a soldier, under fire." He ordered the Tricolor lowered to half-staff throughout France, a tribute his nation usually pays only on the day of funerals for dead chiefs of state.

Along the Champs Elysees, cafes and nightclubs were plunged into gloom. Thousands of Frenchmen and Americans in Paris ignored the rain in their quest of news of the tragedy. One crowd gathered in front of the building housing the Paris edition of *The New York Herald Tribune,* striving to read the latest dispatches from Dallas on a clattering Teletype in the lobby.

In an elegant restaurant, an immigrant Spanish waiter wiped his eyes with a serving napkin and unleashed his emotions in two languages: *"Eso es un chiste malo. Je ne le crois pas. Je n'accepte pas."*

A Paris cabbie said, "All the world will cry."

A French chanteuse, standing alone, leaned against a wall of the Rue de Berri, just a few steps down the street from her nightclub. Her head was bowed, and tears made mascara run down her cheeks.

"It's not so hard to believe," she said in a soft voice to a passerby. "It's just so hard to take."

The heart of France went out to Jacqueline Bouvier Kennedy, the beauteous, French-descended First Lady who had upstaged her husband with impeccable French and Continental grace before General de Gaulle on the President's state visit to Paris, and whose taste in cuisine, coiffures, and clothing had given renewed status to French culture. The French nation watched entranced as television news shows from America via relay satellite brought home the pathos of the tragedy. The scenes of Mrs. Kennedy in mourning prompted one French commentator to describe her as the "Mater Dolorosa."

One of the most moving epitaphs to John Kennedy came from the pen of St.-John Perse, the French poet and former diplomat. In his tribute, entitled "Grandeur de Kennedy" and published in *Le Monde,* the poet wrote:

"History created no myth. Face to face, he was a man, simple, close, and warm, prompt to the activity of each day . . . He was the athlete racing toward his meetings with destiny. He fought always with his weapons unhidden, and in his meeting with death his face was uncovered. Upon events he imprinted a mark of progress that was his own and that leaves us following his path. At the service of a great people in love with liberty, he was a defender of all rights and all freedoms. No one was more the enemy of abstractions or more carried by instinct to the heart of things. He had the clear, direct gaze of those young chiefs formed for friendship with mankind. When fate lifts so high the burst of its lightning, the drama [of death] becomes universal, and the affliction of one nation becomes that of all."

A political crisis gripped Italy. When the news of the shooting broke there, Premier Aldo Moro abruptly adjourned a meeting at which he was struggling to form a center-left coalition to bring Marxist Socialists and Catholic Christian Democrats into a government together for the first time.

Pietro Nenni, the 72-year-old leader of Italian socialism, wept as he emerged from the session. The valiant warrior, who lived in exile to oppose Mussolini and lost a daughter in a Nazi concentration camp, muttered, "These are little affairs, these of ours, in the face of this tragedy for the whole world."

President Antonio Segni, the courtly, white-haired Sardinian landowner who had given up tracts of his private estates as part of an agrarian reform program that he himself sponsored, laid down a pen with which he was signing official papers. Shaking his head, Segni moaned, "No, no, no, no. It cannot be true."

In Rome's Piazza Vittoria Emanuele, the clamoring street peddlers fell silent. Grief enshrouded the Via Veneto. At one Roman cocktail party, the guests set down their glasses and recited The Lord's Prayer.

The mournful words, *"E morto,"* echoed along the elegant avenues of the Eternal City as Italians passed the sorrowful news.

The Rome newspaper *El Giorno* carried the simple headline: "Addio, John, Addio."

Over the Italian Communist party's headquarters in Rome, the hammer-and-sickle was dropped to half-staff.

In Brescia, a 12-year-old boy shot himself to death. He left a letter, explaining that he had decided to take his life because he was so stricken by the assassination.

Tullio Mango, a former fascist functionary who had fought against the United States during World War II, pondered the death in his Rome office. Mango had achieved stature under Mussolini. He had been assistant police chief in Rome, and had remained with the last of the fascist forces that had held out in northern Italy, in a hopeless cause, until the regime completely collapsed in 1943.

Hunted by communist partisans who wanted to kill him, Mango made his way stealthily to Rome. Discredited, a man on the run, he had no one to turn to except his enemies, the Americans. Mango spoke a little English and was an ingenious man. Amidst the confusion following the surrender, he got odd jobs with American organizations struggling to reestablish themselves in Italy. His wife, a schoolteacher, found classroom work. Mango studied law part-time, and after years of struggle he won his degree and became a practicing attorney.

At the time of John Kennedy's death, Mango was doing well. His two daughters were grown and, like their mother, both had become schoolteachers.

Although still a convinced fascist, Mango had long since ceased to hate and fear Americans. Though they had been his foes in the war, they had made it possible for him to survive—a fact that Mango never forgot.

Sitting in his office, thinking of Kennedy's death, Mango suddenly exclaimed to a colleague, "How can such a thing happen in a country like America? In Italy, yes. In France, yes. Anywhere else, yes. But not in America. It's too—it's too Balkan. To such a man? In such a country? I tell you, it must be a plot."

One of Mango's daughters told him that she was going to lead her high school physics class to the U.S. Embassy to place a wreath there. The father approved. The world had come a long way since the guns of World War II were silenced.

From a Roman Catholic convent outside Rome, however, came a blast of bitterness occasioned by a more recent conflict. Exiled Madame Ngo Dinh Nhu, widowed only three weeks before when her husband and his brother, South Vietnam's President Ngo Dinh Diem, were assassinated in a palace coup in Saigon, at first said nothing. Then Mme. Nhu dispatched a cable to Jacqueline Kennedy:

"Though not having the pleasure to know you, or hearing from you personally, I wish to tell you of my profound sympathy for you and your little ones in your time of shock and grief.

"Though I have said that anything happening in Vietnam will surely find its equivalent in the U.S.A., truly I would not wish for anyone what the Vietnamese and myself are now enduring while we were so near our victory against communism.

"But though not being proven alike, I understand fully how you should feel before that ordeal which God has bestowed on you. I sympathize the more, for I understand that that ordeal might seem to you even more unbearable because of your habitually well-sheltered life . . ."

At the Vatican, citadel of John F. Kennedy's religious faith, Pope Paul VI was sitting at a writing desk in his small private study. Pope John XXIII had died earlier that year, and the new pontiff, during a visit by Kennedy to Italy in June, had received in audience the first Roman Catholic to become President of the United States.

That November evening, the telephone on Pope Paul's desk rang, and he was told of Kennedy's death. The Pontiff arose and walked immediately to his chapel to pray for the President's soul. For the first time in Catholic church history, the Vatican's yellow and white banners—which are normally lowered only at the death of a Pope —were ordered flown at half-staff in tribute to the chief of a secular state.

By custom, popes are among the least accessible of all world leaders. They seldom have direct contact with the press. They almost never permit interviews. They never sit for television cameras.

Franco Buccarelli knew this. Buccarelli, an enterprising Neapolitan, worked in the Rome office of the American Broadcasting Company. He had tried for years to wangle a papal interview for ABC. Yet despite the fact that Buccarelli enjoyed excellent contacts in the Vatican, he had never succeeded.

When news of President Kennedy's death hit the Rome ABC bureau, Buccarelli reacted instantly. He picked up the telephone, dialed the Vatican, and managed to reach the Pope's secretary.

"I identified myself," Buccarelli says, "and said the American Broadcasting Company would be honored if His Holiness would make a comment for the American people on this tragic event."

"Just a moment," he was told. "Hold the line."

After a brief pause, the secretary said, "Yes, His Holiness will have something to say. You may come now."

Buccarelli, his boss John Casserly, and their camera crew pounded down the stairs of their office on the Piazza di Spagna, piled into their cars, and sped across town and over the Tiber River to Vatican City. When they arrived, Pope Paul was in his library. He was visibly pale and was caressing an autographed picture of the President and a letter box. Both were gifts from Kennedy.

The Pontiff turned to the TV team and asked, "How is Mrs. Kennedy? Do the children know?" Then, sitting under the klieg lights, the Pope read a statement. His voice wavering with emotion, he said:

"We are deeply bereaved by the tragic and sad news of the assassination of the President of the United States, John Fitzgerald Kennedy, and the grave wounding of Governor Connally, and we are profoundly saddened for such a shameful crime which, through the person of its chief, has struck a great and civil nation, and for the sorrow which it inflicts upon Mrs. Kennedy, their children and their family.

"We deplore this event with all our heart. We express the hope that the death of this great statesman shall not harm the American people, but reinforce their moral and civic sense and strengthen their feelings of nobility and concord, and we pray to God that the sacrifice of John Kennedy may advance the cause which he promoted and defended for the freedom of people and the peace of the world.

"He was the first Catholic President of the United States. We remember having had the honor of a visit by him and having recognized in him a great wisdom and high regard for the well-being of mankind.

"We shall offer holy mass tomorrow for the peace of his soul, for the comfort of those who mourn his death, and that love and not hatred shall reign among mankind."

The ABC crew packed up its equipment and departed quietly with a slightly self-conscious blend of sorrow and elation: the tragedy had given them a journalistic scoop of extraordinary proportions. As it turned out, the beat had also resulted from a quaint misunderstanding. In Italy, as in most European nations, there is only one television network, owned and run by the state. The name "American Broadcasting Company" had sounded to the Pope's aides as though it were the official network in America, state-run and the proper channel for the Pontiff's message.

Later that night, correspondents of other American TV networks besieged the Vatican after they learned of ABC's feat. An uncomprehending secretary told them, "But His Holiness already gave a statement to the American network. It is there for all."

The worldwide hierarchy of the Roman Catholic Church was in Rome for the second session of the Vatican's Ecumenical Council. Word of President Kennedy's murder reached the late Francis Cardinal Spellman of New York while he was in his suite at Rome's Grand Hotel. Spellman could scarcely speak. "He is another martyr of his family of heroes," said the cardinal.

133

The first American Catholic prelate in Rome to hear of the slaying was Bishop Thomas K. Gorman, the white-thatched shepherd of the Dallas-Fort Worth Catholic Diocese. Newsmen rushed to Gorman first for comment because the shooting had occurred in his see.

Voicing sorrow and deploring violence, the bishop nonetheless expressed relief that Kennedy had not died without receiving the final rites of the church. "I am very pleased," Gorman announced, "to learn from the reports that our Dallas priests were alert and able to give this fine Catholic man, the first President of our faith, the consolation of the last sacraments. May God grant this great Catholic man, an historic personage in the history of the United States, eternal rest and peace."

All across Europe, the sorrowful bugle call, Taps, was sounded through U.S. military bases, paying tribute to the troops' dead commander in chief.

In his barracks at Heidelberg, West Germany, a soldier attached to the American Army's European Headquarters mumbled, "This isn't Vietnam, Iraq, or some other damn place. It's America where they've done this. To a man we needed."

Four Negro servicemen were listening to the radio while they played pool in the soldiers' day room at Paris' Supreme Headquarters Allied Powers Europe (SHAPE). When they heard the news that their President had been shot, they put down their cues and stared at each other. When the announcer reported that Kennedy had died, one turned and said, "Who will help us now?"

In the Yugoslav town of Skopje, which had been devastated by an earthquake a few months earlier and to which President Kennedy had dispatched 146 soldiers to help with reconstruction, the American troops were still on hand. After learning of the President's death, they decided to forgo their approaching Sunday off. They kept working that day in his honor.

Ludwig Erhard, Chancellor of West Germany, was riding in his private train, homeward bound from his Paris meeting with President De Gaulle. Within 48 hours, Erhard was scheduled to fly to Washington for his first meeting with President Kennedy. Sipping a Scotch and soda, the rotund German leader briefed himself for that important trip. In Bonn, lights burning late into the night reflected off the shimmering River Rhine as Erhard's officials put finishing touches to position papers for his parley with Kennedy.

Suddenly, a press aide burst into the railway car. Kennedy had been shot and killed in Dallas, he stammered. Erhard was stunned. He sat silently for a moment, then muttered, *"Unfassbar, kaum fassbar* [Inconceivable, hardly conceivable]."

On a brilliant June day earlier that year, communist-surrounded West Berlin had accorded John Kennedy a reception that stamped him as an idol among those inhabiting that outpost of Western society. When the President, his mop of hair waving in the breeze, looked out over an unbelievable throng of 150,000 and shouted to them, *"Ich bin ein Berliner* [I am a Berliner]," their thunderous roar ricocheted through a divided city, even across the wall into the communist sector.

On the evening of November 22, 1963, the people of West Berlin again paid tribute to Kennedy. This time, by contrast, it was with silence and solemnity. The sparkling metropolis dimmed its lights, and countless candles flickered from house windows. An American reporter drove 10 miles through the city and reported, "There was not a window of an inhabited building that did not have at least one candle burning. Even shut-down factories and offices had their candles."

Close to midnight a group of students gathered near West Berlin's Tempelhof Airport. Braving a rain that had begun, they started a march from the Berlin airlift memorial in front of the airport terminal building to City Hall, three miles away. There was no music, no funeral dirge, only the shuffle of marching feet. The students carried torches, casting a golden chain down the wet streets of West Berlin. Through the torch-lit darkness tolled the Freedom Bell, a gift from the United States.

Other West Berliners spontaneously joined the march. The ranks swelled rapidly, until 60,000 Germans reached City Hall, whose steps were soon carpeted with flowers. This was the spot where five months before Kennedy had delivered his speech and encouraged West Berlin's residents to remain steadfast against communism.

Standing before the crowd was Mayor Willy Brandt, taut and weary after having just returned from a trip to Africa. "I know how many of you are weeping tonight," he said, slowly. "We Berliners are poorer tonight. We have lost one of the best."

Shielded by darkness, one daring mourner that night drove a stake into the soggy earth hard by the hated wall and tacked onto it a hand-painted sign that proclaimed:

"J.F.K. Ich bin ein Berliner."

THE
IRON CURTAIN

The death of Kennedy breached both the Berlin Wall and the Iron Curtain. The European communist bloc expressed public commiseration, but also lost no time propounding a propaganda line on the matter: Kennedy was killed in a right-wing conspiracy, a conclusion that was also adopted in many non-communist nations abroad.

In communist-ruled East Berlin, delegates attending an annual convention of the East German Trade Union Movement stood in silence in homage to the late President and passed a resolution that viewed his slaying "with abhorrence and indignation." Morning newspapers in East as well as West Berlin appeared with front-page pictures of Kennedy framed in black borders.

Although Radio Free Europe beamed special broadcasts about the assassination to Hungary, Poland, Czechoslovakia, Bulgaria, and Rumania, the five communist nations maintained their jamming of all American radio reports. At the same time, however, stations inside these Eastern European nations broadcast their own tributes to Kennedy and biographical sketches of him and the new President, Lyndon Johnson.

Yet communism has little room for grief, and even in the face of worldwide mourning, Marxist propagandists strove to make ideological capital out of the tragedy. *Neues Deutschland*, official organ of the East German Communist party, carried the headline, "U.S.A. President J. F. Kennedy murdered by *Ultras* [the German word for extremists]." Hungary's trade union organ *Nepszava* trumpeted:

"The assassination of President Kennedy must be a warning for American labor unions. Only a more vigorous and united fight against anti-Negro banditism can be effective."

American pop singer Paul Anka was in Warsaw that day. He recalls:

"I had been invited to Poland by the Polish government—the visit was approved by the United States government—to tour for eight days. We had toured a few of the major cities, and this was the last day of the tour. We were going to do a concert that night at the new Art Center which had been given by the Russians under Stalin. We were in our hotel room with a few other people—the head of UPI for Warsaw and four or five other associates. We usually had dinner in the hotel room about three hours before a performance about 5 o'clock. I had a nice apartment in the hotel and I had this old radio which I'd been banging on all afternoon trying to get some reception. But I could hardly get anything. We were sitting around the table having dinner and for some reason I got up and started fiddling with the radio. I finally picked up some English and I sat down again. As we were eating we heard the announcer very carefully enunciating each word—'the . . . airplane . . . was . . . landing in Dallas . . . The motorcade . . .' We figured it was just one of those book shows, where they read books in English to the people over the radio on Radio Free Europe. We paid no attention.

"But I was subconsciously attuned to the radio. You really are remote being in Poland. And then I heard the announcer describe '. . . and the President was shot . . .' We all stopped and listened to make sure what we heard was correct. The announcer was reading reports of the assassination. Naturally I cried. It was about 6:30 our time, and by then people had already started going to the theater —embassy people. I went to the theater about 7 or 7:15—in formal dress. It was to be a formal concert, a really gala affair. When we got to the theater we met with the Polish government representatives backstage. We told them there. Then the curtain opened and I went on stage and said, 'Ladies and gentlemen, please excuse me. I won't be performing tonight. The President of the United States has been assassinated.' There was a gasp—they hadn't heard yet—and the whole front section of the theater got up. The embassy people left. I left, too. I flew back to Paris, picked up my wife, and then flew home.

"The Polish people were wonderful. They were terribly upset. The

chauffeur I had during the whole tour couldn't speak English. But on the way to the airport he gave me gestures, with his eyes, his hands to his eyes, he made a gesture like 'All of Poland is crying for Kennedy.' People were very kind. We were trying to assemble facts. Here I was in Poland. You live on the gray side of life. It was like being on another planet. You were wondering whether it was a communist plot. But there were no repercussions with the government. The people were so sad, genuinely. But I was the one who had to go out on stage and announce to the audience that President Kennedy was dead."

In Moscow there was sorrow among rank-and-file Russians and also, if their public displays could be believed, among the Kremlin's communist hierarchy.

Moscow Radio, in a rare move, interrupted its regular program of domestic news to inform the Russian people that President Kennedy had been shot and killed. The radio then switched to funeral music.

The Communist party newspaper *Pravda*, with a daily circulation of 6,000,000, normally refuses to change its pages after they have been made up in the early evening, no matter what the late-breaking news. On the night of November 22, 1963, however, *Pravda* scrapped the entire lower half of its previously prepared front page and substituted details of the death of John Kennedy.

Before dawn, Muscovites braved a cold rain to stand in queues that stretched for blocks, waiting to buy a newspaper. So great was the demand that the kiosks were sold out of papers before it was daylight.

Nikita Sergeyevitch Khrushchev, the swaggering dictator who had tried unsuccessfully to bully the young American President, was visiting the Ukrainian capital of Kiev when he learned that Kennedy had been slain. The Soviet Premier, at the time the only other man in the world besides the President at the head of a world nuclear power, broke off his visit and hastened back to Moscow, traveling all night by train and car.

Politically, Khrushchev had little reason to mourn the passing of John F. Kennedy. Khrushchev's defeat by Kennedy the preceding year in the Cuban missile crisis had been the most humiliating setback in the Russian leader's long and wily career. Nevertheless, early in the morning after Kennedy's death, Nikita Khrushchev, dressed in a black suit, drove to Spaso House, the American Embassy residence.

There, in its big hall, Ambassador Foy Kohler had placed a photograph of President Kennedy, with a black band across one corner of the frame. Beside the picture rested a book in which visitors could write their condolences, and behind stood an American flag touched with black crepe. A Marine guard kept watch over the somber tableau.

The Premier looked grim as he emerged from his limousine. Although his bodyguards usually wore civilian clothes, on this morning, for the first time in memory, he was accompanied by two uniformed security men, one a Soviet Army major. Khrushchev strode into the hall, drew a pair of old-fashioned, gold-rimmed spectacles from the breast pocket of his coat, donned them, leaned over, and scribbled his name and the date in the condolence book.

Khrushchev then turned to Ambassador Kohler, reminisced about the meeting in Vienna in 1961 at which the Soviet Premier and Kennedy had experienced their first confrontation. Khrushchev handed Kohler a copy of a telegram of sympathy that the Premier had dispatched to President Johnson. (Mrs. Khrushchev sent a wire to Mrs. Kennedy.) As he departed, the Red ruler shook hands with the ambassador.

In an extraordinary departure from usual Soviet practice, Khrushchev's visit to the U. S. Embassy was filmed in its entirety by Russian cameramen and broadcast on the Soviet television network.

Moreover, although the U.S.S.R. had for months refused to participate in any exchange of television programs via the U.S.-launched Telstar communications satellite, Kennedy's death broke the resistance. For the first time, Soviet audiences watched live television from the United States, viewing scenes of the aftermath of the tragedy in America. A Russian newscaster in Moscow, hooked into the live pickup, translated the English commentary. As the funereal TV panorama came in from America, one woman commentator for the Russian television network burst into tears.

As the rain turned to snow that weekend, Muscovites sought out Americans to express their dismay, often in halting English.

One man volunteered, "My wife could not sleep all night."

An engineer said, "The whole Russian people is sorry."

On Red Square, a captain in the Kremlin guard commented, "We very much regret this. As we say, each country has its villain. . ."

A cluster of Russians, waiting in the snow at a Gorky Street bus stop, spoke to an American correspondent. One, a waitress, lamented, "He was a good man—it is always the good who must suffer."

A man from the Soviet hinterland, who was searching for a hotel room in Moscow, added, "Write and say we are all sorry. It is a great misfortune."

Within hours, however, the Kremlin developed a split personality regarding the tragedy. While still expressing regret over the demise of John Kennedy, Moscow was quick to react to the revelation that the alleged assassin was a proclaimed Marxist who had defected to the Soviet Union and taken a Russian wife during his sojourn there. Any allegation that communism was responsible for Kennedy's murder, the Soviet intimated, was a capitalist smear.

Initial domestic newscasts to the Soviet people ignored Lee Harvey Oswald's past and his leftist ties. The broadcasts described Oswald simply as a 24-year-old clerk in a textbook store and stressed his denials of guilt during police questioning. Two hours later, Moscow Radio and the Soviet news agency Tass began to accuse the Dallas police of trying to implicate the Communist party in the slaying of Kennedy.

In strident tones, the two official voices for the Kremlin declared in identical statements:

"The more details that are reported, the darker and more sinister this whole case is. Serious commentators are not putting faith in the police version about 'left-wing' elements being responsible for this monstrous crime. They continue to await the results of further investigation."

Tass for the first time then acknowledged that Oswald had spent two years in Russia, that he had a Russian wife, and that he had had links with the Fair Play for Cuba Committee.

The latter dispatch was followed with a nationwide broadcast by Moscow Radio commentator Valentin Zorin, who asserted, "Those who know how the security of President Kennedy is organized, know that it is not possible for a fanatic to commit such an assassination. A political crime, thoroughly prepared and planned, has taken place. It is not accidental that it took place in the southern states which are well known as a stronghold of racism."

Other Soviet newspapers joined the attack, charging that Dallas police and the "yellow press" of the United States were trying to whip up "an anti-Soviet, anti-Cuban hysteria." For a time, Western observers were deeply concerned that an East-West feud over possible political motives behind the assassination could provoke dangerous reverberations.

When Jack Ruby shot Oswald, Tass said, "The murderers of President Kennedy are trying to cover up their tracks." Tass then quoted the Rev. Dr. Martin Luther King Jr. as saying that Kennedy's death had to be viewed against the background of rising violence engendered by racial strife in the South.

In an article entitled "Texas and Telstar," *Izvestia*, the Soviet daily, asserted, "We have seen the grief of the American nation and profoundly sympathize with it. We have seen a mad detective thriller and reject it with contempt and anger."

Back in New York, a veteran AP correspondent, A. I. Goldberg, added another footnote to the death of the President, reflecting on a strange encounter that he had had with Lee Harvey Oswald in Moscow in 1959. That was the year that Oswald had defected to the Soviet Union. At the time, Goldberg was a journalist in the Russian capital.

"Lee was a mysterious character who shunned the American press," Goldberg said. "I finally traced him to the Metropole—an ancient hotel near Red Square where foreigners have been lodged since Czarist days. Oswald confirmed that he had been in the U. S. Marines and had come to the Soviet Union hoping to live and work there. I asked if a woman was involved. He refused to say. I asked what he planned to do, and how he intended to live. He replied, 'I'll get along.' I asked whether the Soviet Union had promised him citizenship. He wouldn't say. And he refused to be photographed.

"I told Oswald there had been a similar case about that time of a Long Island man who thought he wanted to stay in Russia, but found the going was rough and reclaimed his passport, returning to the United States.

"Oswald looked at me and said, 'Maybe he didn't have as good reasons as I have.'

"He disappeared the next day from the Metropole and dropped out of sight."

AFRICA

The word spread through the African continent by the primitive means of tribal councils as well as the modern channels of radio and television. From steaming jungles to sun-baked capitals, there was a sense that Africa's young nations, struggling to survive in a sophisticated world, had lost a friend.

In Kenya, the day had been a scorcher. The sweltering stickiness of the afternoon had lingered long into the night. Nonetheless, the British colony was vibrant with both excitement and tension. It was the eve of Independence. *Uhuru*—freedom—was less than three weeks away.

Most East Africans were sitting down to their evening meals. In Nairobi's bars, customers talked of the impending freedom day. The whites, Asians, and other foreign inhabitants of Kenya were deeply concerned. European farmers, down from the Highlands for the weekend, chatted about that morning's headlines, which had announced the appointment of Kenya's first Governor General, Malcolm MacDonald, who would be merely the Queen's representative after *uhuru*. The white settlers sipped their whiskies and gazed sourly into the future.

On receiving the news of the assassination, the Nairobi *Daily Nation* dispatched its sports editor, Brian Marsden, to the local U.S. Information Service building in quest of some up-to-date pictures of the Kennedy family.

"There were about 20 glum-faced Americans in the room when I got there," Marsden says. "They were sitting, standing, smoking around the radio. Some had shirts and trousers on, but most were in pajamas and robes. They had rushed in from their homes, without even getting dressed, to hear the Voice of America broadcasts."

Nairobi's youngsters were among the first to hear the news of President Kennedy's death. With the weekend ahead, they had brushed aside their homework and were relaxing. By 10 P.M., many were tuned in to the musical "Top Twenty Show" on the Forces Broadcasting radio network, or were watching "Up Tempo," a pop music program on Kenya's only television network. At 10:20, the twanging of guitars and other instruments was stilled on both programs. On the radio, disc jockey Keith Skues switched from his usual breezy chatter to solemn tones, and recited details of the shooting in Dallas. On TV, a woman announcer read the startling news to viewers. Moments later, the television station closed down out of respect for the late President.

A few hundred yards down the road from Broadcasting House, a group of students tramped homeward, dumbfounded. A concert they had been attending in Gloucester Hall at Nairobi's University College had been abruptly terminated without explanation. The perplexed students soon picked up rumors as they trudged downtown to the coffee houses.

One student, Kul Bhushan, recalls that "there was disbelief among the young admirers of the President. I rushed to drop off a girl at her house, and as I drew up outside her place her guardian rushed out to confirm the horrifying news."

Bhushan went to a deserted street outside the offices of *The East African Standard,* another Nairobi newspaper. A van was being loaded with copies of the Coast edition, which would be driven to Mombasa 300 miles away. "We begged a copy of the paper from one of the workers," Bhushan adds, "and soon a large crowd had gathered, all of us craning to read the single copy under the street-light. As I reached home, my parents were still awake and listening to the Voice of America broadcasts. It was unbelievable, but all too true. President Kennedy was no more."

The leaders of Kenya's youth, as a gesture of their affection for Kennedy, sent a giant wreath of 1,700 flowers to the funeral. Their message read:

"From the sunny, warm country of Kenya, the young people who lost so much in losing you send their flowers and their promises to follow your example."

At Gatundu, Jomo (Burning Spear) Kenyatta was getting ready for bed at his country home. Once imprisoned as a Mau Mau leader, Kenyatta had spent most of Friday preparing for *uhuru*. The impending independence celebration was to be his proudest day, the culmination of his lifelong struggle for his homeland's freedom. The old warrior, then in his late 60's, was to become the first prime minister of Kenya. Earlier that day, he had formally accepted the Kenya Independence stands in the arena of the stadium where, on December 12, a quarter of a million people would witness the advent of *uhuru* in a ceremony of explosive gaiety and unrestrained joy.

Kenyatta was a happy man that night—until he heard the news from Dallas. He immediately canceled a scheduled weekend tour of Kenya's Rift Valley, ordered his people into mourning, and permitted a television crew to visit his home. In his brief recorded message of grief, Kenyatta disclosed that President Kennedy had invited him to visit America as his personal guest after independence. That visit would never be made.

At Kapsabet in northwest Kenya, 3,000 half-naked tribesmen stood in silence for one minute in tribute to the President. Home Minister Oginga Odinga, an extreme leftist, had called them together. The natives came, even though most of them had never heard of Kennedy, or much else beyond the problems of their own crops and cattle.

Tom Mboya, Kenya's Constitutional Affairs Minister, and an admirer of America and the West, heard the news on television. He immediately sat down and wrote a personal note to Mrs. Kennedy. Mboya later told a gathering of 5,000 tribesmen how John Kennedy, while a senator, had helped launch their aspiring country's first airlift of students to the United States in 1958.

"When I told Senator Kennedy we needed $2,500 to hire four planes for the airlift," Mboya related, "he immediately got out his checkbook and wrote a check for $2,500 then and there."

Kennedy's name was also associated in Kenya with relief food sent by the U.S. government to help the poor and starving during a famine in Kenya in 1962.

In Katanga, the breakaway province of the former Belgian Congo, President Edouard Bulundwe led his entire Cabinet, along with the members' seldom-seen wives, to the residence of the American consul to express condolences. One minister explained, "This is an old Bantu custom. We Bantus always mourn the passing of a great chief."

One of the mourners was Godefroid Munongo, Interior Minister of the secessionist government who had blamed Washington for attempting to force Katanga's integration with the rest of the Congo. "Mr. Kennedy was the reincarnation of President Lincoln," he said. "There will be mourning in every African village."

Amid the general grief of Africans, some bitter tones emerged. In Ghana, run by leftist President Kwame Nkrumah, the government newspaper *The Evening News* published a letter contending that "President Kennedy's death can only be properly avenged if the American people will find ways and means of ending the free use of the pistol and adoration of gangsterism in films, cinemas, books and other mass circulation media."

President Nnamdi Azikiwe of Nigeria termed Kennedy's death a great loss, but raised the question of whether the United Nations headquarters should remain in the United States. "Slaughter of this typical American reformer shows clearly that among some Americans there is deep-seated hatred of the black man as a human being," he said.

Patrick J. Ryan, a missionary teacher, vividly remembered observing the reactions of African boys in a secondary school. He wrote in the Catholic Jesuit magazine *America*:

" 'Who will care for Mrs. Kennedy?' they asked their teacher. 'Who will buy her food now, and the children's?' Students in Africa were unaware that the President bequeathed a substantial fortune to his family. It made them happy to know she will never want."

More than a year later, Ryan added, the youths would ask, "Why do Americans hate Negroes? Why did Americans kill Kennedy?"

149

THE
MIDDLE EAST

In the warring Middle East, John Kennedy's death provoked a rare unity of grief. Both Israel and the United Arab Republic, the two major powers in the area, viewed the President as a friend.

Israel was at rest when President Kennedy was gunned down in Dallas. The Jewish Sabbath had begun as dusk fell on a cool Friday evening. Enjoying a period of relative calm vis-a-vis their Arab enemies, Israelis were following their custom of relaxing and visiting each other's homes until the Sabbath ended at sundown on Saturday. Streets in the cities were quiet, and little traffic moved through the darkness. From homes, the muted murmur of voices could be heard, mingled with the Voice of Israel, the state radio.

At 8:55 P.M., the radio shattered Israel's peaceful respite. An excited announcer blurted out, "President Kennedy has been shot." At 9:19, Israelis were told that Roman Catholic priests were beside the stricken American leader. At 9:33, Israel heard he was dead.

David Ben-Gurion, the retired Premier of Israel and Jewish elder statesman, was at his lonely retreat at Sde Boker, a *kibbutz* in the Negev desert. In longhand, he wrote a note to the U.S. Ambassador in Israel, Walworth Barbour:

"I can hardly tell how distressed and shocked I am at the terribly tragic loss of the great, courageous, wise and peace-loving President. Not only America but the whole free world has lost a great leader and a true friend. I am asking: Why? . . . why?"

151

That Friday evening the feature attraction playing at the Chen Cinema in Tel Aviv was "The Ugly American," billed on the marquee as "The Most Important Story of Our Time." In Jerusalem, the Eden Theater was showing another Hollywood production, "The Savage Guns," described as "An Explosive Drama of Outlaw Tyranny." As news of the slaying in Dallas swept through the nation, Israelis rushed to their radios, except for the nation's Orthodox Jews, who are forbidden by *Halakah* (Jewish religious law) from turning on electricity on the Sabbath.

Saturday night, *The Jerusalem Post*, for the first time in its 31-year history, published an extra. Thousands of Israelis queued up outside the U.S. Embassy in Tel Aviv to sign a condolence book. Eventually, a second book was opened and in one day 5,000 names were added. Prime Minister Levi Eshkol inscribed:

"A terrible blow for the world. Israel is in mourning."

Shimon Peres, one of Defense Minister Moshe Dayan's closest political associates, was at a party for Prime Minister Eshkol:

"I was called out and given the terrible news. I took a long time to digest what had happened.

"At first, we prayed that he would overcome his injuries. Then we knew he was dead, and we felt the course of the world had suddenly changed. The party came to an end. Immediately."

Dr. Shlomo Avineri of Jerusalem's Hebrew University was at home waiting for guests to arrive:

"I missed the radio news for some reason. Perhaps I was in the shower. I began to wonder about my friends. I called them on the telephone and they asked me, 'Haven't you heard the news?' I said, 'What news?' Then they told me. We called off our dinner date. I was overcome by consternation and shock. People in Israel all seemed to be asking what was going on in the United States."

Ya'acov Herzog, assistant director general of the Foreign Ministry, was asleep "and knew nothing of it at all until I was awakened by a messenger. I immediately went to see the President who was under heavy shock. We all were."

President Zalman Shazar cabled his condolences to the new U.S. President, Lyndon Johnson, and proclaimed three days of national mourning.

Seventeen-year-old Mordechai Eliezer was enjoying a party when someone said that Kennedy had been shot:

"Then we all heard the news on the radio. The party just broke up. Nobody felt like it any more. I went home and sat beside the radio with my mother and father to listen to the Voice of America direct from Dallas. The announcer was crying. He couldn't control himself.

"A Canadian embassy official lived next door. I told him the news and he telephoned the embassy, which confirmed it. Then he went back to showing his home movies. He was always showing home movies."

At Eilat, on the shores of the Red Sea, businessman Izhak Naomi was resting at his home. "We just did not believe it," he recalls. "In such a democratic nation, was this the way to settle political problems? In the Middle East, it is normal that a king should be killed by others for political ends. But we thought a nation like the United States was beyond such behavior."

Marcel Castro, a Tel Aviv messenger and chauffeur, was driving home when he heard the news on his car radio. He arrived to find his family in the dining room, the meal growing cold while they clustered around the radio.

"I turned the sound up. The commentator was excited and tense. My wife, my daughter, and I no longer felt like eating. We just sat in front of the radio until midnight."

Ilana Balaban, a pretty young Israeli secretary, was combing her hair before going to a party given by a wealthy publisher to celebrate his daughter's university graduation.

"A friend telephoned," says Ilana. "I told my parents, who were resting. It was an absolute shock for all of us. We just didn't know what to think first. It was as if someone in the family had died. We thought of his lovely wife and children. Who could have done such a thing to a wonderful family?

"Then I went to the party. All the talk there was of Kennedy, instead of about politics and boyfriends. That night is so alive in my mind. I remember my parents in the bedroom of the old house we had then. I remember the food at the party was terrible—soggy biscuits, cakes from the supermarket, and only two bottles of cognac for 50 people."

Deputy Premier Abba Eban was at home and had turned on the radio a little late and missed the first part.

"I heard later that Kennedy was shot and priests were with him," he says. "Two minutes later, U.S. Ambassador Walworth Barbour called and said that it was his duty to tell me that the President had died. I was absolutely shocked. In addition to the international implications, we had known each other well when I was in the United States and he was a senator. Our families visited each other. My first thoughts were of a personal nature of the tragedy. Of the international aspect, I didn't think predominantly of this area. I felt we had all lost a good friend."

Corporal Arieh Rimon was one of the few Israelis who did not hear of the tragedy immediately. That night, he was manning a lonely military outpost on the Syrian border close to Tiberias on the Sea of Galilee.

"It had been a long night," he recalls. "As dawn broke, I could see a group of Syrians moving across the border. They looked harmless enough. Perhaps their patrol was as routine as my watch. Suddenly, a United Nations jeep rolled up behind me in a cloud of dust. UN observers often came past and I usually waved them on their way. This time they stopped.

"One of them—an Australian, I think—jumped out and said in English, 'Hey, what do you think about Kennedy?' Of course, I didn't know what he was talking about. I asked him what he meant. I told him he was the first person I had talked to since Friday afternoon.

"He shouted, 'I tell you President Kennedy's been shot. He's dead. He was killed in Dallas in Texas by some man with a rifle.'

"I just said, 'Oh, my God.' I thought what a shame. He was so young. What a terrible thing. Then I thought, 'If America collapses, what will happen to us?' "

The assassination occurred several hours after sundown in Cairo, and the streets of the Egyptian capital were chilly. Nevertheless, hundreds of men and women thronged the sidewalk cafes, seeking more news of the event. In Egypt, the young men had grown to follow Kennedy's hair style, and the girls imitated his wife in their makeup and fashions. Many Egyptian youths had also adopted the custom of adorning themselves with neck chains and bracelets bearing the American President's picture.

When the Cairo radio announced Kennedy's death, cries of grief, in guttural Arabic, went up from the city's streets. Then angry shouts were heard as crowds argued over possible culprits.

One businessman remarked, "The Russians have avenged the humiliation Kennedy inflicted on them in the Cuban naval blockade. I swear they killed him for revenge."

A school teacher, Mrs. Mofieda Hassan, said, "Jealousy caused his death. He is rich, handsome, and intelligent. His wife is pretty and charming. It's envy, believe me."

Ibrahim Abdel Fatah, a Cairo police sentry on the Nile River bridge, said, "I would sacrifice my only son if they could retrieve Kennedy to life. He was a great man. He was very friendly with our President Gamal."

The police reported that Nefissa Mohamed, a housemaid, tried to commit suicide by drinking half a bottle of insecticide on hearing that the doctors in Dallas had failed to save Kennedy's life.

President Gamal Abdel Nasser of the United Arab Republic was at his plush villa in the Cairo suburb of Manchiet El Bakria when the word arrived. Nasser's secretary was summoned to a newsroom situated near the room where the Egyptian leader normally pores over affairs of state. The secretary ripped off the first bulletins and ran in to Nasser, then shuttled back and forth as details poured in over Teletype machines. At 9:38 P.M., Cairo time, Nasser received the news that Kennedy had died. Aides reported that he covered his face with his hands for awhile, then looked up with a pensive stare on his broad face. The expression turned to one of dismay and anger.

Nasser dictated a cable of condolence in English to Mrs. Kennedy:

"I was shocked, as were the people of the UAR, by this terrible crime which killed your husband when he was full of youth, hope and zeal to struggle for the sake of his people and for the sake of humanity. I believe the loss which befell the hopes for peace and progress in the world is no less than the loss which befell the American nation and you personally."

To President Johnson, Nasser cabled that Kennedy "fell in battle while carrying the flag."

Across Cairo, church bells tolled their dirge. Roman Catholic churches held special services. The Coptic Orthodox Church held a three-hour mass, and Archbishop Istaphanos wept. Black-clad women, Moslem and Christian alike, mourned. For the first time in recorded history, a non-Moslem, John F. Kennedy, was praised by Moslem mullahs in sermons that Friday as "the humane leader who preached peace." In Cairo's main mosque, mullahs opened an old, festering wound, charging that "the Jews who crucified Christ in the past have today crucified another advocate of love among mankind, John Kennedy."

The accusation was picked up by Egyptian citizens, repeated, amplified.

"The Jews killed him because he wanted to return the Palestine refugees to their homeland," Mohamed Abdel Azis, a shopkeeper, said. "They killed him because he insisted that Egypt should continue to receive American wheat. Wait till tomorrow and you will see how right I am."

Saturday morning, throngs of students, workers, and businessmen demonstrated before the U.S. Embassy in Cairo, shouting slogans against the American people, the Jews, the Russians, the "war merchants" of America, and the American Mafia—all of whom the demonstrators accused of killing Kennedy. Police cordoned off the embassy grounds and kept vigil, fearing that the confused, angry Arab mobs might explode into violence.

Predictably, echoing the Egyptian mood, a headline in Beirut's daily, *Al Massa*, shrilled:
"Zionism Is Behind the Kennedy Assassination."

ASIA

Communist China greeted the news from Dallas with inscrutable silence. Then, 24 hours after the rest of the world reacted, Radio Peking devoted exactly 103 words to the event. The broadcast said merely that President Kennedy had died of a bullet wound in the brain after being shot while riding through Dallas in a car, and that Lyndon Johnson had assumed the Presidency. However, Red China's newspapers ignored the assassination for four days, not mentioning it until after Peking Radio reported that Kennedy had been buried in Arlington National Cemetery.

The only surprise in Red China's reaction was the initial absence of Peking's customary vitriolic slurs against Kennedy, whom Mao Tse-tung's propagandists had scornfully pilloried as a "warmonger" and "Enemy No. 1 of the world's people."

This uncharacteristic restraint soon passed. The official Peking paper *Tao Kung Tao* (*Worker's Daily*) featured a cartoon that portrayed the slain President lying face down on the ground, blood gushing from his head. The caption read, "Kennedy Bites the Dust."

The Communist New China News Agency chimed in, "When the monopoly capitalists and their class allies hail Kennedy as a 'man of peace' . . . one can only be filled with revulsion."

In a neutral Asian nation, a diplomat reported that one of his Chinese translators grinned and said, "Very good news. He was a very wicked man."

In Hong Kong, the communist *New Evening Post* sneered:

"Kennedy used a two-faced policy to promote an imperialist war course."

A Red Chinese delegation in Warsaw stridently protested when a world peace council opened in the Polish capital with a moment of silence for Kennedy. The chief Peking delegate, Tang Ming-chao, pointedly noted that the Soviet delegation was the first to rise. A continent away, a seven-man Peking delegation to an Afro-Asian conference in Conakry, Guinea, stormed out of the hall when the chairman asked the delegates to rise for a moment in memory of Kennedy.

In neutralist Cambodia, Prince Norodom Sihanouk had just concluded a week-long tirade against the United States. After abruptly ordering a halt in all American economic, education, technical, and military aid to his tiny nation, Sihanouk, in a series of speeches, had bitterly denounced the U.S. government and accused Washington of conspiring to oust him. For good measure, he had hailed Red China as "Cambodia's best friend."

In line with his latest stance, "Yankee Go Home" signs glared from walls and posts in the steaming tropical heat of Cambodia's backwater capital, Phnom Penh.

On learning the news from Dallas, however, the Prince decreed three days of national mourning. All Cambodian newspapers and Radio Phnom Penh paused in their verbal assaults on the United States, and Sihanouk also ordered the anti-American posters stripped down—possibly the first time in his reign that the garrulous Prince had chosen to be silenced.

In Ceylon, another neutralist leader, Mrs. Sirimavo Bandaranaike, had succeeded to power as prime minister after her own husband's assassination. In a cable to Mrs. Kennedy, Mrs. Bandaranaike said:

"It is with profound shock that I have learned of the tragic death of your husband. As a wife and mother who herself lost her husband in such tragic circumstances, I know how you feel in this hour of grief. The entire Ceylonese people send our heartfelt sympathies in your tragic bereavement."

In populous India, emotions over the slaying of Kennedy were compared to those that swept the nation following the assassination of the great Indian leader, Mohandas K. Gandhi, in 1948. Gandhi's image, however, was that of a father to his people; India felt orphaned by that deed. Kennedy's image was one of youth, and India's younger generation felt deprived of their inspirational mooring and leadership.

From the perpetual snows of the lofty Himalayas to the heat-parched plains stretching away from the sacred River Ganges, the Indian people exhibited the greatest mass outpouring of sentiment ever seen for a foreigner. Prime Minister Jawaharlal Nehru, in failing health, was informed at 7 A.M. after he awoke.

Arriving at the Foreign Office two hours later, looking deeply saddened, Nehru remarked helplessly to newsmen, "What can I say? What can I say?" He paused, then added, "It is too much, is it not? Too much."

The Indian Parliament paid homage to Kennedy, then adjourned as a mark of respect.

The American President's death coincided with a major domestic tragedy for India. Five of India's senior military officers—an air vice-marshal, two lieutenant generals, a major general, and a briga-dier—were killed in a helicopter crash in Kashmir State on the same day that Kennedy was shot. Normally, the crash would have been the lead story in the Indian press, but it was given a distinctly secondary position under the news from Dallas.

In the summer of 1966, a visitor to Kabul, the capital of Afghan-istan, found an Afghan copper artisan hammering out dinner plate-sized plaques bearing the likeness of President Kennedy and the inscription, "John F. Kennedy, American President." The humble craftsman explained that he had felt the need to preserve for the memory of Afghans some tribute to the "great American." Yet, when asked, the man could not locate the United States on a world globe.

North of Tokyo, a pre-dawn mist shrouded the village of Shiokawa. A neighbor ran to the home of the town chief and rapped on the *shoji,* the sliding panel doors.

Kohei Hanami awakened. Ex-Lieutenant Commander Hanami had gone into politics after leaving the Japanese Navy and became mayor of his home town. When John Kennedy was inaugurated and Hanami learned who was skipper of the PT boat that his destroyer had cut in half in August of 1943, he told a newsman, "It stuns me to think how close we came to destroying the new President of the United States."

Now, in Shiokawa, half a world away from Dallas, it already was Saturday morning, November 23, 1963, when the news of Kennedy's assassination reached Hanami.

"I was shocked beyond words," he said. In Japanese tradition, Hanami maintained, death in the service of one's country is the highest honor one can earn, not a tragedy.

A Catholic priest from the United States was waiting for a train that Saturday morning in Tokyo. It was a national holiday in Japan, called *Kinro Kansha No Hi*, a combination Labor Day and Thanksgiving. The priest, the Rev. John Blewett, turned at the startled voice of a Japanese friend: "*Sensei* [Sir], your President *ansatsu sareta.*"

Ansatsu. Assassination. Literally, the Japanese ideographs mean "killing in the dark." As Father Blewett wrote a few days later, "it is a word all too familiar in Japan, where in the 1920's and 1930's to rule or to lead involved the terror of sudden death. The spectacular assassination some three years ago of the leader of the Socialist party, Mr. Asanuma (who was stabbed to death on a political platform); an unsuccessful attempt on the life of former Prime Minister Kishi; a recent knife thrust at the present Prime Minister . . .

"All at once, a group of schoolboys surrounded me. 'We are very sorry, sir,' a pudgy lad stammered as he thrust an 'extra' before me. There before my eyes was a picture of the Kennedy car in Dallas, taken five hours earlier, seconds before the fatal shots were fired. I had to say something to these youngsters, whose incredulity that *this* could happen in the model democracy of America filtered through their kind expressions of regret.

" 'To die fighting for justice is not such a bad end,' I ventured. 'Mr. Kennedy's New Frontier spirit will not die, you can be sure. Be confident of that.' Luckily, my train slid into the station as my throat tightened."

By coincidence, technicians had arisen before dawn that very morning in Tokyo to prepare for the world's first across-the-Pacific live television broadcast. President Kennedy had taped a personal message to the Japanese people for the moment when video images would be beamed from a station in California's Mojave Desert to the Orient.

But the historic transmission was inaugurated with a far less festive broadcast. When they switched on their sets, startled viewers in Japan saw instead the grim face of a Japanese correspondent in New York who was reporting Kennedy's death.

Tokyo's normally chaotic traffic was light that holiday morning. Then throngs of Japanese began to appear on the streets, sighing "*Taihen, taihen* [Terrible, terrible]," as they rushed to buy extra editions of the city's multimillion-circulation newspapers. Mrs. Hachi Okubo, operator of a newsstand by the Yarakucho rail station in downtown Tokyo, remembers that "the newspapers were selling so fast that morning I didn't even have time to fold them."

The tragic events evoked an outpouring of Oriental ecumenism. Dressed in black mourning kimonos, Crown Prince Akihito and Crown Princess Michiko, although they are Buddhists, led 3,000 mourners who crowded into St. Ignatius Roman Catholic Church in Tokyo for a mass. Other Buddhists—including monks in saffron and black robes—were on hand to kneel with Christians in meditation.

The widow of Inejiro Asanuma, the Socialist leader stabbed to death by a 17-year-old rightist fanatic, mailed a letter to Mrs. Kennedy, offering an unusual condolence. Wrote Mrs. Asanuma:

"The road of a politician's wife is rough and painful. You may think me impudent to say this now, but I believe it will be a consolation to you as the wife of a politician to have been able to stay with your husband until the end. When I arrived at the hospital, my husband was already dead."

"How many years will it require for your lovely smile to return to your face?" she continued. "I learned after my husband's death that it was people's goodwill and encouragement that makes a wilting tree regain life.

"Mother is the sun to her children. Please be brave for your children's sake and recover as soon as possible your bright expression."

In Tokyo Bay, where almost two decades earlier Japan had signed her surrender, the flags of 42 visiting warships from the U.S. Seventh Fleet flew at half-mast for a President who had served the U.S. Navy with bravery and honor. Tiny Japanese fishing boats soon sailed alongside the American vessels, displaying their lowered Rising Sun emblems as partners in sorrow.

There were 16,500 American military "advisers" in South Vietnam that November of 1963 assisting in the struggle against the communist-led Vietcong guerrillas. The immediate reaction by the local American armed forces radio in Saigon to the shooting of the U. S. President was hardly its finest hour in broadcasting.

Admittedly, it was early on Saturday in Saigon and no one could have been expected to be overly alert. A disc jockey was spinning pop records on the station. One American listener who was tuned in that morning said that he heard, "Stick around. We really have some news for you this morning." Five minutes more of popular music followed. Then the announcer said, "John F. Kennedy, the President of the United States, has been assassinated." This was followed by the latest football scores. Then the usual beat of rock 'n' roll blared on until the officer in charge of the station decided that such a repertoire was in bad taste, and the radio switched to classical music.

Later, General Paul D. Harkins, commander of the American forces in South Vietnam, issued a statement broadcast over the Saigon radio. Harkins, who had been instrumental in organizing and expanding the U. S. military assistance program in South Vietnam, declared:

"News of the assassination . . . comes as a great shock to all of us stationed in the Republic of Vietnam, as it does to all Americans throughout the world.

"The bold decision to come to the aid of the Republic of Vietnam in its fight against the communist Vietcong was one of the highlights of President Kennedy's tragically abbreviated but illustrious term as our chief of state. In all his actions he strongly supported the forces of freedom in their struggle against the communists' goal of world domination.

"As a memorial to him, let us strive even harder in all that we do supporting the fight against communism by the forces of the Republic of Vietnam."

The American ambassador to South Vietnam, Henry Cabot Lodge, was en route from Saigon to the United States to confer with the President when the assassination occurred. Arriving in San Francisco, Lodge, a Republican from Massachusetts, commented with an enigmatic slip of the tongue, "I was very fond of him and knew him intimately. Lately we have been particularly close because he followed—no, not followed, but guided—America's foreign policy."

Because of the chaos in South Vietnam at the time, the assassination of the President did not have the emotional impact there that it exerted elsewhere; in politically embattled Saigon, one more crisis —a far-off one at that—made little difference. Three weeks earlier, a military coup had overthrown the regime of President Diem. In an ironic parallel, Diem and his controversial brother, Ngo Dinh Nhu, were murdered. The toppling of the Diem government initiated a long-run series of palace upheavals.

Malcolm W. Browne, who shared a Pulitzer Prize as a correspondent in South Vietnam, was in Saigon on the day of President Kennedy's death. "Vietnam was in turmoil," he says. "The coup and assassinations of November 1-2 that ended the Diem regime ended an old order but did nothing to establish a new one. The popular South Vietnamese who had led the coup was General Duong Van Minh (Big Minh), a large, taciturn Buddhist with sort of an Eisenhower amiability but absolutely no political savvy.

"The reaction among all the Saigonese I knew was that the Kennedy assassination was in some way related to the Diem coup, since the Vietnamese assume that the universe rotates around Saigon. But there was no agreement as to how this might have occurred.

"It would be hard to say that Saigon really reacted to the Kennedy murder. At the time, mobs were still roaming the streets, looting offices and raising hell—partly as acts of political revenge, but mostly in the same way that looters in the States these days are breaking into stores in the name of Black Power. There were massive desertions from the army, especially from units that had been loyal to Diem.

"Big Minh and the civilian prime minister, Nguyen Van Tho, both made statements of public sorrow over the assassination. Stationery from the U. S. Embassy, including Ambassador Lodge's correspondence, was bordered with black. Well-wishers went around to the embassy to give their condolences. Roman Catholic Archbishop Paul Nguyen Van Binh of Saigon said a special mass. And several weeks later, the square in front of Saigon Cathedral was renamed John F. Kennedy Square.

"But the last thing on most people's minds was the assassination itself. To say that there was sorrow or strong feeling in Saigon would be an exaggeration. A bronze plaque for Kennedy went up in cathedral square, but police later discreetly removed it when it appeared that a predominantly Buddhist crowd was on the warpath. It wasn't so much that they were either anti-Catholic or anti-Kennedy, but it

was one of the frequent waves of anti-Americanism that come over Saigon.

"There were mixed feelings about Kennedy in Vietnam. While his youth, vigor, and honesty were admired by many, he was blamed on the one hand for supporting Diem, and on the other for Diem's murder. It was a common complaint that 'your President obviously doesn't know anything about Vietnam.'

"In short, Kennedy never enjoyed the kind of personal popularity in Vietnam as that of, say, Lodge. Everything Lodge did in Vietnam during his first tour there was regarded (erroneously) as personal diplomacy."

The news caught thousands of American military advisers in South Vietnam sloshing through the rice paddies of the Mekong Delta or shoring up outposts in the Central Highlands. This, after all, was "Kennedy's war" (before it was rechristened by its critics as "Johnson's war"), and the Americans involved had lost their commander in chief.

"American GI's were naturally deeply interested in the news of the assassination, but they, too, had other things on their minds," Browne continues. "The Vietcong, who were caught off guard by the November 1 coup, finally began to get into action again along toward the end of the month, and, from that time on, government forces and the Americans took one beating after another.

"Kennedy's death hit the U. S. Army Special Forces hardest. Kennedy had been their major protector against efforts by the Pentagon to absorb them into the Regular Army hierarchy, and with Kennedy's death, the Special Forces ceased to exist. A Special Forces colonel complained to me some time later that his organization had been 'emasculated' now that the generals had their way, and he forlornly added, 'If only JFK had lived another year or two.'

German-born Horst Faas, who won the Pulitzer Prize for his photography in Vietnam for The Associated Press, also remembers the day vividly:

"Most American servicemen, mission officials, and other civilians heard the news about the assassination of President Kennedy on the 7 o'clock news of the military radio station. It was November 23, Saturday, a bright, pleasant morning, relatively cool for Saigon and ideal for helicopter operations and bombing strikes. This first presentation of the assassination news was a real flap. I listened on my car radio while driving to the airport for a helicopter assault. Pop music preceded the newscast—there was no indication that such sad news was coming. The news started with some meaningless item. The third or fourth item was the story of a Greek ship that ran aground somewhere and was sinking, then the announcer said, 'President Kennedy was shot and fatally wounded by a sniper's bullet today. . .' Then came a blast of music and—as every morning—some disc jockey started his daily morning program with a cheerful shout about 'another sunny day in swinging Saigon.' Some rock-'n'-roll hits followed.

"I tried immediately to get some other radio station—the short-wave BBC or the English-language or French-language broadcasts of the Vietnamese government radio. I think others tried the same—the MP guards at the entrance to the Tan Son Nhut military airfield were all huddled over a transistor radio, and I passed unnoticed.

"At the operations desk of the armed helicopter company where I checked in for the upcoming military operation a sergeant asked me excitedly, 'Hey, you're from the AP? What was that about Kennedy?' Several pilots stood in groups. Everybody had heard it on the radio but none could believe it, especially as it was presented in such a casual way. One of them suggested it was a black joke. The operation that was to begin with the pilots' warming up the engines at 0730 was delayed. No pilot wanted to walk out of the briefing room without knowing exactly what had happened. Some of the crews came to the operations room to find out from the officers.

"At about 0720 the silly, happy music suddenly changed into serious, slow tunes—evidently somebody at the station had found out the full story and set the newscaster straight. Everybody hung around the transistor radios for the 0730 broadcast. It carried a few minutes of still fragmentary reports, but it was now clear that Kennedy had been assassinated. The pilots and their crews said nothing—just walked off to their helicopters. A few minutes later the engines started, the hellish noise of a score of swirling rotor-blades made any talk impossible and then the copters took off for their combat assault west of Saigon.

"I did not go along—the impact of the news was such that I did not want to go on a routine combat assault. And it would not have been of any news value that day. Leaving the airfield was as easy as getting in—the MP's were now busy talking, gesticulating. A large group stood around an MP jeep which had its radio tuned in, waiting for the next newscast.

"There were large groups talking excitedly at the bus stations.

168

At home I told my 74-year-old cook that Kennedy had been killed. He is a very good Catholic and admired Kennedy, mainly because he was also Catholic. He asked me in French, 'Was it the Vietminh?'

"I woke up some other correspondents by phone, then drove to the office to answer a score of calls, mostly from U. S. servicemen, most of them unknown to me, trying to get more information from the AP.

"For the rest of the day a veritable cloud of gloom settled over the billets and mess halls. For one morning the bars were nearly empty.

"The Vietnamese, who had just gone through a violent revolution, were in full and open sympathy with the Americans. Vietnamese office workers would come up to their bosses and say, 'I'm sorry.' Vietnamese officers would tell that to their U. S. advisers.

"Vietnamese—in a typical Asian way—would not discuss the matter with their American bosses, counterparts, or friends and argue history. They just showed that they felt sorry with the Americans.

"It was quite different when Martin Luther King and Robert Kennedy were assassinated. Then the expression of condolence was much more formal and one could hear it—said or unsaid—'You see, your house is in disorder, too. So don't you Americans blame us too much for failures because we are inefficient, brutal or corrupt.'

"A monument was set up for John Kennedy—a simple stone piece in front of the Saigon Cathedral. A metal plate gave the name, date of birth, and death of Kennedy. The place in front of the cathedral —the center of Saigon and Indochinese Catholicism—was renamed from Hoa Binh [Peace] Square to John F. Kennedy Square. A mass for Kennedy was said by the Apostolic Nuncio attended by many Vietnamese generals and their wives.

"Later, in 1965, Buddhists and students demonstrated against the fact that the church place had been renamed. Police had to protect the monument as gangs tried to attack it with picl s and paint. It was one of the worst moments in U. S.-Vietnamese relations and the Buddhists, followed by many difficult-to-identify groups, staged daily anti-American demonstrations.

"American GI's correctly assumed, especially after President Johnson's reassuring speech about continued American support for the war, that the war would go on, and their jobs would not change. As you know, the Army is a world apart, and while there is much talk in barracks and tents about events back home, in my experience, it never affects morale in a way that has any bearing on military performance.

"I remember a GI saying at the time, 'So it's really true. Boy,

I'll bet all hell's breaking loose back home. In another four months and twenty-three days, I'll be there to see it.'

"Later, ironically, a group of radical Catholic demonstrators paraded against an American sellout to the Buddhists and stole the Kennedy nameplate. The monument was shortly thereafter removed. However, the name of the square was not changed back, and the place with the tall, white statue of the Hoa Binh Madonna [Madonna of Peace] in front of the cathedral is still the John F. Kennedy Square.

"The popularity of Mrs. Kennedy in Vietnam became even greater after her husband's death. Side by side, pictures of Vietnamese singers or mythological folk heroes and Jacqueline Kennedy can be found in many remote villages, including those under Vietcong control. I often find these pictures when out on military operations."

Despite the momentary shock, on that Saturday morning, as every day in Vietnam, American helicopters whirred into the sky. The war for freedom went on, missing hardly a bloody or heroic beat.

The Vietcong, for their part, chose that day to release a young American civilian from jungle captivity. The prisoner, a technical adviser, had been captured while driving a jeep along a desolate coastal road, and held for five months. However, in case anyone interpreted his release as a gesture by the Reds in recognition of Kennedy's death, the Vietcong indicated that there was no such motive; the prisoner quoted his captors as saying that he had been freed because it was his birthday.

In communist North Vietnam, from which the Vietcong receive their orders, the official newspaper *Nhan Dan* jeered:

"Kennedy is dead. But the imperialist policy of the United States will remain the same."

Far away to the north, on another testing ground between the forces of reason and regression, a shivering dawn was breaking along the truce lines in Korea. Portable radios spread the news to 55,000 American troops still manning the bleak, windswept outposts of an almost forgotten battlefront.

AFTERMATH

THE NATION

There has long existed the school of thought—of which Disraeli was a principal exponent—that holds that assassinations have never affected the mainstream flow of human history. Those who hold this viewpoint cite the fact that many, if not most, assassins—an appellation derived from a secret order of Moslem fanatics, the Hashshahin, addicted to hashish—fail to achieve their political objectives. Undeniably, there is some evidence to support this line of thought.

Perhaps history's first political assassination, at least in Biblical terms, was Cain's killing of Abel; living in a theocracy, Cain became jealous of what he deemed God's preference for Abel and possibly hoped to succeed to Abel's position of pre-eminence. If such was Cain's reasoning, it failed disastrously, because God, according to the Book of Genesis, pronounced a curse on Cain and declared him "a fugitive and a vagabond . . . in the earth."

Nor, as another example, did the assassination of Caesar contribute much to solving the problems of Rome, although one argument cited by the assassins was that Caesar's liquidation would preserve the Roman republic by preventing him from becoming emperor. Twenty-one years later Julius Caesar's nephew, Augustus, became emperor, and Rome continued its political decline.

In feudal Europe, political assassination was virtually a way of life. Food tasters were common, and no medieval nobleman traveled without a bodyguard. Yet, as some experts on the subject point out, despite such political mayhem, the mixture of philosophical inspiration, scientific and artistic achievement, economic transformation, and other cultural forces that produced the Renaissance and Enlightenment continued to grow and develop.

The argument can also be advanced that political murders have often led to consequences that the assassins did not envision but that have had their effect on history. Although John Wilkes Booth failed to revive the defeated South by killing Lincoln, was not American history perhaps changed, to at least some extent, by the fact that Lincoln was prevented from living out the last three years of his second term? Might not the victorious President, who was at the peak of his power and prestige, credited with saving the Union, quite possibly have curbed radicals from destroying the culture of the Confederacy and thus ameliorated at least somewhat the South's bitterness after the war?

It is also argued by some students of history that the Slavic conspirators who assassinated Austrian Archduke Franz Ferdinand and his wife at Sarajevo, Yugoslavia, on June 28, 1914, failed in their goal of achieving freedom for the Slavic people held subject by the Viennese Hapsburgs; in modern Yugoslavia, the Slavs are still a minority, dominated by the ruling Serbs. Yet, the assassination at Sarajevo, by helping touch off World War I—which in turn rearranged the map of Europe, enthroned communism in Russia, and sowed the seeds of an even more disastrous World War II—had a cataclysmic effect on human affairs.

To posit, therefore, that no political assassination ever changes anything of historical significance would seem to be a rather simplistic statement, open to question.

Indubitably, there is plentiful evidence that—whatever the objectives of the assassin who killed John F. Kennedy—there is much in contemporary history that has *not* been changed as a result of the President's assassination.

In the United States, the struggle to achieve a morally perfect and materially equable society continues. The struggle, which was revived and given new urgency by Kennedy, has run into the disenchantment of practical realities. The nation is beginning to perceive, for example, that welfare checks alone cannot wipe out poverty, that it will require more than inflammatory rhetoric to better the lot of the less fortunate, under the American system. There is still apathy and escapism. "Pete and Gladys" have left the CBS television network, but "Lucy" is still popular, and "As the World Turns" still turns. Rifles are still as numerous as fishing poles, with the accompanying toll of accidental shootings and sniper sprees. The nation continues to take for granted the fact that thousands are killed in automobiles on the nation's highways every year, that so many American children are mentally scarred by the breakup of parents.

On the other hand, it might be difficult to substantiate, but one can speculate whether subconscious nostalgia for the New Frontier has been a catalyst in the increasing bitterness against President Johnson over Vietnam. As sincere as the critics' opposition to the conflict may be, could it be fueled by the unspoken—if imponderable—assumption that had John Kennedy lived the United States would not have become so deeply involved? That such nostalgia for the Kennedy era exists was undeniably born out by Robert Kennedy's strong, if tragically truncated, bid for the Presidency, which *Time* magazine aptly christened "the politics of restoration."

One might also ask whether the take-history-into-your-own-hands logic employed by Kennedy's assassin may have played some part in the anarchy that has beset the United States since. Repulsive as the assassination was, there are some who suspect that it may have engendered a reverse lashing out among those who felt politically victimized by it. Clearly there is a Pandora's box of other factors behind the nation's current social unrest, ranging from poverty to communist subversion, and the controversy over the Vietnam war has been a special cause of friction.

In the space of a few years following John Kennedy's assassination, Winston Churchill died; so did Nehru of India and Adlai E. Stevenson. There is, of course, no connection between the tragedy in Dallas and their passing. But it is a truism to say that the moment of 1:33 P.M., November 22, 1963, did change the lives of millions of persons. By political definition alone, every life was altered, because those who had been living in the Kennedy era found themselves automatically shifted into the Johnson era. Lives—big and small—*were* changed in myriad ways.

One month after the assassination, Al Rike, who had helped carry the President's body out of Parkland Hospital, quit his job as an ambulance driver. "I had been pretty tired of picking up babies killed in car wrecks and such things," Rike explains, "and then that afternoon with the President was just too much." Rike went to work in a bakery for awhile, then became a policeman. He is now a night police dispatcher in Highland Park, a fashionable residential sector in the northern part of Dallas.

Levi Deike has been postmaster at Hye, Texas, for 34 of his 57 years. In Hye (population 140), this is an important position. But John Kennedy's death made Deike an even bigger personality. Deike was a personal friend of the new President. When he was a boy, he used to play baseball with a lanky youngster named Lyndon Johnson.

The town of Hye is just a cluster of houses, a filling station, and a general store along US 290. Deike's post office is off in one corner of Hye Store, which trades in such staple merchandise as groceries and overalls, and big sacks of feed. The town rests deep in the heart of Texas, in the rocky hill country made famous by the LBJ Ranch, the Texas White House that lies only three miles east of Hye.

"I turned on the television right after we heard what happened in Dallas," Deike recalls. "I realized immediately that my long-time friend was now my boss, he being President and me postmaster."

Deike, a tight-lipped man of German descent, says Johnson "has dropped by to see me quite a few times. One time the President asked me who was the postmaster general when I was appointed postmaster on June 19, 1934, and I couldn't remember.

"Not a lot has changed really," Deike reflects, "but I guess it has made the job a little more pleasurable."

An obscure but pretty Russian girl named Marina, who was born in Minsk and married a young defector from America named Lee Harvey Oswald, is now known throughout the world—as is her former mother-in-law, Mrs. Marguerite Oswald, once a virtually unknown widow in Fort Worth, Texas.

A writer named William Manchester became famous, and was involved in one of history's most celebrated controversies over what was fit to print by agreeing to a procedural arrangement with the Kennedy family for writing a book on the assassination.

The lives of already well-known persons were inevitably touched. Arthur Goldberg, for example, President Kennedy's Secretary of Labor, was appointed to the Supreme Court by Lyndon Johnson, then later persuaded by Johnson to step down from that lifetime post to become the U. S. ambassador to the United Nations, a position he ultimately resigned from.

Bill Don Moyers, a one-time Marshall, Texas, newspaper delivery boy who was an aide to Vice-President Johnson, became White House press secretary and utility man in the Johnson Administration, then publisher of *Newsday*.

Jack Valenti, a Houston public relations man, became a Presidential aide under Johnson, won brief notoriety for his proclamation that he could sleep better at night knowing that Lyndon Johnson was in the White House, then moved on to become czar of the American motion picture industry.

John-John and Caroline Kennedy were cloistered with all the attention of orphaned royalty. Their mother became the perennial object of the inevitable questions: Will she marry again, and if so whom?

But, perhaps, the forces at work following the tragedy in Dallas have exercised their most dramatic effect in the murders of two other liberal American leaders—the Rev. Dr. Martin Luther King Jr. and Robert F. Kennedy. The latter died while campaigning to restore the Kennedy name to the White House, leaving a younger brother, Ted, now heir to the family's political aspirations.

How, indeed, the question arises, did the slaying of John Kennedy affect everyone's life? "The tragedy of John Fitzgerald Kennedy," James Reston of *The New York Times* declared, "was greater than the accomplishment, but in the end the tragedy enhances the accomplishment and revives the hope."

As a social group, Negroes were the most affected by John Kennedy's death—and then by the subsequent deaths of Dr. King and Robert Kennedy.

In the late 1950's and the first year or two of the 60's, many American Negroes, especially those in the South, wondered bitterly whether there was hope for them. The years following the Supreme Court decision of 1954 that outlawed segregated schools had brought one legal evasion after another. It was in this period that President Kennedy eventually came to represent genuine hope to Negroes throughout the nation.

Five years after Dallas, Charles Evers, whose own brother was slain by a hidden rifleman, looked back and saw a change in his state of Mississippi. "Kennedy's picture is in practically every [Negro] home around. Negroes really appreciated him. He really started clearing the climate, making people think we exist, that somebody could give a damn. The same feeling had already grown up about his brother. I remember before Bobby became Attorney General, we couldn't even get a postcard from the Attorney General's office."

Evers echoes a feeling, shared by other civil rights leaders, that the Kennedy brothers really did not initially understand a great deal about racial problems. He remembers vividly a private gathering that Robert Kennedy, while Attorney General, held with a group of Negro leaders during one school desegregation crisis. One Negro who was present suggested that the Attorney General consider asking the President to fly to the scene and, with whatever armed guard necessary, personally take the Negro children by the hand and lead them safely to the school. According to Evers, Bobby Kennedy laughed, evidently because he thought that the idea was being proposed humorously. To Evers, Robert Kennedy at the time simply did not understand the deep symbolic significance such a gesture from the President of the United States might have for civil rights leaders.

Evers now believes that one measure of both Kennedy brothers was their ability to grasp quickly the depth of the racial problem. "That's what made them so great. They admitted they knew so little about Negroes. He [the President] wasn't a champion of civil rights at first, but he learned—unlike those who'd been around for a long time and knew about the problem. John and Bobby were both champions of human rights. Some who knew more were still willing to keep us down."

Terrell County is a case in point. It is a predominantly farming county in southwest Georgia, not far from the Alabama line. It is a "Black Belt" county, one of about 30 in Georgia with populations that are more than 50 percent Negro. Terrell County, as its chief claim to fame, was the first county in the United States named in a federal court suit involving voter registration.

These same counties have Negro populations so large that substantial Negro voter registration could change the entire political structure in the state. Terrell County's entire voting-age population totals only a little more than 7,000—roughly 3,000 whites and 4,000 Negroes.

On Sept. 14, 1962, President Kennedy, at a news conference, declared, "I don't know any more outrageous action which I have seen occur in this country in a good many months or years. Cowardly as well as outrageous." The President was referring to the night-rider burnings of two small Negro churches in Terrell County, both used for voter registration meetings. Kennedy promised that all citizens who wanted to vote would be protected, by force and additional legislation if necessary.

As Kennedy indicated when he denounced the church burnings, it did take more federal administrative action and legislation to guarantee Negro voter registration. He was not to live to see that legislation become law. But the passage of the Voting Rights Act of 1965—which had much of its inspiration in the Kennedy Administration's early battles with southern white racists—spelled the final breakthrough in counties like Terrell. Where earlier civil rights legislation had failed to ensure southern Negroes access to the ballot box, they could now realistically aspire to be part of the democratic process.

"That did more good than anything," was the way Charles Evers expressed his satisfaction with the Voting Rights Act.

A similar feeling was shared by Thomas C. Chatman, an Albany businessman involved in voter registration drives in an area that includes Terrell County. By the spring of 1968, according to the U.S. Civil Rights Commission, Negro voter registration in Terrell had grown from less than 100 to 2,188.

"To my own knowledge," says Chatham, "there's been a great easing of tension insofar as allowing people to vote. It's much more free, say, in a county like Terrell. There's been a positive effect. Some people still operate under fear. They're still afraid. But it's older people. Among young Negroes, the late President's memory is fresh. They—the younger people—idolize the man. When they think of him, they certainly do not hesitate to go in and register."

Chatman says that the same feeling clings to the memory of Robert Kennedy. "Everybody admired the Kennedy brothers. They stimulated and motivated people. At voter registration meetings, we tell them these men gave their lives to help make them first-class citizens, and the first thing is to vote."

Throughout the South, the Negro reaction has been the same, as witness the situation in Selma, Alabama. In the early spring of 1965 Negro and white demonstrators tried to march from Selma to Montgomery, the state capital, to dramatize their appeal for Negro voting rights. All news media, including live television, covered the confrontation on a small bridge at the edge of downtown Selma when the procession of demonstrators was halted by Alabama state troopers. The marchers were given two minutes to turn back, then were broken up with teargas and clubs.

A Baptist preacher, the Rev. Frederick Douglas Reece, the president of the Dallas County Voters' League, was there that day on the bridge. Looking back, the clergyman says that "the average Negro in the South felt this great loss—felt that many things had come about on behalf of Negroes, and the loss of John Kennedy somehow gave the feeling that this was the end, in a sense."

Yet, on the contrary, Kennedy's death was followed by the beginnings of success in southern Negro voter registration. In all of Dallas County, for example, only 300 Negroes were registered at the time of the President's slaying, even though the Negro voting-age population totaled nearly 15,000. By mid-1968, according to Reece, there were approximately 11,000 registered Negro voters out of that 15,000.

The new ballot power, the preacher points out, has made many things possible in Dallas County. "It has caused the white community to give a little more attention to the segment of the community predominantly Negro. It's even meant jobs; Negroes were hired in stores just in the last year."

As in the South, the legacy of John Kennedy and his heir, brother Robert, affected Negro lives in the North.

Bob Mosely was born in Harlem, a name that symbolizes the deprivation and squalor of America's Negro ghettos. Pulling himself out of poverty, Mosely became a statistician for the New York State Department of Labor in 1953 and promptly moved his wife and three children to a suburb in New York's Westchester County where he could provide them a better education. One of his daughters earned a Ph.D. and the other a master's degree. His son has a degree in business administration. But Mosely maintains a loyal link with the teeming city blocks where he was reared. Since 1962, he has conducted beauty pageants in Harlem.

The day that President Kennedy was shot, Mosely got sick to his stomach and cried. In the years since, he notes, "there's been a greater awareness on our part that we must get a better control of the economics of the communities in which we live. Because if we don't, the monies spent in the community will be taken out by people who don't spend in the community. In these five years, the black man has become fully cognizant of his identity and he's proud of it. When this happens with our people, there's no looking back. This is the change. This is the big change."

Livingston Wingate is a symbol of black leadership in Harlem, now director of the New York Urban League, a former executive director of Associated Community Teams, a Harlem antipoverty agency, and president of the Harlem Youth Opportunities Unlimited.

Recalling the Kennedy years, Wingate says:

"We [Negroes] were at the height of what might be termed the second revolution, which started in 1954 with the Supreme Court decision, Brown v. the Board of Education. It was the era of the wade-ins, sit-ins, marches, the great appeal to the conscience of white America. It culminated in the white backlash.

"A few more blacks could go to the theater; a few more could ride public transportation; a few more blacks could vote. But for the majority of blacks, their living standards in the area of housing, health services, education, in comparison to their white brothers, had not improved. As a matter of fact, the gap had widened."

Wingate knew Robert Kennedy as a friend, and says that his slaying in Los Angeles has "shaken me, for some strange reason, even more severely than that of the President. Perhaps because I knew the Senator. I knew him well. Bobby Kennedy was assassinated in what may be termed the era of the white backlash and the era of black disillusionment. We had witnessed the failure of integration as an effective strategy for black freedom. The civil rights movement has been replaced by a strong emphasis on the black man who has accepted the reality of his political, economic, cultural and geographical separation. It is marked by a black man's search for his own set of values which emanate from his struggles to survive. It is marked by a realization that he is neither fully African nor American, but instead is reflecting the isolated geographical turf which a racist America has carved out for his residency."

The focus now, says Wingate, "seems to be on converting the ugly black slum into a beautiful black community. No longer is the emphasis on busing the black child into the white neighborhood. Instead, it is upon developing quality schools within the black ghetto, which are compatible to the unique style and rhythm of the black ghetto child. The emphasis seems to be on controlling the services: health, police, educational, and so on, within the geographical area. The black man must have control of all things within his area which affects his life. The test of well-meaning whites is to bring their technical know-how into the black community, but on the black man's agenda just as they would do for underprivileged foreign nations."

There was also an area of American life, often overlooked, that was touched and altered by John Kennedy. Much of the new social consciousness of Big Business dates from the Kennedy Administration, and most significantly from the confrontation between the late President and Roger Blough, chairman of the U.S. Steel Corporation. Blough touched off one of the most dramatic tugs-of-war in recent Wall Street history the day he drove to the White House with a message for Kennedy. Blough did so on the heels of union-management negotiations in the steel industry, during which the Administration had pressed labor for a noninflationary settlement.

As Kennedy read Blough's message, he learned that U.S. Steel

was at that moment announcing an across-the-board price increase
for its steel products. The President exploded. To a startled nation,
Kennedy denounced U.S. Steel, portraying the giant corporation as
an example of selfishness and greed in Big Business. The intimation
was that U.S. Steel was a corporation without a conscience, and that
in modern times no company could endanger the economy or hold
itself more important than the national interest. U.S. Steel hastily
backed down.

A few years after this celebrated clash, a reporter was talking
with a top executive of U.S. Steel at the corporation's New York
offices. "No corporation, no matter how successful," the executive
said, "can continue to remain so unless it aligns its aims with the
national interest."

It was newly understood that Big Business and Big Government
must cooperate. That need for cooperation was soon reflected in the
speeches of virtually every major corporate executive. So common
did the theme become that Henry Ford II, chairman of the Ford
Motor Company, felt compelled to introduce his speech to the National Retail Merchants on Jan. 12, 1967, this way:

"I plan to speak to you this evening on a well-worn subject—the
relations between government and business. If anyone were to keep
track of the top 10 subjects for business banquet speeches, government and business would probably be Number One, year in and
year out."

No less a figure than Roger Blough himself devoted his address
to the 76th annual meeting of the American Iron and Steel Institute
in New York on May 23, 1968, to the subject of "The Public Life
of Private Business." John D. Harper, president of the Aluminum
Company of America, whose price increase was slapped back by
Kennedy's successor, Lyndon Johnson, was soon to cool his anguish
and address a meeting of the National Association of Manufacturers
on the subject, "Private Enterprise's Public Responsibility." Said
Harper:

"Great tides of change are on the move today, and the business
system of this nation must move with them, must help to direct
them through the exercise of its public responsibility. We cannot
shirk or evade that responsibility."

Swiftly, as the idea grew that Big Business must cooperate with
Big Government, it also became apparent that to do so Big Business
must also expand its social horizons in the interests of a balanced
and just economy, that it had to, in fact, join in a partnership with

government to tackle the problems of air and water pollution, crime, urban decay, public transportation, better schooling, more jobs. The Job Corps, business participation in the problems of the ghettos, and special training programs for Negro workers are partly the result of this new spirit of business-government cooperation for the good of society. The participation of business in areas where it once thought that profits could not be made—that is, in improving the social environment—in part emanates from its attitude of social responsibility, which was given major impetus during, and after, the Kennedy years.

Undoubtedly one of the most significant effects has been the change in style in the Administration between John F. Kennedy and Lyndon B. Johnson. The Boston rocker is gone, and the Texas hat that John Kennedy had declined to don publicly in Fort Worth became symbolic of the United States government. There was a new brusqueness in style. The urbane, well-born easterner gave way to the rough-hewn, country-bred southwesterner, whose compulsive energy and readiness to make the fullest use of Presidential power was typical of the often ruthless dynamism of the Texan.

The Administration has to a degree lost its sense of humor, or at least the easy-going wit of a President who was able to laugh at himself. If one wished to make an unkind comparison, he could quote the words of Horace Walpole, "The world is a comedy to those who think; a tragedy to those who feel."

Notwithstanding the emigration of Jack Valenti to Hollywood, and Lyndon and Lady Bird Johnson's own sincere interest in encouraging the arts, the relationship between the White House and filmdom has never been the same; movie celebrities no longer enjoy informal entree to the Presidential circle. And although the Johnson Administration utilizes its own breed of staff intellectuals, there has been a notable estrangement between the White House and left-wing thinkers. The major cause has been the Vietnam war, but a contributing factor is simply that the most avant-garde intellectuals do not take to Lyndon Johnson's form of hard-headed liberalism.

Indeed, Camelot died hard for many in Washington. Although a surprising number of the New Frontiersmen who came in with Kennedy stayed around, not only in the top spots but in second, third, and lower echelon jobs, many did not.

A favorite indoor cocktail sport became the unchivalrous one of shooting at the Birds—Lady Bird and Lynda Bird. As for Johnson himself, few presidents have been on the receiving end of as much ridiculing innuendo as LBJ, from his accent to the size of his ears, from his ego to his degree—not from Harvard, of course, but from Southwest Texas State Teachers College.

Yet, Camelot was not all rosy to some Washington observers, who saw Johnson's style of Texas openness and hospitality as a refreshing change from the stuffy Boston airs.

"Yeah," says one Congressman, "you read a lot about what Jackie did down at the White House—the decorations, the new air, the smart parties with the chic menus and oh-so-right entertainment. But my wife never saw it. Not many wives of Congressmen did."

"You know what's different with Lady Bird?" he continued. "My wife don't have to read about the White House now. She's being invited down there all the time. So am I. You just ask a congressional wife and she'll tell you that Lady Bird's tops."

If congressional wives liked the new Administration, so did most of their husbands—in the beginning.

"Hell, you had to go along with Lyndon that first couple of years in office," says one veteran legislator. "He had the nation with him. If it hadn't been for Vietnam, if it hadn't been for the money crunch, if it hadn't been for the riots, if it hadn't been oh, hell. Look at what's happened in the last three years. Take any of those ifs out and Lyndon would probably have had it made."

More important has been the effect of the assassination on the nation's politics. Almost surely, the disaster engendered a desire, conscious or subconscious, among political leaders to make restitution for such a national tragedy. The national feeling of guilt may well have helped persuade a previously recalcitrant Congress to steamroll through the historic social reform legislation that distinguished the Johnson Administration's first years. That legislation included some of the most far-reaching proposals ever written into the statute books—chief among them the civil rights and antipoverty programs. The first gave new hope to the American Negro fighting for equality and justice, and significantly shifted political power in the South by enrolling unprecedented numbers of Negroes on voting lists. The second gave federal sanction to a concept radically new in American philosophy: that other taxpayers, through their government, owe the poor a living, and that the poor themselves have the right to "maximum feasible participation" in local antipoverty projects. Both series of legislation were in part posthumous paeans to

John Kennedy, laws won in death that he had been unable to gain in life. Thus, his assassination broke the legislative logjam that had so frustrated him, and helped set the nation on a radically different course in its social relations.

This phenomenon is readily confirmed by Washington observers today.

"This nation put on a hair shirt," says a veteran congressman. "Maybe it was because this was the first great national tragedy you could see and feel in your home because of television. But whatever the reason, we wore a hair shirt. I don't think you'll get much argument on that. Certainly I think that was one of the reasons for so much legislation that was passed in the second session of the 88th Congress and in the 89th Congress."

Many in Washington frankly think that the myth that has grown to surround Kennedy's 1,000 days in office have created Camelot where there was no Camelot. Perhaps it was the contrast—memories of the youthful Kennedy compared to the man from Texas, in age only a few years older, in manner generations apart. Perhaps it was a yearning — for something young, now lost, for something different, not cut to the mold of established politics. Few remember how much trouble John F. Kennedy had with Congress, how little of his legislation actually became law, how much of it was bogged down and seemingly never destined to move.

Certainly there is doubt that the Civil Rights Act of 1964 would have ever passed in its final form had Kennedy remained alive. Johnson urged passage as a memorial to Kennedy. By itself, that may not have cut much ice with a hard-bitten Congress. But the mood of the nation, a nation wearing a "hair shirt," had changed. And Congress does react to the moods of the nation, although, admittedly, it often does so weeks and months after it is obvious that there is a change of mood.

Everett Dirksen perhaps expressed it best, perched on a rickety table in the Senate press gallery, holding one of his periodic "moments with the press."

Why was he supporting the civil rights bill? Did he think it would pass? Could that 100-day filibuster be choked off?

"Yes, I do," he said. "And, I'll tell you why.

"In history, there is a time and a place when every idea must come to its destiny. On this civil rights bill . . . the time and the place has come."

There was other legislation that John F. Kennedy had proposed and had seen wither in the recesses of Senate and House committees.

He had a dream of helping the poor people of Appalachia, a dream born from that West Virginia primary against Hubert H. Humphrey that was his catapult into the Presidency.

The Appalachian Regional Commission became law in 1965.

The war on poverty, a war that Kennedy had preached must be won, passed in 1964 in the wake of the assassination. Again, the now-dead shining knight's memory was invoked.

"Look," says a Democrat who has served 14 years in Congress, a man of social conscience from a basically conservative state, "OEO, Appalachia, civil rights, aid to education, Medicare, health research, Social Security amendments, teacher corps, Vista, housing — all of these things probably would have come, but it would have taken a lot longer.

"Kennedy's assassination jarred the nation's conscience. Now don't ask me why. Maybe it is because basically in this country every one admits that every man should have a right to a job, medical care, a good education, a decent living in his old age. None of these things is brand-new, you know. They're extensions of FDR's days — oh, tricked up here and there, yet basically extensions.

"But I think that when Kennedy was killed, people felt something should be done, and now. That tomorrow is too uncertain.

"All of this is damned hard to put into words. It's just a feeling I have. And I think that's the only way you can say it: there was a feeling after the killing that what he said was morally right, and the time to do something was right now."

Dirksen's "the time has come" philosophy might well have been a collective label for the huge stack of legislation passed by the 89th Congress. Of course, Republican ranks had been decimated by the Goldwater debacle, but the shadow of the assassination was present just the same. In the second session of the 89th a mood began to develop that perhaps Congress was going too far, too fast. The Senate majority leader, Mike Mansfield, at the outset of the 90th session in 1967, urged Congress to slow down on new laws, that it was now time to make the glut of social legislation work. Nevertheless, Kennedy's historic proposals were law.

Before his death, John Kennedy's sole major accomplishment with any real public impact had been the Peace Corps, and there is plenty of argument that the idea was originally that of Hubert Humphrey. In either case, Kennedy got it through. Aside from the dramatics surrounding it, the Peace Corps was the first attempt to give college youths something concrete on which to hang their ideals. Although the bloom of the corps has faded in the fact of antiwar demonstrations and campus revolt, it demonstrated that there is a role for idealistic youth.

If it was short on legislative accomplishments, the Kennedy Administration was certainly long on mood — freshness, new thinking, new directions. Perhaps, this was really what Camelot was — not a place, but an idea. Because of this, whether mystic place or mood, the lives of every American have been changed, and by extension the world. Civil rights is law; so now is open housing. That the last vestiges of second-class citizenship, by law, have been stricken is evident in the switch in goals among the Negro leadership, from rights to economic fulfillment. The omnibus aid to federal education bill struck down the barrier to some help (in textbooks and materials) to church schools. And not a thunderbolt was unleashed.

The seed that was planted that every man, woman, and child has a right to a decent life is nurturing. The guaranteed income — be it called income maintenance, negative income tax, or whatever — is becoming more and more accepted, and there are some in Congress who predict that the idea will be fact by 1970.

Certainly the "get this country moving" belief of Kennedy did stir the nation into new directions that became turnpikes in history only after his death. That much of this was escalated because of his death is a tribute more to what Kennedy stood for than for the fact that he was a giant as a statesman.

Perhaps this is true of any controversial figure whose place in history is marked by martyrdom. (Martin Luther King, many believe, was a waning figure, scorned by many of his own race and fast losing much of his white liberal support in the months before this slaying.)

To be sure, the nation's new course has cost dearly those who bear the tax burden. The American Medical Association's Dr. Edward Annis has been proved right in his warning that the Kennedy-proposed Medicare program would cost far more than originally estimated. Federal spending in other areas has also risen to unprecedented heights, in large part because of the Vietnam war, but also because of social betterment programs.

Unanswerable, but nonetheless intriguing, is whether Kennedy would have pursued the same course as Johnson has in Vietnam. He had already begun the buildup of U. S. "military advisers" there.

In any event, Johnson, elevated to the Presidency by Kennedy's death, has pursued the war with stubbornness, dividing the nation as rarely before. The lives of thousands of American young men have been redirected, if not lost, in the savage conflict.

The war has also reshaped the American military establishment. The United States has had to withdraw troops from Europe. Whereas in the 1950's and early '60's, most of the Pentagon's attention centered on the push-button missile and age of retaliation, Vietnam made it necessary to return to the concept of classic troop warfare; the infantry again prevailed over Buck Rogers.

"The Army's always changing its concepts," one articulate colonel says. "We had the square division, then the triangular division, the battle group concept vs. the regiment. You went from horses to tanks and now you've gone to helicopters to take the place of parachutes for quick mobility.

"Remember that old saw in every western cavalry movie you ever watched: the sergeant (usually played by a Ward Bond type) is chewing out the rookie lieutenant (Audie Murphy or Tab Hunter or one of those types) and he says, 'Mister, in this man's army you adapt to the terrain. You don't play hero and stand up and do it like they do in those manuals at West Point. You fighting injuns, mister; in rocks, you become a rock. They may have told you a good officer stands up and is counted. Mister, a dead officer ain't no good officer. He's a stupid officer. You do what you have to do — and you do it now.'

"The military does what it has to do — now. That's what changes military thinking."

And the President, Johnson, has stamped his brand on everything the government does, much to the annoyance of many federal officials.

"Hell, the White House is now even announcing routine appointments and changes in assignments of Army generals and Navy admirals," one jealous government public-relations man grumbled.

Another protested, "If it's good, the White House will tell you about it. If it's bad, we get stuck with the announcement."

The most widespread and persistent effect of the assassination on the United States has perhaps been psychological. The immediate, most acute emotional reactions soon disappeared. But indications are that the tragedy engendered in the American people more deep-seated feelings of guilt and blighted hopes. In short, the assassination of President Kennedy *did* something to the nation from which it has yet to recover. The disaster shook America's confidence in itself as no previous event in this century—introducing a mood of bewilderment and despair.

The hospitality and good-humored politicking that characterized John Kennedy's last trip to Texas seem to have vanished in large measure from the American political scene. The President now rides around in a covered limousine, and often cannot show himself at ceremonies because of hostile mobs. To many Americans, even the promise of the United States has palled, and its fruits no longer seem so precious. A note of foreign-ness has crept into American culture; the narrow-brim hat has given way to the Nehru jacket. The nation as a whole no longer has a feeling of well-being and contentment; a sense of sickness fills the soul of many Americans while unbridled violence stalks the country's streets. There is a new and uncharacteristic fatalism—a willingness to accept the view that political assassination in the United States is not just something for the history books, but is a fact of modern American life.

The mass guilt growing out of the slaying of John Kennedy has been evident ever since the first rushed indictments by politicians and pundits, charging that the nation at large was somehow responsible for the crime. Illustrating the chorus of self-incrimination, Arkansas Senator Fulbright, in a speech two weeks after the assassination, called for "a national self-examination." Declared Fulbright:

"It may be that the cause lies wholly in the tormented brain of the assassin. It may be that the nation as a whole is healthy and strong, and entirely without responsibility for the great misfortune that has befallen it. It would be comforting to think so. I for one do not think so. I believe that our society, though in most respects decent, civilized, and humane, is not, and has never been, entirely so. Our national life . . . has also been marked by a baleful and incongruous strand of intolerance and violence."

This mood was perhaps most dramatically expressed in the initial reaction of J. Irwin Miller, president of the National Council of Churches, who said:

"This young man, our President, rests now in the care of his heavenly father. He came to responsibility in a time of difficulty and peril, and he led the nation with courage and dignity. . . We who live on stand, every one of us, under terrible judgment. His martyrdom resulted not alone from the dreadful act of one person but equally from the accumulated acts of all of us, who have hated when we should have loved."

In sum, millions of Americans had drilled into their consciences the idea that they were in some way silent accomplices in the murder of their President. A symptom of this attitude is perhaps reflected in still another finding from the survey of the National Opinion Research Center: three-fourths of those questioned about their reactions to the assassination "thought some kind of lesson had been learned, 25% specifically stating that there must be less hate and intolerance, more love and understanding, among all Americans."

Nowhere has the national mood of bewilderment at the assassination been more pronounced than in the city where it occurred. And probably no American metropolis in modern times has undergone such a scathing and often bitter reexamination of what it was and what it ought to be as did Dallas in the aftermath of John Kennedy's death. Dallas civic leaders even held a formal conference in the central Texas town of Salado to ponder future goals for Big D; the proceedings of the Salado conference were published in book form and sold at Neiman-Marcus for $1 a copy. Editorials in both of Dallas' daily newspapers held to the consistent view, "It could have happened anywhere."

Obviously, it could have. But the indelible fact was that it had happened in Big D, perhaps the proudest and most image-conscious of Texas' major cities.

Moreover, the assassination of John Kennedy had a major political impact on Dallas, and indeed throughout Texas: the Republicans, who had entertained high hopes of making major gains in the Lone Star State in the elections of 1964, were thoroughly routed. Sympathy for the slain President, coupled with the fact that a Texan, and Democrat, occupied the White House, proved disastrous to the GOP. One newspaper, analyzing that year's general election, described the results for Texas Republicans as an "unmitigated disaster." In Dallas County, after the votes were in, only one Republican public official remained in office. He felt, he said, "like the last survivor of the Lusitania."

GOP Congressman Bruce Alger of Dallas, who had been a spokesman and unofficial leader of the city's conservative bloc, went down to defeat before the Democratic mayor, dairyman Earle Cabell. In the state as a whole, prior to the November, 1964, election, the Texas delegation in the U.S. House of Representatives had contained two Republicans; afterward, the Lone Star contingent was solidly Democratic. By 1967, the GOP had regained two seats in the 23-man

Texas delegation, but neither district that voted Republican was near Dallas.

Yet no city changes completely, and Dallas has retained its own personality. Dallas' economic boom, grounded in banking, insurance, and aerospace-electronics, continues to flourish. Job hunters from the piney woods of east Texas and the open plains of west Texas still flock to Big D. Although the city's leaders and newspapers eulogized John F. Kennedy regularly after he was dead, as late as the summer of 1968, nearly five years after his death, there was still no memorial to him completed in the city, or any local freeway, park, or other public facility named for him — an amazing lack considering the wholesale renaming of streets, parks, and airports across the nation and throughout the world. A Kennedy Memorial Plaza is scheduled to be finished in 1969, but the newest major freeway being built through the city bears Johnson's initials. There is a small bronze plaque with a brief inscription in Dealey Plaza, adjacent to the site of the assassination, but about the only reminder of November 22, 1963—except what residents carry locked within their hearts—are the ever-present gatherings of curious tourists at the plaza, with license plates from as far away as New York, Iowa, and Oregon. One out-of-town housewife, who visited the site in mid-1968, wrote a relative:

"They are still putting wreaths near the inscription about him. It was so sad."

Some place flowers at the bronze plaque, some take pictures, and all have to move quickly to stay out of the way of busy traffic.

THE WORLD

As it has in the United States, the assassination of John F. Kennedy has worked its influences in the rest of the world.

Naturally, there is much abroad that has not changed. The Cold War, despite premature announcements of its death, continues to be a live corpse. Although the Atlantic partnership has been strained by Europe's resurgence of nationalism, notably in Gaullist France, the North Atlantic Treaty Organization still functions as a shield against Soviet designs on Western Europe. Western access to Berlin is still an issue.

Closer to home, only 90 miles from American shores, communist dictator Fidel Castro has clung to his Cuban stronghold. Although still frustrated in repeated attempts to export Peking-style revolution to the rest of Latin America, Castro has been undaunted in his fanaticism and seemingly immune from American attack. He has even been trying to subvert the United States through its Black Power extremists and student anarchists.

Rafael Gonzalez Labrada, now an accountant in Manhattan, was an officer of Brigade 2506 in the disastrous Bay of Pigs invasion in 1961. He spent 20 months as a prisoner in Cuba, and was in the next-to-last group of survivors exchanged by Castro for American drugs and medicines. On December 27, 1962, Gonzalez Labrada joined a multitude of Cubans who massed in Miami's Orange Bowl to watch President Kennedy receive a Cuban flag that had been carried into battle at the Bay of Pigs. Kennedy proclaimed to the cheering throng that the banner would one day be returned to a free Havana.

"But we didn't know then," says Gonzalez Labrada, "that the President had already made the Kennedy-Khruschev pact against invasion of Cuba. Before Kennedy was assassinated, we had all learned of the pact. It was only natural that we Cubans had grown to expect nothing more from the Kennedy Administration in our struggle. With President Johnson, after the Gulf of Tonkin and his intervention in the Dominican Republic, we saw some hope of freeing Cuba. But Johnson inherited the pact. His isolation with respect to the Cuban problem must be rooted in that agreement."

And what of John Kennedy's inspiration, the Alliance for Progress? By 1968, seven years after its founding, the United States had pumped more than $7 billion into the visionary effort to bring a better life to Latin America's 200 million inhabitants. Unquestionably, there have been results—new schools, new housing, and, most important of all, a new realization among Latin American leaders of the need for at least a start at reform.

Throughout the hemisphere, however, critics have wondered whether Kennedy's noble program has achieved anything approaching the aspirations it had aroused. Poverty is still widespread south of the border, and Latin America's cultural ills—the root of its poverty— are largely untouched. Striving to pump new life into the alliance, President Johnson held summit meetings with Latin American presidents. He drafted Sol Linowitz, the dynamic captain of the Xerox Corporation, to go to Washington as U.S. ambassador to the Organization of American States. In other ways, he has eloquently carried forward with the *Alianza*. But there still seemed to be more alliance than progress. "The Alliance for Progress has left us a name, and nothing more," declared Costa Rican President Joaquin Trejos Fernandez.

The slaying of John Kennedy has likewise had its repercussions in other areas of the world. One of the most interesting effects has occurred in the Middle East. For David Ben-Gurion and his Israeli people, the assassination, paradoxically, produced a sense of warmer relations with Washington. For Egypt's Nasser, the death of the American President was a blow to the aspirations of Arab nationalism.

As the Arabs tell it, the day President Kennedy was assassinated

marked the beginning of a sad ebb in Arab-U.S. relations. The tragedy, one Egyptian official contends, started a "steady switch from a positive, balanced attitude between the Arabs and Israel to an open, hostile policy against the Arabs." An Arab League leader, reflecting on John Kennedy's murder, comments sadly, "His death was not merely the end of one man's life, but it constituted the death of reason and fair play of American policy in the Middle East."

Officially, the Arabs refrain from linking Kennedy's death to any political coloring. Privately, however, many an Arab official points a finger of suspicion at Israel and its Zionist backers in the United States. The belief that seems to underlie the general thinking in Cairo is that the Jews were duly alarmed by Kennedy's "cordial dialogue" with Nasser, and that they plotted and assassinated the President.

Kennedy's "understanding" toward the Middle East, a confidant of President Nasser has written, was demonstrated in many instances. The confidant, Mohammed Hassanein Haikal, editor-in-chief of the Cairo newspaper *Al Ahram*, recalled that under Kennedy the United States had been one of the first Western powers to recognize the republican regime in Yemen. Moreover, Haikal noted, Kennedy had resisted Congress' decision to bar American wheat shipments to Egypt, and had submitted to the United Nations a draft proposal calling for the return of Palestine's Arab refugees to their homes, or alternately compensating them. Most importantly, Haikal added, Kennedy had initiated a "warm and friendly" dialogue with Nasser.

The Arab League has described the Kennedy era as "one of understanding and realism" toward Arab problems, particularly Palestine. It has praised Kennedy as "sympathetic with Arab problems" and declared that Kennedy's thinking had led him to abolish "such myopic strategies as the Eisenhower doctrine and Dulles' policy of brinkmanship." In the words of the Arab League, the Eisenhower doctrine was predicated on an imaginary vacuum created by the downfall of the British Empire in the Middle East, purporting to fill it either by an actual American presence in the area or by creating "puppet" regimes in Arab states. Kennedy, by contrast, was portrayed by the Arab League as beginning anew to enhance nationalistic feelings in the Arab world by showing respect for Arab nationalism. This, the League contended, drove communism away from the Arab East and projected a popular, respectable image of the United States in the Moslem world.

In sum, as the Arabs picture it, they saw nothing from Truman or Eisenhower but smiles for Israel and a rigid military policy that culminated in the landing of American Marines in Lebanon in 1958. In a policy reversal, the Arabs assert, Kennedy wanted to protect American interests in the Middle East by befriending rather than intimidating the Arabs. A league report conceded that Kennedy's Middle East dilemma was to balance his friendship with the Arabs against his obvious desire to keep Israel alive. But after Kennedy, Arab diplomats say, the "ebb" began in Arab-American relations because of "Washington's flagrant flirtation with Israel."

In an unusual confluence of opinion, Israeli leaders confirm the Arab view—that Kennedy was closer to the Arab world than President Johnson. Officials in Tel Aviv believe that President Johnson has given Israel firmer support than Kennedy did.

Israeli Foreign Minister Abba Eban emphasizes, nonetheless, that "there has been no sharp deviation. Policy has moved along the same lines. The friendship which Kennedy enunciated toward Israel has not only been maintained but has flowered further. On the balance of forces, Kennedy made significant moves: he agreed to supply Hawk missiles. Johnson developed this further with the supply of tanks."

"Kennedy once even used the term 'ally.'" Eban recalls. "This has been fully supported by President Johnson, who would himself agree that he has acted with continuity. He put his own special zeal into it."

Dr. Shlomo Avineri, lecturer in political science at Jerusalem's Hebrew University, views the switch from Kennedy to Johnson more in terms of personalities:

"The change has affected the relationship of leaders more than the direction of policies. On a personal level, Prime Minister Levi Eshkol may feel easier with Johnson than he would have with Kennedy. Eshkol, like Johnson, is chummy and folksy. He would find more in common with Johnson than with the sophisticated, New England, Harvard aloofness of Kennedy. The Johnson Administration leaned over backwards in 1964-65 to help the Israeli government. I think Kennedy would have done the same."

Mark Segal, a leading Israeli political commentator, points out that the agreement allowing Israel to acquire U.S. Hawk antiaircraft missiles went through under Kennedy. "But on the other hand," Segal says, "Kennedy was rather charmed by Nasser. He was more sympathetic with the Egyptian president than Johnson has been. Johnson is a different kettle of fish altogether. He calls a spade a spade. Kennedy was more adroit in world affairs."

"But the State Department runs America's foreign policy," Segal contends. "God forbid we should benefit from the assassination, but there is a certain feeling in my country that Johnson is more sympathetic and open-minded to Israel's interests than Kennedy was or would have been. Kennedy was more under the influence of the State Department."

Reuven Barkatt, a member of the Knesset (Parliament) security council, observes:

"The U.S. attitude to Israel has not exactly been one of pure, altruistic friendship. There has been an identity of interests vis-à-vis the Soviet Union. I don't think the assassination changed this attitude considerably. I sincerely believe that Kennedy understood the humanitarian value of our enterprise. Maybe he was more rational in his approval. Johnson has been more emotionally involved in this friendship."

A colleague of Barkatt's, Shimon Perez, assistant secretary-general of the powerful Labor party, thinks that if Kennedy had lived there possibly would have been a better rapprochement between the United States and Russia that, in turn, would have affected the Middle East.

"Also," says Perez, "Kennedy would have tried to convince Nasser not to do all those foolish things in May, 1967. Then again, I don't think he would have been successful."

Probably the greatest single effect of the assassination abroad, taken together more recently with the assassinations of Martin Luther King and Robert Kennedy, has been to raise questions about the stability of the United States as a nation. From foreign lands whose traditions of cloak-and-dagger political bloodshed are far richer than America's has spewed a cacophony of contempt for American culture. Foreign politicians and commentators began describing Americans as a breed of lawless gunslingers. To what degree the assassination may have affected official relations between the United States and other nations is difficult to assess, but the fact that President Kennedy's murder occurred at a time when several American allies were showing greater independence of the United States may have been significant. The disaster in America could hardly have helped those foreigners striving to maintain intimate ties with Washington.

At the U.S. State Department, the "nuts and bolts men"—lower echelon personnel charged with executing policy work—take a more sanguine view of the effects of the assassination on world affairs. They profess irritation and surprise at questions suggesting that there have been any major changes in foreign policy as a result of the slaying. "The same people who made foreign policy for Kennedy kept on making it for Johnson," says one. "It was their policy. Why change it?"

The big change, of course, was the decision by Johnson to escalate the war in Vietnam. But, as he and others in his Administration have been wont to point out, he inherited Vietnam, as well as the Joint Chiefs of Staff and other advisers already committed to the war.

Furthermore, the State Department policy implementers argue that, essentially, the world does not view the United States any differently. "The world basically looks at the U.S. as a great civilized society," says one Foreign Service officer. "For us to have a grubby little assassination is not civilized. That was why it was such a great shock. Most people in the world look on the U.S. as some place they would like to go to live or like their country to be—just like in the movies."

Another State Department officer points out that many of the attacks on the United States by foreign leaders are motivated by internal political agitation; the slaying of President Kennedy, according to this view, is ready ammunition for a broadside against the United States that will divert attention from the problems of one's own country.

What about the differences of the Kennedy and Johnson images abroad? American diplomats note that Kennedy's mystique for foreign nations, as in the United States, was that he was young and different. One could translate it like this: When Kennedy said, "Let's get this country moving," the rest of the world read it, "Let's get this world moving." On the other hand, Johnson, to foreigners, represents a return to the "old guard" political establishment. Because most people in most foreign nations do not really trust their own "old guard" political establishments, it is easy to "distrust" Johnson.

"We're still the dream world for most of the world's citizens," sums up one State Department foreign pulse-taker. "There are some who are dissatisfied with us. But then they're dissatisfied with their own government. You can look at their own internal troubles to see this."

THE REASONS

The reactions were mixed—grief, fear, a sense of loss, the desire for revenge, shame, guilt—and they were almost universally applicable to Americans. Why, indeed, did Americans react as they did to the death of a President?

Fear and revenge, sometimes the first emotions expressed, were the quickest, on the surface at least, to dissipate. For some there had been a nameless, haunting dread that the world might be falling apart, that they might get killed in the process—an understandable reaction, perhaps, in view of the facts of the nuclear age that were fresh in the minds of all following the brink to war that the United States and the Soviet Union had edged toward during the Cuban missile crisis a year earlier.

It was perhaps a combination of both feelings that prompted the new President, Lyndon Johnson, to speed his return from Dallas to Washington after being sworn in as Kennedy's successor. And, in Washington, moments after the shooting, an aide to Johnson instructed the National Cathedral School for Girls, where 16-year-old Luci Johnson was in class, "to release her to nobody but the Secret Service."

The facts of the case quickly dispelled fear, although a foreboding about the stability of the world was to linger both here and abroad and was to be revived less than five years later with the assassinations of Martin Luther King and Robert Kennedy.

Revenge, interestingly, was never a powerful factor.

In a preliminary report on its survey of reaction to the assassination of President Kennedy, the National Opinion Research Center pointed out that those interviewed reacted more in personal terms than in any other. Only one person in nine hoped that the killer would be "shot down or lynched," and "the 'lesson' of the assassination was seen much more often as the evil harvest of hatred and intolerance than as a demonstration of need for harsher security measures and stepped-up efforts to 'catch the communists.'" Although noting that "it is good to document the relative infrequency of ideological fervor in the public's replies," the report raised the question, "one wonders what would have been the reaction ten years ago, in 1953, if an active leftist with a Russian wife had been charged with the assassination of the President of the United States."

Similarly, the report found that "Americans did not change their views of the world. The assassination of their President did not seem to make them more or less anti-Communistic, it did not affect their attitudes toward civil rights, nor did it erode their basic optimism about other people's motives." By way of suggesting an explanation for this, the survey paper cited the sudden, 10-point increase in the proportion of Americans who thought it "more important to help England than to keep out of war" during a brief period in July-August, 1940, immediately after the initiation of mass air raids on Britain.

"A possible explanation," it suggested, "lies in the fact that responsible leadership—notably Roosevelt—interpreted the events of the summer of 1940 to the public in a way that made wartime intervention seem more relevant and necessary. . . In contrast, no responsible leader interpreted the assassination to the public in a way that made changes in the items we are here considering seem relevant or necessary. Had a responsible Senator or FBI official urged the need of an anti-Communist crusade; had a charismatic evangelist used the occasion to call for a 'return to religion'; had some leader on either side of the race issue managed to relate the assassination to civil rights in a way that the public could comprehend—then, some of these items might have changed."

Tragic as the assassination of John Kennedy was, it provided a major impetus for additional research into the emotional factors that link Americans to their chief of state. Two days after his death a group of behavioral scientists held a hurriedly organized meeting in Washington, at the National Institutes of Mental Health, to plan a series of studies of how Americans were responding to the terrible event. The assassination, those who were present agreed, fitted into a category of events classified technically by social scientists and psychiatrists as "disasters," a category that also includes catastrophes such as fires, floods, tornadoes, and wars. Formal investigation of reaction to the murder of the President, explained one spokesman for the group, could "add to the tradition of research on the reactions of normal people under stress."

The most comprehensive study was carried out by the already cited National Opinion Research Center of the University of Chicago. The center's director, Dr. Peter Rossi, had attended the Washington session and returned to Chicago Sunday evening with a preliminary questionnaire. Under his direction, the center's staff worked around the clock to finalize the formulation of the questionnaire and to dispatch it to field canvassers. In all, the NORC interviewed 1,384 adults across the nation, 97 percent of them by Saturday, November 30. The national sample encompassed both Negroes and whites, farm dwellers and city inhabitants.

In a report on the survey, published in 1964, researchers Drs. Paul B. Sheatsley and Jacob J. Feldman elaborated on the reasons for conducting it:

"As unique an event as the assassination was, it nevertheless provided an opportunity to learn something about more normal phenomena. For instance, we know surprisingly little about the meaning of the presidency to the American public. Many studies have been made of electoral behavior with respect to that office, yet we haven't much idea of just what it is that people feel they are electing. . . .

"A survey of reactions to the assassination could also contribute to our knowledge of the bereavement process. Although mourning and grief have been studied intensively in highly select populations, they have not previously been investigated epidemiologically over a broad population. . . .

"There was a golden opportunity, then, to collect a body of data with both immediate and long-term significance. None of the other major events of our time had been subjected to detailed investigation."

The NORC canvass impressively corroborated the breadth and depth of the emotional response to the shooting of President Kennedy. During the four days following the assassination, 68 percent of those interviewed "felt very nervous and tense," 57 percent "felt sort of dazed and numb," 53 percent cried, 48 percent "had trouble getting to sleep," 43 percent "didn't feel like eating," 42 percent "felt more tired than usual," 26 percent reported rapid heart beats, 25 percent had headaches, 22 percent had upset stomachs, and 17 percent reported that their "hands sweat and felt damp and clammy."

Moreover, 54 percent reported that they did not continue their usual activities after they heard the news. A similar percentage of those interviewed said that they "felt like talking with other people about it," while 40 percent "felt more like being by myself." "It appears," Sheatsley and Feldman noted, "that the more people admired the late President, the more likely they were to want to be alone after they heard of his death."

"The majority of all respondents," the NORC report continued, "could not recall any other time in their lives when they had the same sort of feelings as when they heard of President Kennedy's assassination. Of those who could think of such an occasion (47%) the majority referred to the death of a parent, close friend, or other relative. . . Negroes and pro-Kennedy Northerners were much the more likely to compare Kennedy's death with that of a close friend or relative; a full 80% of the Negro references were to such an occasion of personal grief. . . .

"Perhaps the most striking finding . . . is the immense tide of grief, loss, sorrow, shame, and anger that people felt when they first heard the news, and the relative frequency with which political or personal concerns were mentioned.

"The first reactions of nine out of ten Americans were sympathy for Mrs. Kennedy and the children and deep feelings of sorrow that 'a strong young man had been killed at the height of his powers.' Four out of five 'felt deeply the loss of someone very close and dear.' Five out of six admitted to deep feelings of 'shame that such a thing could happen in our country,' and approximately three out of four 'felt angry that anyone should do such a terrible deed.' These feelings were characteristic, in only slightly less degree, of those who opposed the late President politically as well as those who supported him. . . . Almost half the *volunteered* comments to the question, 'Were you more or less upset than most people' included some reference to . . .: 'I couldn't believe that he was dead,' 'It seemed like a bad dream,' 'It couldn't happen,' 'We thought it must be a joke,' etc.

"The three next most frequent reactions were of sorrow and concern about the future of the nation. Forty-seven percent immediately worried about the effect of the assassination on 'the political situation in this country'. . . . Forty-four percent worried about 'our relations with other countries' and 41% about 'how the United States would carry on without its leader'. . . . One American in five 'wondered if anybody could be really safe in this country these days, when the President himself can get shot.'

"The Presidential assassination seems clearly to have engaged the 'gut feelings' of virtually every American. . . . It is important to note that even political opponents of the late President shared the general grief. . . Sixty-two percent of the Southern whites who opposed Kennedy in 1960 'felt the loss of someone very close and dear.' "

The survey also indicated that there was a considerable amount of individual prayer. "In response to the question, 'Did you yourself say any special prayers at any time during this period?'," the NORC reported, "three-fourths of the national sample answered 'Yes.' By far the most frequent objects of prayer (by 59% of those who prayed) were the late President's wife, children, and immediate family. One-third of those who prayed said their prayers for the repose of the late President's soul. About a third of the group prayed for the country, the welfare of the nation, and about a fourth for the new President."

Apart from the increase in private prayer, the loss of the nation's leader engendered no great boom in public worship. "Probably from very earliest times," the NORC report said, "a major function of religion has been to provide solace to the bereaved; and the United States, at least as far as church attendance is concerned, is a more religious nation than most. Even aside from the spontaneous prayers and meditation occasioned by the violent death of a beloved President, the frequent references to the deity by national leaders and the ecclesiastical elements of the funeral would lead one to expect an upsurge of religious feelings and behavior among the general public. . . Yet, in contrast to the impression one may have received that the churches were flooded with people during this period and that there was a deepening of religious conviction among Americans as a result of the event, neither of these seems to have occurred."

Among regular churchgoers there was some increase in frequency of attendance during the period. "Almost half of those who did attend said they went to more than one service, and a third of the attenders . . . said their attendance was greater than usual," reported the NORC. However, among the overall population sample, it noted, "when asked, some days after the post-assassination Sunday and the national day of mourning on Monday, 'Have you attended any church or religious service since President Kennedy was assassinated?' half the sample answered 'No.' The 50% affirmative is thus very little higher than the 46% average church attendance reported by Gallup in 1962 and 1963."

The national grief that followed the slaying of John F. Kennedy was by no means the first time that Americans had reacted similarly to the loss of their President. Historically, the death of any President in office, whether by assassination or natural causes, has exerted a traumatic effect on the American populace. The phenomenon appears to be more pronounced when the President involved exudes a particular charisma, when the times are particularly tense, or when the circumstances surrounding his death are especially tragic.

After Lincoln was shot, a man on a Washington street shouted, "I'm glad it happened!" and in a trice "he was scuffed underfoot, most of his clothes ripped from his body, and he was carried toward a lamp post. Three policemen drew revolvers to save his life." Following the shooting of President James A. Garfield by a disappointed officeseeker in Washington's Union Station on July 2, 1881, mass indignation ensued. The death of William McKinley on September 14, 1901, after he had been shot eight days earlier by an anarchist at the Pan-American Exposition in Buffalo, New York, also precipitated widespread grief and anger. McKinley's successor, Theodore Roosevelt, proclaimed a day of national mourning and prayer, and crowds jammed New York City for McKinley's funeral procession. The anguish precipitated by the death of Franklin D. Roosevelt, who guided the United States through the Depression and World War II, was of epic proportions, exceeded perhaps only by the dolor engendered by the murder of Kennedy.

Nevertheless, shattering national shock was also touched off by the passing of Warren G. Harding, who died in office in 1923 of pneumonia. A newspaper account of the reaction in New York City related:

"People in the streets around Times Square could hardly believe the news. A man in evening dress said, 'It can't be true.' There was a steady stream of telephone calls to newspaper offices by persons seeking to verify the news.

"[A congressman of an opposing party said]: 'Oh what a calamity. This is a tremendous shock. Politics are now forgotten in the love all factions had for him as a man.'

"[On the official day of mourning] public activity was suspended; banks, stores, theaters, and movie houses were closed. At noon, the entire nation observed two minutes of silence in honor of the dead President."

There seems little doubt that the massive, spontaneous tributes to the relatively colorless Harding amounted to further evidence of the powerful psychological hold that the Presidency maintains over the American people. Dr. Fred I. Greenstein, associate professor of government at Connecticut's Wesleyan University and visiting professor of political science at Yale, a leading scholar on the relationship between the American populace and the Presidency, writes:

"The descriptions of psychological responses to presidential deaths are, in general, so identical as to be interchangeable. In each instance the same sense of shock and loss, the public weeping, people acting dazed and disoriented, and showing the symptoms of anxiety."

Yet the question remains: Why are Americans, with what they have traditionally considered the world's most stable governmental structure and most secure constitutional channels for the orderly transfer of power, so deeply affected by the demise of their President? The precise factors that link people emotionally to their leaders are still the subject of conjecture and debate among behavioral scientists. Research into the phenomena that has been carried out to date is far from conclusive. Nonetheless, enough evidence has been collated to permit psychologists, sociologists, and political scientists to suggest some tentative hypotheses.

A measure of the President's importance as a social nexus may be seen in the fact that, when he dies, Americans seem to experience a need to communicate with each other. After Kennedy's assassination the nation's telephone lines were clogged with calls, and persons who would otherwise have passed on the street without paying the slightest attention to each other found themselves engaging in earnest conversation, often confiding their most intimate responses to total strangers. For example, one New Orleans housewife, who heard the news in her upstairs apartment, ran compulsively downstairs and into the street because, she said, "I needed someone to talk to."

One of the most widely held views among psychoanalysts is that human beings tend subconsciously to regard national leaders as parental surrogates. To Sigmund Freud, politically popular "great men" represent father images upon whom the people could project their sense of need for protection and material fulfillment.

In his essay, "Moses and Monotheism," Freud contends that the title of "the great man" is not conferred simply because "a man possesses to a specially high degree qualities that we value greatly." To argue such, wrote Freud, "clearly misses the mark in every respect. Beauty, for instance, and muscular strength, however enviable they may be, constitute no claim to 'greatness.' It would seem, then, that the qualities have to be mental ones—psychical and intellectual distinctions. As regards these, we are held up by the consideration that nevertheless we should not unhesitatingly describe someone as a great man simply because he was extraordinarily efficient in some particular sphere. We should certainly not do so in the case of a chess master or of a virtuoso on a musical instrument; but not very easily, either, in the case of a distinguished artist or scientist. In such cases we should naturally speak of him as a great poet, painter, mathematician or physicist, or as a pioneer in the field of this or that activity; but we refrain from pronouncing him a great man. If we unhesitatingly declare that, for instance, Goethe and Leonardo da Vinci and Beethoven were great men, we must be led to it by something other than admiration for their splendid creations."

"Let us, therefore," Freud says, "take it for granted that a great man influences his fellow-men in two ways: by his personality and by the idea which he puts forward. That idea may stress some ancient wishful image of the masses, or it may point out a new wishful aim to them, or it may cast its spell over them in some other way. Occasionally—and this is undoubtedly the more primary case—the personality works by itself and the idea plays a quite trivial part. Not for a moment are we in the dark as to why a great man ever becomes important. We know that in the mass of mankind there is a powerful need for an authority who can be admired, before whom one bows down, by whom one is ruled and perhaps even ill-treated. We have learnt from the psychology of individual men what the origin is of this need of the masses. It is a longing for the father felt by everyone from his childhood onwards, for the same father whom the hero of legend boasts he has overcome. And now it may begin to dawn on us that all the characteristics with which we equipped the great man are paternal characteristics, and that the essence of great men for which we vainly searched lies in this conformity. The decisiveness of thought, the strength of will, the energy of action are part of the picture of a father."

Political scientists have noted with interest the speed and spontaneity with which American children become aware of the President and begin to think of him as a favorable and benevolent figure, long before they are formally taught about the Presidency in school. As

Professor Greenstein says, "These early childhood attitudes provide a fascinating problem for analysis. They evidently develop quite subtly, in ways not easy to untangle or explain. Young children are apparently not *taught* to believe the President important and virtuous. In fact, they are ordinarily not explicitly taught about the presidency at all in the early school years. Rather, the notion that the President is 'very important' seems unconsciously to build up in the child's mind from casual exposure to such sources as the mass media and adult conversations."

The positive attitudes that children adopt so early toward the President, some psychological and political analysts believe, are an important contribution to political stability, in that they help create a generally favorable predisposition toward the nation's governmental system.

A further indication that the President effects a subconscious influence on people is suggested by the intensity of reaction to his loss. Greenstein points to "the seeming paradox of emotional reactions that are out of proportion to the individual's prior attitudes and behavior—for example, intense mourning at the death of an individual one had expressed little feeling toward. In such a case the psychiatrist expects to find that unconscious feelings had been present all along."

Noting surveys indicating that the majority of the populace is usually relatively indifferent to politics—80 percent of the electorate do not discuss politics regularly and 90 percent do not write to public officials—Greenstein asks:

"How do we account for the seeming inconsistency between public indifference to politics and the profound emotional outpouring that results when the nation's chief political figure dies in office?"

Still other possible explanations for the "gut feelings" that President Kennedy's death aroused may lie in the fact that man is a social being. It would seem axiomatic that man's tendency to adhere to leaders is an important means by which he constructs his social organization. And for man, unlike many other beings, that organization must be consciously built.

"*Homo sapiens* occupies a peculiar position in the animal kingdom," notes sociologist Peter L. Berger of Manhattan's New School for Social Research. "Unlike the other higher mammals, who are born with an essentially completed organism, man is curiously 'unfinished' at birth. The non-human animal enters the world with highly specialized and firmly directed drives. As a result, it lives in a world that is more or less completely determined by its instinctual structure. Consequently, each animal lives in an environment that is specific to its particular species. There is a mouse-world, a dog-world, a horse-world, and so forth. By contrast, man's instinctual structure at birth is both underspecialized and undirected toward a species-specific environment. Man must make a world for himself."

Part of the building of man's world is the organization of society, and in this, as in other cultural endeavors, he reveals himself as a social being. "While society appears as but an aspect of culture," says Berger, "it occupies a privileged position among man's cultural formations. This is due to yet another basic anthropological fact, namely the essential sociality of man. *Homo sapiens* is the social animal. This means very much more than the surface fact that man always lives in collectivities and, indeed, loses his humanity when he is thrust into isolation from other men. Much more importantly, the world-building activity of man is always and inevitably a collective enterprise. Men *together* shape tools, invent languages, adhere to values, devise institutions."

In his essay "Group Psychology and the Analysis of the Ego," Freud calls man "a *horde* animal, an individual creature in a horde led by a chief," and explains:

"Thus the group appears to us as a revival of the primal horde. Just as primitive man virtually survives in every individual, so the primal horde may arise once more out of any random crowd. . . The leader of the group is still the dreaded primal father; the group still wishes to be governed by unrestricted force; it has an extreme passion for authority . . . a thirst for obedience. The primal father is the group ideal, which governs the ego in the place of the ego ideal."

The social role of the U. S. Presidency is particularly strong, not only because of the power that it represents but because it is intimately bound up—thanks to the American democratic system—with the interests of the people. "The President," Greenstein observes, "is the fulcrum of our domestic political system and a central force in the international political arena. . . In what some consider an ambiguous phrase, the President often is called the most powerful democratic leader in the world. The ambiguity in this characterization lies in both of the qualifying terms, 'powerful' and 'democratic' . . . Both terms refer to interpersonal relationships, not merely to qualities which reside in a single individual. . . When we say that the President is powerful, we are saying that he has been empowered by others. To understand this power relationship we must be attentive not only to the President's actions, but also to others' reactions to him. When we say that the President is democratic, we may mean a number of different things, one of which is the closeness of fit between the President's actions and popular desires."

In addition, Americans have traditionally accepted the Presidency, as well as other institutions of their system of government, as legitimate expressions of public order. "In the United States," Greenstein notes, "the standing decision of the citizenry to accept its leaders as authoritative has an unrecognized, almost atmospheric quality. But we can see the importance of this standing public commitment to the existing political order by reminding ourselves of instances where it has not existed—for example, France of the Third and Fourth Republics, the contemporary Congo, the United States in 1860."

On the basis of available evidence, Greenstein believes that it is possible to draw certain other conclusions about the social importance of the American Presidency:

¶ "The President is by far the best-known figure on the American political scene. . . For some people he is the *only* known leader, and for others one of the few.

¶ "Adult assessments of the performance of incumbent Presidents fluctuate from time to time . . . but in spite of the variation, adults normally have a favorable view of the President's performance. . . The most convenient index is the question asked regularly since the 1930s by the Gallup poll: 'Do you approve or disapprove of the way President X is handling his job?' Most of the time a clear majority of the electorate . . . approve."

¶ "There is a significant tendency for citizens to rally to the support of the President, particularly when he acts in times of international crisis."

¶ "The existence of a single, highly publicized national figure who combines the roles of political leader of the nation and symbolic head of state provides citizens with an enormously convenient vehicle for taking cognizance of government and politics. Even for the politically sophisticated, the existence of this central figure in the political arena helps provide a focus for ordering one's thoughts and perceptions about public affairs. For the politically inert, the Presidency may provide the only basis for connecting the citizen to his government."

¶ "By personifying the complex process of government and politics, the President becomes a potential object of identification. To the degree that the President's actions are effective, citizens who identify themselves with him may experience heightened feelings of potency—of being in a world in which one is not completely dependent upon external circumstances and events."

¶ "We may assume that the Presidency normally helps to signify social stability. . . Again, the ease with which even the most apolitical citizen can personify the government in the President is probably significant. Our own lack of interest in the details of how the nation is governed becomes more acceptable if we feel that *someone* is attending to such matters. The assumption is that events are being controlled, that life is not whimsical and dangerous."

Greenstein concludes that "the public reaction to a presidential death is a grim instance of the unifying power of the presidency. Whether or not one psychically takes the part of the President, it is clear that he serves as a reassuring *symbol of social stability*. For many people, one of the most disturbing aspects of President Kennedy's assassination was the implication that went with it of lack of control—of possible national and international disaster."

"This, in effect," he adds, "is the direct opposite of the crisis situation in which a calm and decisive President, by seeming to be in firm command, enhances the citizens' feelings of confidence and security. It is a caricature of the complex, sprawling, uncoordinated nature of the American political system to see it as a great ship of state, sailing on with the President firmly at the helm. But a great many people find comfort in this oversimplified image."

An explanation of the effect of the assassination of President Kennedy on the American younger generation and other, older, Kennedy supporters is given by Dr. Benson Snyder, psychiatrist in chief at the Massachusetts Institute of Technology:

"In order to examine reactions to the Kennedy assassination you first have to examine the preconditions that exist for the person.

"How do people maintain their self-esteem so that they do not feel helpless?

"It is one of the ways of politics in the United States that people get a sense of worth by identifying with a charismatic leader, one who is young and doing things, and who gives the illusion of being able to translate your private wishes of what will happen into reality. John F. Kennedy was one.

"When that [charismatic leader] suddenly is removed, there is an enormous sense of loss. It's not just the loss of a person. It is the whole business of having to say, 'Who is going to listen now? Maybe I won't be heard.'

"For many people there is an urgent wish to get a lot of simple answers. It is as if there were an equilibrium by which an individual has built up a sense of worth for himself. A part of that equation is his leader. When that is removed, the search begins for a simple model of what the world is like. It makes the blinders that people wear even larger. They seek an explanation of their loss of worth outside of themselves. They seek a scapegoat. They say, 'If we get rid of permissiveness, or Communists, or dirty words, then everything will be all right.'

"There is also a sense of disillusionment, of de-idealization. There is a loss of faith that is associated with a sense of helplessness. If you think a man has the right ideas, you identify with him as a leader and then he gets popped off.

"There is a long-term reaction of apathy and alienation. The person says, 'Well, I got burned. I'm not going to care any more.' This is a Hippy philosophy; Hippies are a caricature of this feeling. It is also part of suburban culture. The suburbanite is saying, 'I won't be bothered. I'm going to cool it.'

"The process of grieving is a painful one. But if the person does not go through it, it festers."

Snyder recalls that one student came to him after the assassination because something bothered him. He believed that the academic world concentrated too much on the brain while ignoring the heart. He was in a professor's office when he (the professor) heard from a secretary that Kennedy had been shot. The professor didn't react. A few days later the student watched the funeral on TV. He saw video tapes of people bursting into tears. He was hit by the difference between the rational efforts to accept the death of Kennedy at school and the other people who reacted emotionally."

"The way that the Kennedy assassination relates to the young people is important," Snyder declares. "Most of these kids were 14 or 15 or 16 at the time of the assassination. They were at an important point in their adolescence. The guy who really spoke to them is gone. It is a difficult thing to have to deal with at that time of your life. . . They say, 'Who is going to listen to my voice? No one cares.' When someone does listen, he gets picked off."

Further, Dr. Snyder believes that the assassination of John Kennedy occurred at a particularly crucial point in American history. "Usually, the world undergoes a slow, steady rate of change," he observes. "The successful transmission of that change depends greatly on what strains are put on a system. We have seen a great change between one generation and another. It is like nothing we've seen before. It means that many of the cultural and psychological ways that we have of dealing with the world are obsolete. They actually get in the way of our view of the situation. Man has not been able to keep up with his environment. Throw in something like the loss of a major leader and the strain on the system is that much more difficult."

President Johnson, while drawing no such specific parallel, nonetheless gave a graphic description of the contemporary temper of many Americans in an address to the American Bar Association in 1968. "Our old institutions today are under serious challenge," he said. "There is tension between the generations, between the 'haves' and the 'have nots,' between the schooled and unschooled. The line between freedom and license has become unclear to many people. Threats and counter-threats fill the air every day. There is a degree of intolerance and almost totalitarian vehemence that says, 'Either see it my way or you will be sorry.' "

Such varying emotional responses were reflected in the reaction of psychiatric patients to Kennedy's death. Identification of the President with parents has been reported by psychiatrist David Kirschner, based on observations of eight female patients. They described their initial reaction to the news as "exactly the same" as their responses to their parents' deaths. This was typically one of disbelief, followed by depression, grief, mourning—and the identification of the death of the President with the symbolic loss of a father figure, a feeling of being "orphaned." Kennedy served as an idealized parent symbol, compensated in these patients' fantasies for the felt or real deficiencies of their own parents. One woman, who perceived her father as a passive, dull nonentity, discussed her feelings as follows:

"He [Kennedy] represented to me the things I always wanted my father to be—a great intellect, forceful, a person of dignity who commanded the respect and esteem of others."

It was even possible, Dr. Kirschner reported, for patients to express more grief and tears for Kennedy than they had for their own parents. But despite the intensity of their reactions, he concluded, "it is also felt that the response of these patients to the assassination may have differed only in degree (if indeed at all) from that of similar non-patient groups."

Even if one does not accept the parental substitute theory, notes Greenstein, "psychiatric case histories of patients in treatment give unusual insight into feelings and responses that cannot readily be observed in more formal interviews.

"For example, when President Roosevelt died a number of psychoanalysts reported that their patients reacted in ways that clearly indicated they identified him with one or both of their parents. One analyst found similar associations among his patients even during the less extreme circumstances of the election campaigns of 1948, 1952 and 1956. President Kennedy—in spite of his youth—affected some patients in the same manner, both before and after his death. The deaths of other public figures, political leaders, ex-Presidents, religious leaders, entertainment celebrities do not produce similar reactions, except in very specialized segments of the population."

Sheatsley and Feldman, commenting in the NORC report on the theory of "the displacement of childhood feelings of dependency from one or both the subject's parents onto the incumbent chief of state," concede that "anxiety, the manifestations of which are difficult to distinguish from grief, is practically an inevitable consequence of the separation through death from the source of succor," and that it may "give us insight into the feelings of certain limited parts of the general population." Although it would have been more difficult for the youthful JFK to be a father figure than an older man, they note that there are "various explanations for the intensity of effect brought out by the death of a 'ruler.'" Sheatsley and Feldman cite a thesis of New York University philosophy professor Sidney Hook, who has argued:

"Perhaps a more important source [than the parental surrogate function] of appeal made by the leader to his following lies in the vicarious gratification of their yearnings through his presumed traits and achievements. The splendor, the power, the flame of the leader are shared imaginatively. New elements of meaning enter the lives of those who are emotionally impoverished. The everyday disparities and injustices of social life, and sometimes the lacks and incapacities of personal life, fade out of the center of concern . . ."

In other words, the attractiveness and magnetism of John Kennedy may have been almost as great a factor in the reaction to his death as his high office. Moreover, Sheatsley observes, "the feelings of grief were accentuated by the prior tragedies in the Kennedy family."

The national leader, analysts generally agree, can also become the object of ambivalent feelings of hatred and revenge, growing out of childhood repression and hostility. "Early conflicts with parents, who are the ultimate authority in a young child's life, produce much of this repression," Greenstein explains. "Typically there are two inconsistent impulses toward family authority that the child forces out of consciousness—the need to be excessively submissive and the need to express hostility, to rebel. In later life, according to this line of psychiatric reasoning, these repressed feelings toward the private authorities of childhood are expressed in citizens' reactions to public authorities such as the President."

Still another set of intriguing insights into the reactions set in motion by John Kennedy's death was provided by psychoanalyst George Krupp, who has carried out special studies on bereavement:

"On November 25, 1963, the day of the funeral of our late President, I went to the office to keep my regular appointments. My patients talked of nothing but the death of John Kennedy. . . Finally I saw how the reactions of my patients to the death of the President were different in degree, perhaps, but not in kind, from the reactions of my family, of my friends and of my neighbors. . .

"A young, unmarried schoolteacher, for example, found it difficult to talk about the President without weeping. 'The whole world is rotten,' she said as she dabbed at her tears with a handkerchief. 'Nothing that is any good ever lasts for long.' Later, after a fresh outburst of tears, she asked: 'What's wrong with me? Why am I crying so much? He wasn't a member of my family; he was a stranger to me. Why do I feel so awful?'"

"She was crying," Dr. Krupp explained, "because she had been overwhelmed by a sense of loneliness that left her frightened and confused. She was crying, as all human beings cry, whether the tears are visible or not, because she had lost something . . . dear to her. . . To avoid the pain she tried to define it out of existence by calling President Kennedy a stranger; the death of a stranger, after all, should cause little pain. But he was no stranger, this vital, charming man who entered her world almost everyday of the week, whether on television or the radio, in movie newsreels, daily newspapers or weekly and monthly magazines. He had played a more important role in her life than she was aware of."

Referring to the comment, frequently expressed after Kennedy's death, that when he died "a bit of us died with him," Krupp continued:

"But what happens when 'a bit of us dies?' . . . Even as adults we continue unconsciously to identify with others. Bits of their personalities become deeply embedded in our sense of our adult selves —and this is the part of us that is threatened by their deaths. When a man like President Kennedy dies, a man whom we may never personally have met, it is difficult to understand that we have nevertheless identified with him and that consequently our grief stems from a feeling that something within ourselves has withered. Literally millions of people reacted to the news of the shooting of John Kennedy with expressions of bitter anger that, although they were unaware of it, primarily reflected their rage at feelings that they themselves had been shot. When we mourn someone's loss, we mourn for ourselves."

Dr. Krupp found this response strikingly evident in the words of one of his patients, a young business executive, who said of Kennedy, "He reminded me of myself. He was young, he was good-looking, he had a beautiful wife, lots of money and plenty of faith in himself. He was the new modern age. He was all the things I wanted and needed."

"The funeral bell that tolled for the dead President," observed Krupp, "certainly tolled for this man, who saw in John Kennedy an ideal self, an image of all his own secret hopes."

By way of contrast, Krupp also cited the case of another young man who bitterly criticized the Dallas police after the shooting of Oswald. "His criticism may well have been largely justified; the vehemence of his attack, however, betrayed a personal involvement that he himself did not understand. All his life this young man has suppressed his resentment of his father. . . . His unconscious wish to be rid of his father finds its fantasy counterpart in the actions . . . of Oswald, and my patient . . . defends himself by defending Oswald." This patient, added Krupp, "struggles with an unacknowledged sense of guilt, even as you and I. Few among us have not at one time or another wished we were rid of our fathers, our bosses or any other individuals with authority and power over us. Thus a sense of shame, if not guilt, troubles us when to our horror we experience even momentary kinship with any person who uses violence to settle a score as we may fleetingly have fantasied doing ourselves."

Death can also cause emotions to well up that are associated only indirectly with the person who dies but are nonetheless acute. Some persons, for instance, relive their personal losses and concerns. Another of Krupp's patients, a young woman, "freely expressed her sorrow over John Kennedy's death."

"When I asked her initial reactions, however, she recalled that on hearing the first news bulletin she had thought not of the President or of his wife or baby son but instantly had begun worrying about little Caroline. This identification is not difficult to trace, since both parents of this particular young woman had been killed in an automobile accident when she was very young."

A lawyer discussing the assassination with Krupp "felt great concern about Lyndon Johnson's ability to handle the nation's affairs. He said little about John Kennedy. . . His identification with President Johnson was logical. This man's father, a prominent lawyer, had recently had a heart attack, and as his son he now faced the frightening responsibility of taking over his father's entire practice."

Noting that "pets have been known to waste away and die after the death of a master" and that "husbands and wives have been known to die within a short time after the death of the partner they loved," Krupp finds that "a meaningful distinction between healthy and unhealthy mourning suggests itself. . . Grief that becomes fixed in despair, that surrenders to apathy, is a symptom of illness. Grief is healthy when it gradually diminishes in intensity, increasingly accepts the absoluteness of this final separation and commits itself once again to the mainstream of life."

Similarly, Freud, in his essay "Mourning and Melancholia," written in 1917, interpreted mourning as a normal and necessary means by which human beings adjust to the loss of someone for whom they yearn. Freud labeled this process "the work of mourning," and described it as the repeated, painful, involuntary reminding of oneself that the lost one is, in fact, dead, until the psyche ultimately accepts the fact. "Although grief involves grave departure from the normal attitude of life," he wrote, "it never occurs to us to regard it as a morbid condition and hand the mourner over to medical treatment. We rest assured that after a lapse of time it will be overcome, and we look upon any interference with it as inadvisable or even harmful."

Freud, however, distinguished between such healthy grief, whose function is to restore one's psychological equilibrium, and "melancholia." The latter he described as a morbid, pathological condition characterized by "a profoundly painful dejection, abrogation of interest in the outside world, loss of the capacity to love, inhibition of all activity, and a lowering of the self-regarding feelings to a degree that finds utterance in self-reproaches and self-revilings and culminates in a delusional expectation of punishment."

Concluded Krupp:

"There are many other emotions, some hateful and humiliating, that may involuntarily sweep across our consciousness before we can banish them. They merit mention, if only to clear the air. There may be, for example, a feeling of relief when we think of how fortunate we are—we didn't die, and neither did we kill. There may be an awareness of personal gain, material or otherwise. There may be a fear that we cannot deny, the fear of death. All these feelings and many other similar ones evaporate quickly, leaving a stubborn residue of such troubling emotions as anxiety, depression and guilt. This is almost universal and this exists even when denied. For identification, being unconscious, follows its own dictates and expresses itself in our fantasies, daydreams and nightmares."

Such individual feelings may help to explain the complex mass reactions to the death of a popular national leader. Writing in the winter, 1964, issue of *Psychoanalytic Review*, New York psychologist Dr. Joseph Katz likens the shockwaves that followed President Kennedy's assassination to the original social repercussions felt after the murder of Christ. The pattern of reaction in both instances, Katz suggests, included a sense of mass guilt, with people eulogizing the slain leader and magnifying his virtues, and a need to pay penance, to make restitution, to immortalize him, and thereby negate or deny the final deed. Instead of ancient altars, Katz points out, contemporary men substitute the eternal flame, the hasty naming of airports and buildings, the setting up of foundations and libraries bearing the lost leader's name.

Katz likewise conjectures that, from the scanty data available, it would appear that persons with deep homosexual problems had the most disturbing dreams following Kennedy's death. The probable reason was that they were more fully able to identify with both the alleged assassin and victim; their impulses to kill the hated father were the most intense, and correspondingly they feared being killed themselves in return.

Katz, unlike some other experts, found an almost too quick recovery of the mourning masses to normalcy. Such very fast forgetting, he contends, lends a certain note of hypocrisy to the initial period of intense grief and perhaps exposes the unconscious satisfaction in the fulfillment of the original death wish toward the leader. Thus, a few days after the assassination business was as usual, and the stock market had recovered. Occasional anger and contempt were

219

expressed toward the fallen leader, for example, to the effect that he was so erring in judgment as to cast aside precautions and permit himself to be killed.

In any event, the murder of John F. Kennedy clearly had for Americans a very personal effect. Summarizing the National Opinion Research Center survey, Sheatsley and Feldman reported:

"We may note the tendency to personify the event. . . Perhaps great events can be meaningfully grasped only through personal symbols, such as . . . General MacArthur in the Philippines defeat, or Dwight D. Eisenhower on D-Day. The multitudinous political ramifications of such events are too complicated and diffuse to comprehend; we seek instead a more familiar referent. At such times, too, our attitudes are strongly swayed by emotion, and our emotions tend to seek a human object rather than an abstraction."

In the aftermath of the assassination of John Kennedy, there were those who refused to agree that the entire nation should be blamed and sought to allay the pervading atmosphere of guilt.

"It was not a flaw in the American system or the American character that struck down John Kennedy," declared Senator Thruston Morton, a Republican from Kentucky, in a speech on the Senate floor. "It was not the sin of a city or of its citizens. It was not a tragedy that struck from some dark stain of violence on the American system or in the American soil. . . Let us mourn the terrible event, but let us not mourn for the American soul—for that soul is stout and lighted by truth and faith."

"There is guilt," the House Republican Policy Committee declared, "but it is not American guilt, but the guilt of the murderer. There is hatred, fanaticism, and bigotry in the world, but America is not its source, or loyal Americans its practitioners."

More recently, as Senator Robert Kennedy lay on his death bed in Los Angeles, President Johnson stated the issue even more straightforwardly:

"Tonight this nation faces once again the consequences of lawlessness, hatred and unreason in its midst. It would be wrong, it would be self-deceptive, to ignore the connection between lawlessness and hatred and this act of violence.

"It would be just as wrong and just as self-deceptive to conclude from this act that our country itself is sick, that it's lost its balance, that it's lost its sense of direction, even its common decency.

"Two hundred million Americans did not strike down Robert Kennedy last night, any more than they struck down President John

F. Kennedy in 1963, or Dr. Martin Luther King in April of this year.

"But those awful events give us ample warning that in a climate of extremism, of disrespect for law, of contempt for the rights of others, violence may bring down the very best among us."

One of the most perceptive prescriptions for the American people, in the wake of John Kennedy's assassination, was offered by Dr. Krupp, who urged Americans to "learn to distinguish between guilt and responsibility." The notion of guilt, he noted, is the basis for that of blame, which he termed "a futile emotion" that is, in turn, linked to the idea of punishment. "This, of course, is the philosophy of 'an eye for an eye,'" counseled Krupp. "Feelings of *guilt* seek relief in punishment, either of oneself or others; feelings of *responsibility* seek relief in restitution, the righting of a wrong. I do not believe that as a democratic nation we can permit self-blame to be the form in which our grief over the loss of a gallant and courageous leader expresses itself. This would indeed be a shabby tribute. We require a heightened sense of responsibility for the death of the President. If nothing else, we are responsible because we failed (and are still failing) to help those in our midst who are raging with hate and who must sooner or later strike to kill—either an innocent bystander who may happen to be the President of the United States, or themselves."

Writing five months after Kennedy's death, Krupp added:

"The 'work of mourning' in the months that lie ahead still remains to be completed. By now most of John Kennedy's fellow Americans have progressed to the point at which, although sudden and unexpected moments of remembering create thrusts of pain, the acceptance of his death and of our emotional separation from him and his family has been achieved. There remains the greater challenge. How can we transfer the loss of this man—indeed, the loss of anyone we love—into an increased sense of our own capacities for living, an increased sense of the many purposes and meanings of life? For in the final analysis this deeper commitment to life is the only creative response to death that the living can make."

As for the overall political effects of the assassination of President Kennedy, some interesting observations have been made by Dr. Henry F. Graff, professor of history at Columbia University and one of the nation's most distinguished political historians. In a special interview for this book, Professor Graff declared:

"I'm not sure I could describe the chemistry of the moment, and it may be that no one can at this time. It may very well be that future historians will see some elements that we're too close to the event to be able to see. I've always thought that Kennedy's death had the effect of updating the democratic ideal so far as it is able to be embodied in a single person.

"What I have in mind is this: George Washington belonged to the 18th century and he was cold, cold to the touch. He was always a marble statue to Americans. You didn't approach him. Gouverneur Morris tells of how he once slapped him on the back in a kind of Rotarian greeting—though that's my phrase and not Gouverneur Morris'—and got a cold, icy stare that he was sure would remain with him the rest of his life. And I think that, nevertheless, that was acceptable to Americans, as the embodiment of the American ideal white man. And an enormous number of American counties, rivers, bluffs were named for Washington in a long generation that followed his death.

"And then that got outdated. That was no longer satisfactory. You get Lincoln. Lincoln is in the age of the photograph and everybody can see him. He's the first president of whom everybody could own a picture and he was like Uncle Sam himself—tall, cadaverous, slow to anger, rich in mercy, like God of the Old Testament. And he represented a lot of things for Americans—even being shot on Good Friday enabled him to occupy a place that was appropriate to the second third of the 19th century. And I think that we carried Lincoln a long time.

"I was always aware, whenever I went into a school auditorium, that you had Washington on one side, Lincoln on the other—that's standard all around the United States. I remember when Eisenhower was in the White House. As you know, it's customary to have the predecessors' portraits on either side of the entrance of the White House. And I remember the first time I was in the White House, after Eisenhower became President, whoever it was had changed this tradition, had done the most unimaginative thing. He'd put Washington and Lincoln there. Well, somehow, I had come to the conclusion, just in ordinary conversation, that we'd run the string on Lincoln now. They have a Lincoln penny. Even when one talks of the Lincoln Center, one no longer sees Lincoln. One may see the Chagalls in one's mind's eye or think of the awful food in the Philharmonic cafe—it's no longer Lincoln. We went through that. And while it's true that Lincoln was assassinated while wearing a Brooks Brothers' suit, one didn't think of him as the modern Brooks Brothers type.

"And Kennedy seemed to have suddenly brought us up to date, the embodiment of what it is we think we are. I think Lincoln represented hard work, seriousness of purpose, pleasantness, wit, kindliness, determination—a variety of goals that may even be the goals that are Uncle Sam's. I think that we've changed a little bit—a good bit. And I think Kennedy represented a new kind of hero. As a handsome man, he's assimilable to the theater crowd, particularly the movie crowd. He's wealthy—having money is a greater ideal than rising from poverty—he had that. I mean it's a more insistent dynamic in our society. I wouldn't say it's a greater ideal—more dynamic. I think that the sophisticated *joie de vivre* that Kennedy projected conforms with the view of how life ought to go, in a generation that has become, in a surface way, acquainted with the international set, with other culture groups than their own via newspapers, by the national weeklies, via 60 years of muckraking journalism, 60 years of the violation of the privacy of public figures. And he was married to a lady who matched him in these qualities which represented something very special.

"And I think he was able to convey in some way the opposite of what Lincoln conveyed which also had usefulness—the sense that 'I don't have the answer—I think I know what the questions are.' And his youth made him a symbol of a nation that likes to think of virility. I think that one could extend this sense of what Kennedy was. I think all of this suddenly was precipitated by his passing.

"And the contrast with Johnson I think probably in some measure —probably not in a very great measure but some measure—silhouetted Kennedy. Here was a man who was more like other Presidents we had had, who projected the riverboat-gambler quality which belongs to another age and another part of the country. I think it was very important that, in the making of the public judgment of Kennedy so quickly, that his passing could be shrouded in mystery. The gods all die mysteriously, don't they, in Greek mythology? And we could go on adding some of the things that will make this the stuff for playwrights and poets.

"I had the opportunity to be teaching a survey course in American history at the time of Kennedy's assassination. And that coming at the end of November, just about a week or two before one talked about Lincoln's passing. And I realized how different Lincoln's passing will always be now. And it was this that first taught me, if I can put it, that Kennedy had done something. The ideal Ameri-

223

can was now somebody who looked like Kennedy rather than like Lincoln. And I think this was born out in the way Kennedy's death was received around the world, and in the deification which has taken place in the years that are following.

"It was in his first message to Congress that Kennedy said, 'We still do not know whether our system can work.' He was referring, of course, to the relation between the Congress and the President. I think in some ways he was posing a question about the American political system which was growing very insistent then, but which has grown more insistent since. And in recognizing the question, the importance of the question, I think that he was raising some doubts about the adequacy of the methods and that of the programs which had been up to then addressed to American problems.

"He did not have the muscle up on the Hill that Johnson has had. He was not an insider in the Senate club. It's a commonplace to say now that he didn't draw on his personal popularity. One does not know whether in his lifetime he had that popularity. We don't know what would have happened if he had made an appeal. His great problem as it was being talked about by political scientists was how to expand the mandate of that very narrow victory in 1960. And I remember a Bill Mauldin cartoon which showed him kind of dragging a donkey called Congress and [saying] 'I know you don't want to move but you've got to,' or something like that. His passing broke the dam.

"He was moving toward an embracing of the civil rights movement. He had moved relatively slowly up to that point. You remember the discussion of whether with one stroke of the pen he could eliminate discrimination in public housing. It was some time after he was President. Negro leaders were still asking when he was going to deliver that stroke of a pen. And yet he was moving toward an understanding of the problem of the Negro. I sensed this. The week before the march on Washington, I had the feeling then that we were living in a new time. This was the year of the assassination. The President of the United States was really committing himself to whatever it was that civil rights may be said to have been at that time. I'm not saying that he envisioned the subsequent legislation, that it is what he would have advocated, or that it is what he would have urged in that next message to the Congress. But I think that he was moving here.

"I think he was an understander of the problem of the city. I am not of the opinion that his plans were far-reaching. I think he put a lot of things on the rails and Johnson gave them a push—and, of course, added some ornaments, too. I think that American presidents had to be educated to the problems they face. Remember that they're used to dealing with a Congress that had been largely rural until the one-man, one-vote case. It is very hard to talk about urban problems in a rural Congress. If you have a very thin mandate as Kennedy did and you have to deal with a rural-based Congress, it is very hard to say you're going to get going on urban problems. I remember in the campaign of 1960 hearing Kennedy over in the Bronx saying, 'Well, you know I'm really a Bronx boy myself.' He once lived in Riverdale, which is technically part of the Bronx—but he wasn't really an urban type.

"He was learning how to deal with ethnic groups. He knew a great deal, of course, about the Irish-American but it didn't come out of his pores to deal with the others. I think he was learning that very fast. And I am sure that even before the assassination, there were a great many people in the Kennedy entourage who were aware that history had somehow been unkind to Kennedy. Others were going to get credit for a lot of the things he began. And history is mean. And I think within the family, the official family, in the frustration over the lack of movement, lack of ability to move that donkey, there was an awareness that the ideas were right, but you weren't going to be able to move them far enough.

"How is Kennedy going to be judged? I think some day when we've had many more Presidents than we've now had, we won't be able to know all their names. We will be more like the French when they talk of the early Merovingian kings, late Carolingian kings. We'll talk about the Virginia presidents, political presidents, and we'll probably talk about the Cold War presidents—lump them together. I think more and more Americans are coming to recognize that there are more continuities from one Administration to another than was formerly the case. When you and I first learned history, I think we thought history came in four-year chunks and we kind of tore off a piece of history on the dotted line on Inauguration Day. There is still a lot of that in American thinking about politics. There'll be a lot of it in the press when the next president is inaugurated. And I don't think this is true. I don't think any historian can believe this is true. I don't think any good observer can believe this is true. I think that it's being assumed then we're going to talk about Truman, Eisenhower, and Kennedy as a group. And those are hard words to say when we still all feel the anguish of the loss of this enormously gifted man, the warmth and gaiety he brought to the White House. But we're now five years after the event, close to five years. Look at the problems that are still with us—Cuba, Middle East, Congo, Berlin, Vietnam. The difference between Vietnam and Korea will dim just as the difference between Pitt the Elder and Pitt the Younger has long since disappeared for British schoolboys. And we're going to see problems of American power in the world, see a collection of styles, Trumanesque, Eisenhoweresque, Kennedyesque. But I think we'll always want to have for Kennedy the might-have-been.

"Among the assassinated Presidents, Lincoln had, as it were, done his work. Garfield had just begun it. McKinley was at the end of the line—he'd 'saved' the currency, won a war. And you think of the people who've been incapacitated or died in office. Wilson had done the job, maybe he hadn't finished the League [of Nations]. With Kennedy, everything was in full swing. He was taken at the flood tide rather than the ebb tide—which made this in a way a special kind of disaster. He was full of youth and vigor, his own word was a symbol. Bad history, to talk about the ifs. I don't think I ought to talk about the ifs. But Kennedy's being youthful leaves a kind of glow. And I think the result is we tend to resolve what the ifs would have turned out to be on the favorable side rather than on the un-favorable side: he wouldn't have escalated in Vietnam; he would have found a way to reduce the Cold War even further; he would have been able to get along with de Gaulle; he would have saved, I don't know how, the gold outflow. My own feeling is that the problems of international affairs particularly, to say nothing of domestic affairs, are so enormous that we aren't likely to see startling new solutions for problems that men of good minds and will have been wrestling with for a long time. But the very toughness of these problems forces us to want to believe there was at least some hope of solution.

"And I don't think I'm very optimistic that these problems are going to go away. But it's somehow comforting to us to think that somehow they would have gone away. I think this is very important for America. It's a little bit like the isolationists of the late 1930's who created the impression that we did have options when in fact we didn't. And people don't like to think of themselves as floating along on an endless cosmic sea. They like to think they have options. And this is the marvelous historic role which at the moment is Kennedy's."

Thus, for whatever psychological and sociological reasons, a president of the United States occupies a position of towering importance in the minds of the American people, and his death precipitates near-trauma or serious disorientation among virtually the entire population. By the same token, the demise of other particularly charismatic political leaders, although not evoking precisely the same type of emotional outpouring as the death of a president, can also trigger intensive reactions commensurate with their importance —as illustrated by the assassinations of Martin Luther King and Robert Kennedy.

In effect, people become themselves for a brief time. Their defenses and barriers are temporarily down. The mighty become humble, and the humble rise to participate in the mass grief with egalitarian abandon. Mankind, ever lost without someone or something to hold onto, is reminded with painful and almost unbearable force of his essentially lonely state.

Despite the evolution of democracy, with its concept of each man being a free and equal political entity, man is still intrinsically wedded to his leaders—even to leaders of other cultural groups when they are eminent enough to represent an element in the structure of world order.

TV'S IMPACT

A far-reaching question posed by the slaying of John Kennedy is what special effects, if any, the televised assassination has on national and international order. Given the fact that the assassination of any major political leader is a jolt to the status quo, does the presence of the electronic eye, absorbing the shattering details into millions of minds at home and abroad, shake the social equilibrium even more— or, conversely, perhaps cushion the shock? There are those who maintain that the latter effect, surprising as it may seem, is actually the more probable, at least in the immediate sense.

Marshall McLuhan, in his book *Understanding Media: The Extensions of Man*, defines TV as "a cool, participant medium," observing:

"The Kennedy assassination gave people an immediate involvement, on the one hand, and a numbing effect as deep as grief, itself, on the other hand. Most people were amazed at the depth of meaning which the event communicated to them. Many more were surprised by the coolness and calm of the mass reaction. The same event, handled by press or radio (in the absence of television) would have provided a totally different experience. The national 'lid' would have 'blown off.' Excitement would have been enormously greater and depth participation in a common awareness very much less. . . .

"Most of all, the Kennedy event provides an opportunity for noting a paradoxical feature of the 'cool' TV medium. It involves us in moving depth, but it does not excite, agitate or arouse. Presumably, this is a feature of all depth experience."

There is evidence tending to support McLuhan's thesis. For all the shock and sorrow of Kennedy's murder, the nation did not erupt in senseless rioting or uncontrollable grieving; vicarious participation in the tragedy and the funereal aftermath, by means of video, may well have acted as an emotional outlet.

Moreover, if TV be a "cool" medium, it is also a comradely medium. The same factors by which it heightens the impact of an assassination—such as graphicness and breadth of exposure—also permit television to "purge the shock," as some analysts have termed it, by drawing people more closely together behind a new leader.

It would seem difficult to believe, however, that the sense of loss and anger at the murder of a political leader—and the consequent effect on social stability—is not increased by the psychological power of the video tube. The rioting by Negroes that followed the assassination of Martin Luther King had, of course, the special motivation of racial injustice and frustration. Yet the scenes of Dr. King's shaken comrades telling of the shooting only moments after it occurred, of the slain Negro leader lying in his coffin, of the old-time religious wailing at his funeral, can have done little to still the aroused passions of the Negro community. By the same token, the consternation set off by the killing of Robert Kennedy undoubtedly resulted in great measure from the fact that it was the third assassination of a major American political figure in five years. The sense of national anguish must certainly have been deepened by the spectacle of John Kennedy's younger brother lying in his own blood on a hotel kitchen floor, by the vivid scenes of hysteria and tears among his supporters, by the instant lectures on the intricacies of brain surgery—complete with skulls and visual aids—delivered by neurosurgeons invited before the national TV audience.

In all three tragedies—that of John F. Kennedy, Martin Luther King, and Robert Kennedy—it would seem reasonable to suggest that television made its special contribution to the national sense of guilt and anxiety.

Thus, judged over a longer view, the televised assassination may be something more than a completely "cool" political event. Even if it should not touch off an explosion of popular chaos—and there would appear little guarantee that such is not possible—the televised assassination possibly adds to the lengthier, debilitating effects on a society, precisely because the video murder is a participatory happening. The viewer is not only a firsthand witness to the circumstances surrounding the event and possibly to the actual assassination, but also a participant in the national disaster. An assassination today, in effect, takes place in each citizen's living room. To the extent that the more closely one experiences an event the more closely involved he is in its ramifications, assassination-by-television involves the American people more intimately in the anguish created by the murder of their leaders.

This phenomenon would seem to be a manifestation of a larger transformation, that of the television revolution amounting to a re-defining of the body politic. The framers of the United States Consti-tution envisioned a political system in which the exercise of power would be reasonably removed from the immediate emotions of the populace. Wisely realizing that pure democracy equals mob rule, the founding fathers placed institutional buffers between the people and their government; the American system is neither a dictatorship of the guillotine nor of the proletariat, but a tempered democracy based on government by representatives. The television era threatens to weaken the buffer zone between the people and power by effecting a return to an almost Athenian democracy through the new participa-tory nature of the body politic in events. McLuhan has posed the possible evolution somewhat differently, suggesting that TV "poten-tially . . . can transform the Presidency into a monarchic dynasty. A merely elective Presidency scarcely affords the depth of dedication and commitment demanded by the TV forum."

Still, the end result is perhaps not all that dissimilar: in either case, the people are more deeply and personally involved with their leaders and affairs of state, are gallery spectators of politically sig-nificant happenings as never before. A case in point is the war in Vietnam. President Johnson himself has raised the question of whether the conflict, long and frustrating as it has been, would have caused such controversy among Americans had it not been history's first "televised" war, with the people back home exposed in evening newscasts to the painfully real sights and sounds of their sons dying in battle.

In addition to shifting the presence of the electorate from the forks-of-the-creek to front-row-center, the electronic age also has the effect of increasing the size of the operative body politic. Citizens, such as rural southern Negroes or Appalachia mountain dwellers, who, in the past, might have had only a distant appreciation of na-tional issues, can today, for the price of a down payment on a TV set, become privy to events and interpretation of events that vitally affect their lives.

The Rev. Vernon F. Miller of Indiana, a Church of the Brethren minister and student of current social trends, even foresees the rebirth of the town meeting on a mass scale. This would come about by means of push-button response by viewers to national questions posed on TV. Writes Miller:

"Contemporary mass media have been accused of creating a mass culture in which the individual is lost in a depersonalized society of unrelated persons. But reversal of this prospect is possible. Mass media can be the vehicle for individual involvement in modern life. . . The combination of mass media with the potential of computerized response can bring every citizen into as vital a relationship with his government as was possible in town meeting days."

Few events affect Americans' lives more than the death of their president, and the American people's reactions to the nation's assassinations of the '60's almost certainly reflect the added impact of today's cathode democracy. As McLuhan writes:

"As electronically contracted, the globe is no more than a village. Electric speed in bringing all social and political functions together in a sudden implosion has heightened human awareness of responsibility to an intense degree. It is this implosive factor that alters the position of the Negro, the teen-ager, and some other groups. They can no longer be *contained*, in the political sense of limited association. They are now *involved* in our lives, as we in theirs, thanks to the electric media. . . .

"Perhaps it was the [John] Kennedy funeral that most strongly impressed the audience with the power of TV to invest an occasion with the character of corporate participation. No national event except in sports has ever had such coverage or such an audience. . . . The Kennedy funeral, in short, manifested the power of TV to involve an entire population in a ritual process. By comparison, press, movie and even radio are mere packaging devices for consumers."

It would also appear logical to say that the televised political murder is a special menace to social stability, in terms of either immediate reaction or longer-range effects.

When the populace is so instantly, vividly, and massively moved by the liquidation of a leader, the inevitable potential for pouncing on a scapegoat would seem almost certain to be enhanced. The dangers inherent in the instantly and visually communicated assassination would appear to surpass national boundaries. Television thrusts the tragedy not only into the living rooms of the citizens whose leader has been killed, but into foreign nations as well—thus helping undermine confidence abroad in the stability of the state whose leader has been killed. The historic first Pacific-spanning TV transmission pictured the brutal assassination of a president of the United States. Since that chilling day, foreign lands have also viewed the tragedy of Martin Luther King, the racial rampages that followed, and an incredible repeat of the Kennedy nightmare in the shooting of Robert Kennedy.

Moreover, because violence engenders violence, there are indications that one assassination can lead to others—as witness the shooting of West Berlin's leftist student leader, Rudi Deutschke, by a gunman who said he had been inspired by the assassination of Martin Luther King in Memphis, Tennessee, a few days earlier. The murder of Bobby Kennedy followed King's by only two months. Says Dr. Joseph Satten, a psychiatrist at Topeka's Menninger Foundation:

"Clinical experience does suggest some sort of contagion phenomenon. The more people see of these things, the more they tend to increase."

An interesting analysis of the possible infectiousness of political murder in the United States is given by Dr. John P. Spiegel, director of the Lamberg Center for the Study of Violence at Massachusetts' Brandeis University. The center was formed in 1966 and, although it has made no in-depth study of the assassination of John Kennedy, it is carrying out a survey around Atlanta of reactions to the killing of Martin Luther King. To the question of whether the murder of President Kennedy may have contributed to the violence that has swept the United States since, Dr. Spiegel observes:

"It is difficult to say anything that represents firm knowledge on this subject.

"We do know for certain that certain dramatic events do serve as models for later actions. There is a contagious element to violence. It is plausible that once an event happens and is dramatically represented on television, as was the Kennedy assassination and the killing of Oswald, it can have a contagious effect.

"Sometimes we get direct evidence of this. The fellow who shot Rudi Deutschke actually said that he was motivated by the assassination of Martin Luther King.

"There were people in the United States who poured gasoline on themselves and turned themselves into human torches. They saw it happen in Vietnam on television. [Anthropologist] Margaret Mead said the other day that self-immolation is a cultural practice in Buddhist countries. No one intervenes because it is regarded as the individual's right to immolate himself. The act has meaning in that culture. But it has no meaning to us as an act of protest. It has no cultural acceptance with us. The acts of self-immolation that took place in the United States were clear cases of people acting out the example of a model. There was no previous model here or even an understanding of the act.

"A dramatic act serves as a focus of contagion by providing the person who plans an act of violence with a scenario. We can assume that if an assassin goes in that direction it promotes further assassination.

"I hate to use the word epidemic, but one sets the style. There is a repetition. The next act is in a similar place and the same way. A person in public office who represents issues that are in controversy in a dramatic fashion is picked as the victim, and the assailant performs according to scenario. He appears in a public place with a gun and shoots the victim. I think our scenario was handed down by John Wilkes Booth.

"There could have been other models for assassination. There is poison. They [assassins] could try to invade the person's home. But always it is a public place with a lot of people around. It is very dramatic."

There are those who fear that exposure to televised assassination has, moreover, inured the American people more deeply to political violence. Some believe that they saw signs of such a hardening of sensitivities in the reaction to the murder of Robert Kennedy. "I had the feeling that this was such a familiar routine," says Miss Barbara Amazaki, a Hawaiian-born resident of Chicago. "We're inured to this. I got the feeling that though there was some genuine sorrow, it was mostly an orgy of self-pity. There was something about the crowds. . ." Mrs. W. Miles Burns of Chicago, a Negro college graduate, was "sick" and "shocked to pieces" at the news of Bobby Kennedy's death, which like millions of Americans she heard in the middle of the night. Even so, adds Mrs. Burns, "I was surprised at my own self, because I was able to go back to sleep."

Paul B. Sheatsley of the National Opinion Research Center, who was instrumental in conducting the NORC's survey of responses to the death of John Kennedy, comments regarding the assassination of Robert Kennedy:

"This was quite a contrast to five years ago. In my experience talking with people, it seems we are all becoming more calloused, less sensitive. I do not know the answer. The assassination of the President seemed a unique event. It now seems commonplace to assassinate public figures."

As part of the national mourning, the Chicago Historical Society closed its privately supported museum of local history following the deaths of John Kennedy, Dr. King, and Robert Kennedy. Since the latter event, however, officials of the museum have decided that henceforth it will be closed only if a president is assassinated in office. The prevailing view now, explains Fred Gotham of the museum's education department, is that "it's foolish to be closed. We shouldn't shut it up. People have no place to go."

Despite the beginnings of callousness that some suspected were present in the reaction to Bobby Kennedy's death, there has also been ample evidence that the tragedy heightened people's concern about the nation. A discerning view is expressed by Dr. Hamid Mowlana, a 31-year-old Iranian who holds master's and Ph. D. degrees from Northwestern University, and who has taught journalism since 1965 at the University of Tennessee in Knoxville.

"I'm comparing this with what I've seen in Europe," he says. "One of the greatest things here was that people didn't worry. They didn't have doubts about their society. They believed in it. It was a big thing for me, this country. Now people have doubts about their country, their jobs, their future. They are worried.

"In Iran, when I was young, I saw our prime minister assassinated. Then six of them were assassinated. But I always thought that kind of thing was the problem of a small country, Iran. Can you imagine these American kids today—what they will think, what they will do, having grown up with these assassinations?"

Speaking of his own generation, Bill Newell, 28, a Chicago computer salesman, observes:

"We were brought up in the days when there wasn't really violence. We have never really experienced any violence at home. We've never really had to scrounge. We don't remember going through the Depression. We were flower children, you might say. JFK was the first President to be assassinated in our lifetimes. It was once unthinkable —I mean, to murder a president used to be out of the range of possibility." Nevertheless, Newell does not think that there is cause for panic. "I don't think the country is on the brink of going down the drain."

Speaking in the wake of the Bobby Kennedy's death, Jim Parden, a Chicago stockbroker in his early 30's, comments:

"I'd hate to be named Abdul now and try to buy a drink in a bar. I was a history major and assassinations are part of history. Our history has been barbaric. But how many assassinations can you take in a year?

"I think we are developing a fetish for the dead. It's like we were living in Bulgaria in 1908 or in one of the banana republics. I think the country is becoming a little paranoid. Maybe it's cathartic to watch a train go by [a reference to the train bearing Robert Kennedy's body from New York to Washington]. Everybody stands together, black and white, abhorring death. Within minutes after the train passes, they're at each other's throats again."

Finally, there is the rather obvious consideration that the televised assassination, in an age of push-button nuclear war, constitutes a special potential hazard. One of the almost instinctive initial reactions to an assassination is the suspicion that it may be the dark deed of a foreign power, as part of a plan of subversion or eventual aggression—all of which does little to ease international tensions. Throughout history, the murder of a political leader has been dangerous to national and international stability. One need not be an alarmist to suggest that, in an era when nations are linked together by both the electronic tube and atomic terror, a shattering event such as a major political assassination is potentially capable of triggering Armageddon.

What measures might be taken to reduce the shock of assassination in the television era? Such a question could form the topic of a major study, but a few practical proposals would seem to merit consideration. To state one of the more obvious, radio and television staffs should be consciously prepared to report assassinations as coolly and intelligently as possible—as TV did notably in the aftermath of the slaying of Dr. King, somewhat less after Robert Kennedy's death. In a time when, quite literally, Walter Cronkite can be the arbiter of social and political stability, such thought would seem well within television's acceptable professional code, without restricting the freedom and responsibility to give the news. Local, state, and national governments might profitably draw up contingency plans for use in the event of a major assassination—including special riot-control preparations and psychological measures to reassure the populace. The United Nations might well consider drawing up its own specific procedures for allaying international tension, perhaps by setting up an assassination investigatory commission that would adjudge charges of foreign instigation of a murder and decree sanctions.

The theory could also be advanced that today's video-democracy makes the choice of the No. 2 person in any area of political responsibility—be he the vice-president of the United States, or the successor to any other important leader figure—more important than ever before. To be sure, as political scientists point out, people automatically rally to a dead leader's successor. But because of the greater emotional impact lent by television to the loss of the original leader, and the closer and wider scrutiny by the populace of his successor likewise afforded by the electronic eye, it would seem vital that the successor be capable of exuding confidence and capability.

Few would deny that the take-charge attitude of Lyndon Johnson following the death of John Kennedy—an air of confidence relayed into American homes by TV cameras—went a long way toward assuring a stricken people as to the stability of their government's institutions. The impression among American businessmen that Johnson would pursue essentially sound fiscal policies, for example, was instrumental in the nation's rapid economic recovery. *Business Week* reported a week after the assassination that most economists believed Johnson's "overall monetary and fiscal policies will be calculated to sustain national and international business confidence." Typical was the verdict of Gabriel Hauge, president of the Manufacturers Hanover Trust Company and a former economic adviser to President Eisenhower: "The new President has moved with great skill in his first trying days, and one cannot doubt that he will continue to do so, reinforcing confidence in the future as he proceeds." The New York Stock Exchange report on the effect of John Kennedy's assassination on the stock market echoed the result: "The impulse to sell which had seized some people when they learned of the tragedy had disappeared by Tuesday morning. The quick, orderly transfer of the reins of government to President Johnson brought a renewal of confidence in the fundamental stability of our government."

Still another means of ensuring stability might be a self-imposed moratorium on inflammatory rhetoric by all citizens in the wake of an assassination. An impressive example was the call for nonviolence and calm made after the death of Dr. King by his successor in the Southern Christian Leadership Conference, the Rev. Ralph Abernathy.

Naturally, the best way to soften the jolt of an assassination is to prevent the assassination itself. As demonstrated by President Johnson's decision, motivated by the shooting of Robert Kennedy, to assign Secret Service guards to all major Presidential candidates, the security of leader figures must be taken far more seriously. Although the Secret Service and other law enforcement officials emphasize that it is impossible to guarantee the safety of any public figure, surely more security measures can be taken. The Secret Service cannot prevent a president from riding in an open car or plunging into crowds, but responsible presidents might refrain from doing so. Lacking such a disposition on the part of the chief executive, Congress might ponder legislation that would require a president to forgo unnecessary risk-taking. Such restrictions might appear Draconian, but they would improve a president's actuarial probabilities. Besides, in today's television era, a president has instant access to, and thus is an omnipresent guest in, every citizen's living room anyway. On the day that Senator Kennedy died, CBS commentator Eric Sevareid observed that "we will probably have to conduct our political campaigning in a different way. This past year President Johnson has avoided exposure to most crowds; his opponents derided him for this, but he has surely been right."

Moreover, local police departments might benefit from improved training and preparation for the care of visiting public figures. Martin Luther King might be alive today had the Memphis police more efficiently secured the neighborhood surrounding the motel where he was shot. In the wake of President Kennedy's assassination, Police Superintendent O. W. Wilson of Chicago ordered his force to conduct a review of circumstances under which the deed took place, in order to guide Chicago in planning security for future Presidential visits.

Gun control laws more befitting a civilized society are another must —as Congress finally seems to have realized after the murder of Bobby Kennedy, by making at least a start on improved legislation. However, the National Rifle Association and other Americans wary of blanket restrictions on firearms would appear to have a point in one argument: that it makes little sense to disarm the law-abiding public if punishment by the courts of the criminal element for gun violations is lax. Therefore, enforcement of existing firearm laws should be vastly toughened—along with sentences for violations. Further, a society that outlawed gun silencers as a measure against organized crime in the 1930's should find it possible to regulate the import, manufacture, and sale of telescopic rifle sights.

Although a democratic country must proceed with caution in such areas, there should be better means of spotting and controlling the psychotic potential killer. The most basic security against assassination, at least from within the ranks of a society, is, of course, the healthiest possible society—morally, materially, intellectually.

It may come to pass that the video tube will so inure the populace to political assassination that people will take in stride this new experience in violence. Moreover, man may ultimately reach the day when—with the help of electronic circuitry—power is so organized and applied, when heroes are so outmoded and individual reactions so controlled, that the death of a leader will cause hardly a ripple because his loss will be automatically compensated for by a far more efficient and dispassionate society. But for the present, there seems little doubt that the element of TV participation has given political assassination a dimension never before recorded in history —a phenomenon that will provoke questions by sociologists, psychiatrists, political scientists, and historians for a long time to come.

Whatever their final conclusions, it would appear that in an era when a chief of state could be assassinated in full view of a worldwide TV audience, when the teetering of stability in one nation is of concern to all, the world would do well to interest itself in the memories and meanings of that cataclysmic moment, 1:33.

It was John Fitzgerald Kennedy who once said, "The only two dates that most people remember where they were are Pearl Harbor and the death of Franklin Roosevelt." To that, regrettably, must be added November 22, 1963.

BIBLIOGRAPHY

Books

Berger, Peter, *The Sacred Canopy*. Garden City, New York: Double-day, 1967.

Bishop, James A., *The Day Lincoln Was Shot*. New York: Harper, 1955.

Freud, Sigmund, "Group Psychology and the Analysis of the Ego," "Moses and Monotheism," and "Mourning and Melancholia," *The Complete Psychological Works of Sigmund Freud*, Standard Edition, London: Hogarth Press, 1956, by permission of Sigmund Freud Copyrights Limited, the Institute of Psychoanalysis and the publisher.

Hook, Sidney, *The Hero in History*. New York: John Day, 1943.

Manchester, William, *The Death of a President*. New York: Harper & Row, 1967.

McLuhan, Marshall, *Understanding Media: The Extensions of Man*. New York: McGraw-Hill, 1964.

The New York Times Company, *Report of the Warren Commission on the Assassination of President Kennedy*. New York: McGraw-Hill Book Company, 1963.

Newspapers

Arizona Republic
Atlanta Constitution
Boston Globe
Boston Herald Traveler
Chicago's American
Chicago Daily News
Dallas Morning News
Dallas Times-Herald
Delta-Democrat (Greenville, Miss.) Times
Des Moines Register
Lewiston (Idaho) Tribune
Los Angeles Times
New York Herald Tribune
New York Post
Oakland Tribune
Washington Post

Periodicals

America, December 14, 1963, "World Resounds—Tokyo," John Blewett; February 27, 1965, "Africa Remembers J.F.K.," Patrick J. Ryan.

Annals of the American Academy of Political and Social Science, March 1966, "Controversies About the Mass Communication of Violence," O. N. Larsen.

Business Week, November 30, 1963, "World Weeps and Waits," and "A Shock, Then Recovery."

Christian Century, December 25, 1963, "Reaction to Assassination."

Good Housekeeping, November 1965, "Day J. F. K. Died; What People Remember Now," Alan Levy.

Nation, October 11, 1965, "One World," David Sarnoff.

New Republic, December 7, 1963, "When Castro Heard the News," Jean Daniel.

New York Times Magazine, November 15, 1964, "What Was Killed Was Not Only the President," James Reston.

New Yorker, December 7, 1963, "Letter from London," M. Panter-Downes, and "Letter from Paris," Genet.

Newsweek, December 2, 1963, "And A Child's Yellow Flowers"; December 9, 1963, "World Mourns in Doubt, Fear, Hope"; December 16, 1963, "Reactions in the South"; March 16, 1964, "How America Felt"; September 14, 1964, "When Kennedy Died; Psychological Impact"; December 4, 1967, "Scene of the Crime."

Psychoanalytic Review, Vol. 51, 1964, "Some Reactions of Patients in Psychotherapy to the Death of the President," David Kirschner.

Public Opinion Quarterly, Vol. XXVII, 1964, "The Assassination of President Kennedy; A Preliminary Report on Public Reactions and Behavior," Paul A. Sheatsley and Jacob J. Feldman for the National Opinion Research Center.

Redbook, March, 1964, "The Day the President Died," George R. Krupp.

Saturday Review, December 7, 1963, "Manner of Speaking," John Ciardi; December 14, 1963, "If You Can Keep Your Head When All About You: TV and News Magazine Coverage of the Assassination Story," R. L. Tobin; January 11, 1964, "A Reporter Must Trust His Instinct," Tom Wicker; January 8, 1966, "One-World Concept of Mass Communication; General Sarnoff's Forecast," R. L. Tobin; July 23, 1966, "The Town Meeting Reborn," Vernon F. Miller.

Science News Letter, December 7, 1963, "Reaction to Killings"; October 23, 1965, "Mass Media Calmed U. S.; Catharsis for National Grief Over President John F. Kennedy's Death."

Television Magazine, January 1964, "The Four Days."

Time, November 29, 1963, "Covering the Tragedy," and "How Sorrowful Bad; World Reactions."

Trans-Action, November 1966, "The Best-Known American," Fred I. Greenstein.

Speeches
Greenstein, Fred I., "Popular Images of the President," paper read at 121st annual meeting of American Psychiatric Association, New York City, May 3–7, 1965.

Robinson, G. Wilse, "A Study of Political Assassination," paper read at 120th annual meeting of American Psychiatric Association, Los Angeles, California, May 4–8, 1964.

Sevareid, Eric, from "CBS Evening News with Walter Cronkite," June 6, 1968.

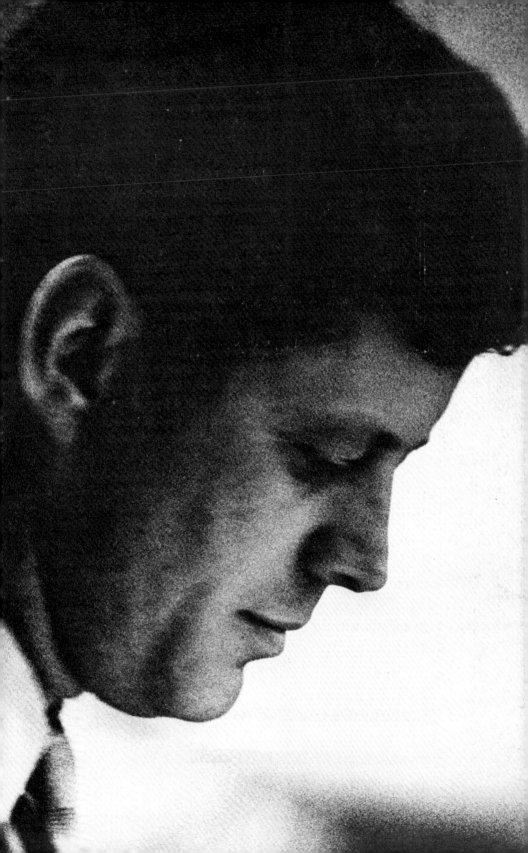